THE DOCUMENTARY AUDIT

INVESTIGATING VISIBLE EVIDENCE:
NEW CHALLENGES FOR DOCUMENTARY

INVESTIGATING VISIBLE EVIDENCE:
NEW CHALLENGES FOR DOCUMENTARY

JANE GAINES, FAYE GINSBURG, POOJA RANGAN, MICHAEL RENOV, SERIES EDITORS

A new series addressing the most pressing questions
for documentary studies today.

Revolutionary Becomings: Documentary Media in Twentieth-Century China,
by Ying Qian

Kill the Documentary: A Letter to Filmmakers, Students, and Scholars,
by Jill Godmilow

THE DOCUMENTARY AUDIT

LISTENING AND THE LIMITS OF ACCOUNTABILITY

POOJA RANGAN

Columbia University Press   *New York*

Columbia University Press
Publishers Since 1893
New York   Chichester, West Sussex

Copyright © 2025 Columbia University Press
All rights reserved

Library of Congress Cataloging-in-Publication Data
Names: Rangan, Pooja, 1984– author.
Title: The documentary audit : listening and the limits of accountability / Pooja Rangan.
Description: First edition. | New York : Columbia University Press, 2025. | Includes bibliographical references and index.
Identifiers: LCCN 2024050307 | ISBN 9780231217972 (hardback) | ISBN 9780231217989 (trade paperback) | ISBN 9780231562003 (ebook)
Subjects: LCSH: Documentary films—Social aspects. | LCGFT: Film criticism.
Classification: LCC PN1995.9.D6 R363 2025 | DDC 070.1/8—dc23/eng/20250113

Cover design: Adam Maida
Cover image: Screenshot from *Shared Resources* (dir. Jordan Lord, 2021). Courtesy of the artist.

GPSR Authorized Representative: Easy Access System Europe, Mustamäe tee 50, 10621 Tallinn, Estonia, gpsr.requests@easproject.com

For a world where Palestine is free

CONTENTS

Acknowledgments ix

Introduction 1
1. Listening with an Accent 27
2. Listening in Crip Time 77
3. Listening Like an Abolitionist 124

Coda: Listening Without Impact 176

Notes 183
Bibliography 233
Index 253

ACKNOWLEDGMENTS

The questions driving this book have preoccupied me since I began writing my first book, *Immediations*, as a graduate student. This book was completed alongside my first term chairing the Film and Media Studies program at Amherst College. I learned, in the process, that producing a second book is as much about building support structures and intellectual communities as it is about finding time to write.

Each chapter of this book emerged from collaborative research. Chapter 1 grew out of my work with Ragini Tharoor Srinivasan, Akshya Saxena, and Pavitra Sundar on the Accent Research Collaborative. Our activities, including our edited anthology *Thinking with an Accent* (2023), were supported by our institutions, the University of Arizona, Vanderbilt University, Hamilton College, and especially Amherst College, which sponsored the conference that launched our publication. Writing alongside these exquisite prose stylists has been a joyful rediscovery of the multiplicities contained in a voice. I developed chapter 2 as a visiting scholar at New York University's Center for Disability Studies during my tenure as an American Society for Learned Scholars (ACLS) Frederick Burkhardt Residential Fellow at New York University's Center for Media, Culture, and History, whose extraordinary director, Faye Ginsburg, arranged an additional visiting scholar appointment at the Center for Disability Studies, which she codirects with Mara Mills. Faye, Mara, Peggy Vail, and CDS fellows Yan Grenier, Laura Mauldin, and Alexis Kyle Mitchell brought me into intellectual and political community during the worst of the COVID-19 pandemic. Chapter 3 grew out of an ongoing research collaboration with Brett Story on documentary, prisons, and carceral common sense and came to fruition during a research fellowship at ConTrust Research Center at Goethe Universität that brought me into conversation with Laliv Melamed, Vinzenz Hediger, and Ra'anan Alexandrowicz around questions of documentary, trust, and conflict.

I have had the immense privilege of building these relationships from the stable perch of a tenured position at Amherst College. Amherst provided me with a semester of posttenure leave, support to accept the ACLS Burkhardt fellowship, and generous research funding courtesy of the Faculty Research and Publications Program, the Language and Literature Fund, and the Provost and Dean's Office. I thank my lucky stars daily for my kind, committed, and intellectually curious colleagues in the English Department and the Film and Media Studies Program. I am especially grateful to Lisa Brooks and Frank Roberts for teaching me what radical mentorship means; Anston Bosman, my favorite accented colleague, for bringing humor and rigor to postteaching office chats; Chris Grobe for always sharing findings relevant to my research; Amelie Hastie for showing me how to navigate the transition to midcareer scholar and teacher; Michael Kunichika for leading me back to my voice at a time when it faltered; Judy Frank for being the senior colleague I want to grow up to be; my writing group Krupa Shandilya, Ingrid Nelson, Yael Rice, and Amelia Worsley for bringing me to my desk even when it hurt and making me feel glad to be there; Josh Guilford for walking the impossible line between colleague and partner every day with patience and love; and the Amherst College Faculty and Staff for Justice in Palestine group for their political sustenance and community.

Every word in this book has been sharpened by teaching. I am grateful to the students in my seminar and colloquium courses

Disability, Media, and the Art of Access; Hearing Difference: The Political Economy of Accent; and After COPS: Police, Media, and Prison Abolition for always asking the difficult questions. Several of my students have worked with me as research assistants, and I am especially grateful to Eniola Ajao, Bebe Leistyna, Jihyun Paik, and Alexandra Kukulina for assisting me during various stages of this book's journey. I have grown as a writer and thinker thanks to my dedicated and brilliant staff colleagues. I never fail to learn something new about writing and research from Amherst's writing specialists Emily Merriman, Kristen Brookes, and Jessica Kem and from our research librarian Sara Smith. I will always be grateful to Emily and Sara for lingering after a class visit to Hearing Difference to have a conversation about research that was utterly transforming for me. Dave Moran in Multimedia Services and the librarians at Amherst have been wonderful partners in locating, digitizing, and making accessible the media and scholarly resources that I relied on to write this book. It has been a pleasure chairing the Film and Media Program alongside our talented department coordinators, Genevieve Sawyer, Danielle Thompson, and Dana Whitney, each of whom modeled how to manage time effectively and graciously.

In addition to longer-term collaborations, conversations with generous interlocutors spurred important insights. Andrew Ritchey, who made the transition from film sound scholar to radical bookshop founder and U.S. postal worker, introduced me to the early films of the British General Post Office Film Unit and shared research copies of the films. Union Docs hosted one of the first illustrated lectures I saw by Lawrence Abu Hamdan, on the politics of listening. Ekrem Serdar at Squeaky Wheel encouraged me to look into Jordan Lord's work and ended up facilitating what has become one of the most rewarding exchanges of my scholarly life. Joel Neville Anderson screened *Goodbye CP* on 16 mm during a visit to Rochester that he arranged along with Almudena Escobar López and invited me into what has become an ongoing conversation about this important film.

Joel also generously pointed me to resources that would have been impossible to find without his expertise and translation skills. Thanks to the curator Shai Heredia, my fellow colleagues at the Flaherty, and the translator Aiko Masubuchi, I was subsequently lucky enough to spend an unforgettable week at the 2019 Flaherty Seminar with Hara Kazuo and Kobayashi Sachiko. Sonali Gulati, Lawrence Abu Hamdan, Jordan Lord, Brett Story, and Ra'anan Alexandrowicz engaged in extensive conversations with me about their practice in both formal and informal settings. The world and this book are undeniably better for their deeply engaged reflections on why they do what they do.

I have had the good fortune to develop the ideas in this book in the company of scholars and practitioners across a range of institutional locations. I found my way to this project in the course of giving talks at Skidmore College's John B. Moore Documentary Studies Collaborative, Rochester University, Princeton University's Thinking Cinema Series, and Lafayette College's Film and Media Studies Seminar Series, thanks to invitations from Jordana Dym, Joel Neville Anderson and Almudena Escobar López, Steven Chung and Zahid Chaudhary, and Katherine Groo. Several parts of this book began as conference papers at Visible Evidence, American Comparative Literature Association, Society for Cinema and Media Studies, Modern Language Association, and European Network for Cinema and Media Studies. Chapter 1 benefited tremendously from feedback from audiences at New York University, Vanderbilt University, University of California Berkeley's Film and Media Seminar Series, Seattle University, and Columbia University's Sites of Cinema Seminar during talks arranged by Toby Lee, Jennifer Fay, Rizvana Bradley, Benjamín Schultz-Figueroa (with an incredible response by Nalini Iyer), and Nico Baumbach (with Lana Lin, who delivered another brilliant response). Jean Ma, Nima Bassiri, Mara Mills and Faye Ginsburg, Stephen Woo and Alex Maxwell, J. D. Rhodes and Peter McMurray, Vinzenz Hediger and Laliv Melamed, and Nicholas Glastonbury and Derek Baron are to thank for invitations to present what eventually became chapter 2 with the help of feedback from audiences at Stanford University Humanities Center's Matters of Voice Workshop, Duke University's Critical Theory Workshop, New York University's Center for Disability Studies, Brown University's Modern Culture and Media Graduate Student Speaker Series, a keynote lecture at the Global Media Conference at Cambridge University, Goethe Universität, and the Properties of Voice Symposium at Rutgers University. Chapter 3 was developed in the company of graduate students at Brown University, as well as through the Kracauer Lecture at Goethe Universität, a keynote lecture at the Forms of (More-Than-Human) Relationality Workshop at the Amsterdam School for Cultural Analysis, and a keynote lecture at the Atmospheres of Violence graduate conference at Harvard University. Stephen Woo and Alex Maxwell, Daniel Fairfax and Vinzenz Hediger, Nadica Denić, and Julia Sharpe and Valerie Werder are to thank for these opportunities.

I am most grateful of all for the fellowship of a small number of trusted readers—Neta Alexander, Laliv Melamed, Brett Story, Tess Takahashi, Paige Sarlin, Josh Guilford, Steve Dillon, Jordan Lord, Genevieve Yue, Mike Zryd, Jennifer Cazenave, and my accented sisters Ragini, Akshya, Pavitra, and Nina Sun Eidsheim—who have read parts of this book in various stages of gestation and helped me improve on it greatly. I am indebted to the four peer reviewers who recommended that Duke and Columbia pursue this project, and I was humbled when Toby Lee, Benjamín Schultz-Figueroa, and Joshua Glick later revealed to me that they had been among these readers. In Jordan's words, the debts I have accrued through your generosity and trust is a bond that grows. Some of the best writing in this book was done during writing retreats organized by Jason Fox. Jason is indefatigable in his efforts to create sustaining structures through which documentary practitioners and scholars can engage in meaningful exchange, and some of my most cherished relationships have been fostered by the community that Jason has built through the journal *World Records*. I am also grateful to Iva Radivojević and Amber Bemak for the restorative energy of our Rhyax symposium gatherings in Eresos, Lesvos, and to Lakshmi Padmanabhan for swimming lessons in the Aegean and philosophy in the kitchen. To my pandemic pod—Josh, Steve, Sarah, Mollykutty, and Pumpkin—my teacher, Rey Chow, and my parents, Girish and Sheela Rangan, and Vijiakka, my second mother, I owe simply everything.

It means the world to have this book appear in the Investigating Visible Evidence series. I am deeply honored that Jane Gaines, Michael Renov, and Faye Ginsburg trusted me to join them in coenvisioning the future of their field-shaping conversation as an editor of this book series. Philip Leventhal has been an incredible partner and editor. I have learned so much about collegiality forged through commitment to humanistic inquiry from Philip and from Courtney Berger at Duke. I was able to see the shape this book needed to take thanks to an early conversation with Courtney, who recognized and reflected to me the kind of writer that I am. The book has assumed the form you hold in your hands thanks to the wonderful production team at Columbia, including Emily Simon, Michael Haskell, and Zachary Friedman; Ben Kolstad and his team at KnowledgeWorks Global Ltd., who oversaw copyedits and page proofs; Adam Maida, who designed a beautiful cover featuring an image from Jordan Lord's wonderful film *Shared Resources* (the deep crimson image, fading to pink, is produced by the filmmaker holding their finger over the camera lens); and Sarah Osment, who created the index. I am especially grateful to Sarah for joining her brilliant editorial voice with mine in the final stages of finessing this book's prose. Working with Sarah has given me an entirely new understanding of what it means to listen.

PRIOR PUBLICATIONS

Aspects of the conceptual frameworks introduced in this book were developed in "Audibilities: Voice and Listening in the Penumbra of

Documentary: An Introduction," in "Documentary Audibilities," special issue, edited by Pooja Rangan and Genevieve Yue, *Discourse* 39, no. 3 (Fall 2017): 279–91; "The Skin of the Voice: Acousmatic Illusions, Ventriloquial Listening," in *Sound Objects*, edited by Rey Chow and James Steintrager (Durham, NC: Duke University Press, 2019), 130–48; "Dossier on 'Documentary' (Adj.)," *Millennium Film Journal* 74 (Fall 2021), with Toby Lee, Laliv Melamed, Paige Sarlin, and Benjamín Schultz-Figueroa; "Documentary Listening Habits: From Voice to Audibility," in *The Oxford Handbook of Film Theory*, edited by Kyle Stevens (Oxford: Oxford University Press, 2022), 403–20; and "Listening Like a Documentary," in *No Master Territories: Feminist Worldmaking and the Moving Image*, edited by Erika Balsom and Hila Peleg (Cambridge, MA: MIT Press, 2022), 81–87.

Earlier versions of excerpts that appear in chapter 1 were published in "Auditing the Call Centre Voice: Accented Speech and Listening in Sonali Gulati's *Nalini by Day, Nancy by Night*," in *Vocal Projections: The Voice in Documentary Film*, edited by Maria Pramaggiore and Annabelle Honess Roe (New York: Bloomsbury Academic, 2018), 29–44; and "Inaudible Evidence: Counterforensic Listening in Contemporary Documentary Art," in *Deep Mediations: Thinking Space in Cinema and Digital Cultures*, edited by Karen Redrobe and Jeff Scheible (Minneapolis: University of Minnesota Press, 2021), 161–79.

A condensed excerpt from chapter 2 appears as "Listening in Crip Time: Toward a Countertheory of Documentary Access," in "The New Disability Media," dossier, edited by Faye Ginsberg, B. Ruby Rich, and Lawrence Carter-Long, *Film Quarterly* 76, no. 2 (Winter 2022): 25–30.

THE DOCUMENTARY AUDIT

INTRODUCTION

Documentary teaches us that listening is the highest ethical act. Listening, we are told, brings the voiceless into the domain of audibility, where their humanity can, however belatedly, be heard, recognized, and admitted. This book is about that domain of audibility and how it is shaped by what I call *the documentary audit*. It concerns the ways that documentaries listen, the tacit habits of listening that they endorse when they beckon audiences to hear the voices of the dispossessed, and what those habits teach us about listening's accountability. It is, above all, a meditation on the relationships, values, and social worlds that documentary forms enable us to inhabit when they train their attention beyond that central, commonplace tenet, "giving voice."

The short film *We Are Going to Record* (2014), directed by Peter Snowdon with the anthropologist Juan Javier Rivera Andía, offers a simple but effective illustration of the documentary audit. The film consists of a series of outtakes shot in an improvised studio where Indigenous people from a small village in the Peruvian Andes have been gathered to record examples of their traditional music. One elder holds a drum, another has a guitar, and a younger man has a book of poems. Rivera Andía and his crew of professional sound recordists from Lima hover nervously around the performers, adjusting postures, straightening mics, and hushing bystanders: "We are ready to record!

Nothing must move! Don't speak! Don't speak! The microphone is very sensitive. Every breath you take will be heard. So breathe very quietly. If you could stop breathing, that would be even better!" An eruption of nervous laughter. Someone hits record then stops. "I can hear a conversation outside . . . a child's voice." The bemused villagers blink, nod, and comply. But we never hear anything they say or sing. Indeed, the film tells us so little about whom, what, and why we are watching that the scene exists in the realm of parable. This is how I hear it: as a parable of a prevailing approach to documentary listening. The film is a record not of the voices being documented but of the record itself or, more specifically, the conventional operations and procedures involved in its production. Let the record show, the film says, that when marginalized people are invited to "speak up," usually as part of a redemptive effort to remedy their existential exclusion, their voices are not freely narrated or indiscriminately captured. They are instead subject to an *audit*—a prior accounting, inspection, or screening process—that shapes their speech in line with the very extractive culture whose dispossession they have been brought in to remedy. The documentary audit rewrites the record in line with its own interpretive logic: It precedes, trains, and narrows the relational horizons of documentary voicing and listenership, all while claiming the mantle of inclusivity and accountability.

Documentary forms signal to their audience their twinned imperatives of listening and accountability in explicit and implicit ways. The field's most prolific theorist, Bill Nichols, has argued that an interpellative address to an attentive but undirected listening public is the signal trait of the documentary mode. "Unexpectedly, someone calls out: 'Hey you!'" Nichols writes, and "to be addressed by a film—to sense that a film seeks to engage and speak to us about the world we share—functions as a hallmark of documentary film."[1] This is a version of what Nichols has argued throughout his career: Despite differences in who speaks and how and whether their address is explicit or implicit, all documentaries share the common denominator of a *voice* that acknowledges the political receptivity and disposition of audiences to act remedially on the world they share, however asymmetrically, with others.

It is thanks in part to Nichols that "voice" rather than "gaze" has become the go-to metaphor for a documentary film's unique worldview or social perspective. When Nichols first wrote his pathbreaking 1983 essay, "The Voice of Documentary"—which he defined, enigmatically, as something narrower than style but broader than any one feature such as dialogue or spoken commentary ("that intangible, moiré-like pattern formed by the unique interaction of all a film's codes" that "conveys to us a sense of a text's social point of view, of how it is speaking to us and how it is organizing the materials it is presenting to us")—he was channeling the prevailing semiotic orientation of narrative film studies.[2] But he was also carving out a disciplinary space for documentary distinct from the former's pursuit of psychic economies, imaginary projections, and the rubric of visual pleasure. By building itself around the spoken word, as he clarifies in *Representing Reality* (1991) and his textbook *Introduction to Documentary* (now its fourth edition), documentary operates in the realm not of story but of reality-attentive, sober, rational discourse, not just of style but of ethics.[3]

Deconstructing the polarity between documentary reality and fictional illusion has subsequently become a central preoccupation of documentary studies. But the rhetorical and rational associations of *voice* and its uses as a metaphor for documentary's pursuit of humanity, truth, and justice have proven harder to dislodge.[4] The subfield has been allergic to the kind of structural analysis that made the concept of the gaze such a generative site of film theoretical debate, in part because of the unquestioned consensus that documentary is a materialist practice of giving voice to real people, issues, and problems.[5] This oppositional narrative has so thoroughly saturated the discourse of documentary scholars, makers, funders, and distributors that few have thought to ask *how documentaries listen*. When did listening emerge as a symptom of documentary's justice-seeking ambitions? Whose listening vantage do we inhabit when documentaries ask us to perform the function of moral or political oversight? What conditions have led documentary listeners to expect that they will be granted access to information and knowledge? How have these listening habits, expectations, and positionalities coalesced into documentary conventions that organize the field of the audible and condition political attention?

The questions that drive *The Documentary Audit* distill over a decade of my research and writing on the reverberations of the voice metaphor across documentary theory and practice. I began this work in my previous book, *Immediations: The Humanitarian Impulse in Documentary*.[6] *Immediations* examines the role of humanitarian structures and sentiments in the late twentieth-century emergence of participatory documentary interventions seeking to "give a voice" to disenfranchised subjects, including the children of Kolkata sex workers, Hurricane Katrina victims, nonspeaking autistic people, and endangered animals. I argue that this gift of a voice, encapsulated in the gesture of handing over the camera, is not always benevolent. Documentary can diminish its beneficiary at the precise moment that it bequeaths visibility and recognition, transforming the speaker, indeed even the speaker's very existence, into a mouthpiece for cherished humanitarian values such as "agency," "resilience," "interiority," and "humanity." Voice is a crucible and master trope for these values; this is why Nick Couldry calls voice a "value about values."[7] When the child protagonists of the photojournalist Zana Briski's Oscar-winning film *Born Into Brothels* speak in the photographic aesthetic of innocence, they are said to have a voice; when the voice actress Juliana Margulies intones Sue Rubin's autobiographical writings as an articulate, intimate first-person voice-over in the CNN documentary *Autism Is a World*, Rubin, a nonspeaking autistic woman, is said to have a voice. The documentary camera functions here as a humanizing prosthesis through which what Brian Winston might call "social victims" of environmental harm, criminalized poverty, and institutional violence can belatedly demonstrate their value—their voice—in terms that are immediately recognizable to humanitarian audiences.[8] "Immediations" is the term I use to identify and theorize documentary tropes that generate a sensation of urgency around endangered life—a sensation that is extraordinarily effective at producing consensus, especially when these tropes are employed directly by disenfranchised subjects. My book investigates what immediations *do*: how they reinforce particular meanings of humanity, justify insidious forms of discrimination, and consolidate neoliberal regimes of power, all under the aegis of the seemingly inclusive gesture of giving voice. In place of this gesture, I seek a more capacious aesthetic and political vocabulary for documentary that opens up the horizons of humanity rather than presuming them in advance.

Since writing *Immediations*, I have discovered that the diminishing returns of voice are a result of documentary listening habits that both tailor and taper perceptual and political horizons. Trinh T. Minh-ha's voice has been a lodestar in my inquiry. Her postcolonial feminist polemic against giving voice appears as the closing salvo of an essay titled "Mechanical Eye, Electronic Ear, and the Lure of Authenticity." Published as part of Trinh's remarkable collection *When the Moon Waxes Red* in 1991, the same year as Nichols's *Representing Reality*, it is worth quoting at some length:

> Making a film on/about the "others" consists of allowing them paternalistically "to speak for themselves" and, since this proves insufficient in most cases, of completing their speech with the insertion of a commentary that will objectively describe/interpret the images according to a scientific-humanistic rationale. Language as voice and music—grain, tone, inflections, pauses, silences, repetitions—goes underground. Instead, people from remote parts of the world are made accessible through dubbing/subtitling, transformed into English-speaking elements and brought into conformity with a definite mentality. This is

astutely called "giving voice"—literally meaning that those who are/need to *be given* an opportunity to speak up never had a voice before. Without their benefactors they are bound to remain non-admitted, non-incorporated, therefore, unheard.⁹

Trinh's critique resounds beyond her immediate target, ethnographic film, a genre that John Grierson famously identified as the wellspring of documentary's liberal humanism.¹⁰ Later, when Trinh names the slippage between ascription (bestowing upon others) and expression (speaking for oneself) characteristic of "giving voice," she identifies a widespread documentary tendency: the asymmetrical relational dynamic between speaker and listener that documentary discourse has largely affirmed as a positivity ("voice"). Documentary forms have been harnessed in neocolonial projects that involve *auditing*—vetting, surveying, appraising, and analyzing—the chaos and unruliness of non-Western modes of speaking and organizing social life by devising abstract forms (commentary, dubbing, subtitling) that make their contents perceptible to and manipulable by those seeking to include or recognize them. What is more, the modes of listening cultivated by these abstract forms have come to be associated with the liberal humanist values of inclusivity and openness. Trinh's words are a potent reminder that every documentary's textual voice is a product of the immiserating maneuver concealed by these values—evident in the screening process captured by Snowdon and Rivera Andía—which separates some "us" from some "them." "When we hear the so-called voice of a documentary and respond to its hail," I hear Trinh ask, with her trademark counterintuition, "aren't we listening through the filter of its listening ear? Aren't we, in effect, *listening like a documentary?*"¹¹

My book enacts the program of study implicit in this provocation. I frame *the documentary audit* as a habitual structure that distributes attentional and material resources and shapes relational and political prospects. *Audit*, like *document*, is both noun and verb. I am interested in the multiple, shifting meanings that result from the fusion of these two grammatically unstable terms. One colloquial meaning of *audit* refers to the informal mode of attending a class in which a student monitors their own learning. In his account of the auditory counterpart of the gaze, the sound studies scholar John Mowitt defines "audit" as "that which exceeds and conditions hearing and organizes the field of the audible."[12] Jennifer Lynn Stoever describes this ideological filter as an aggregate "listening ear" shaped by the accumulation of normative listening practices that channel the polymodal diversity of embodied listening practices into a narrow corridor of "correct" or "reasonable" responses.[13] Following Mowitt and Stoever, I understand the documentary audit as the entrained but not necessarily aware auditory perspective embodied by documentary listenership in the aggregate. Documentary listenership is conditioned by a variety of normative listening habits—informal pedagogies of sorts—that create the reality that they purport to verify, often in the name of progressive or democratic social values.

As a structure upheld by rituals of verification, the documentary audit also shares a rationale with the moral and administrative oversight associated with the more commonly known meaning of *audit*, which refers to an official review of an individual or organization's financial accounts. The word *audit* is colloquially used nowadays as a catch-all for a variety of assessments, evaluations, and measurements that ensure compliance with established standards or best practices concerning the governance of an entity or organization. Historically, the audit as verification process was necessitated by taxation as a state mechanism for extracting revenue and profit from land and labor, both of which had to be stolen in order to make and hoard capital.[14] Audits functioned as a bureaucratic mechanism for ensuring the accountability of taxpayers to the state under circumstances of mutual mistrust. They bore an evidentiary burden, too, in that they had to take a persuasive form capable of convincing those to whom accountability was to be rendered.[15] Conveniently, that persuasion worked in both directions: Procedures and operations that bore the stamp of accountability came to signify progressive values of transparency, openness, and integrity that were as difficult to criticize as they were easy to internalize. Thus, by engaging individuals, corporations, and state-funded institutions in bureaucratic "rituals of verification," audits functioned as a means for the state to evade the very accountability it demanded of others.[16]

This book's main proposition is that documentary operations and procedures have, under the mantle of accountability, provided a moral cover for listening habits that profile, exclude, and incarcerate. In direct and indirect ways, documentary listening habits reproduce the social relations and values that justify linguistic profiling, ableist exclusion, and carceral enclosure. Each of the three chapters of the book develops a theoretical framework for engaging with the origins and afterlives of listening habits that emerged alongside a historically significant and trend-setting chapter in documentary practice: the 1930s expository turn associated with commentary-driven educational and promotional films produced by the British Crown's GPO film unit under the leadership of John Grierson; the post-vérité turn that made a confrontational and performative aesthetic of verbal disagreement and debate a hallmark of documentary film and video in the 1980s and onward; and the testimonial turn, beginning in the 1990s, which seeks to implicate perpetrators of war crimes, environmental harm, police killings, and other acts of violence by speaking truth to power. At each of these moments, I argue, documentary practices schooled audiences in habits of *neutral listening* (chapter 1), *entitled* (or ableist) *listening* (chapter 2), and *juridical listening* (chapter 3).

The association of these listening habits with liberal-inclusionist values such as transparency and fairness have turned them into conventions, understood both as recognizable tropes and as anchors of aspirational values or what Lauren Berlant calls "placeholders for a desire to more-than-survive."[17] As Paige Sarlin has noted, assertions regarding documentary's anticapitalist and humanist vocation—what Marx might term its *use value*—have framed its draw for left-leaning and socially progressive filmmakers dating back to the interwar period.[18] While critiques of documentary's assumed autonomy from the market are at least as old, politically committed filmmakers have recently zeroed in on the coercive dominance of commercially viable "storytelling" (three-act films based on individual characters, with a conflict-resolution narrative arc) and the bourgeois values that they naturalize as the primary obstacle impeding documentary's capacity to intervene in social struggles.[19] I share these concerns regarding the challenges facing political filmmaking today, but my diagnosis is somewhat different: In order to understand the compromised situation of socially committed and justice-oriented documentary forms, I argue that it is necessary to understand the fraught histories and implications of their orienting liberal-progressive values and the listening habits that hold them in place.

My research uncovers the provenance of three of these values, namely *objectivity*, *access*, and *justice*, in pursuit of forgotten chapters and oppositional registers of documentary listening. Objectivity as an epistemological stance is seldom considered in discussions of listening since it is commonly believed that sound cannot be stabilized or "framed" in the manner of an object.[20] In chapter 1 I show how the accent-neutral commentary of early sound films advertising the British Crown's telecommunications services became a familiar marker of documentary credibility and, furthermore, how the raciolinguistic formal system supporting this convention gave credence to a neutral listening vantage that is still employed today in the linguistic profiling of asylum seekers and call center workers. Chapter 2 examines the entitled and extractive listening habits that emerged alongside the midcentury vérité turn, when access to private or intimate realms began to be leveraged as a form of documentary value. This chapter centers the role of disability justice activists in challenging this transactional interpretation of access as a commodity to be traded in exchange for visibility or other individual benefits, rather than as a shared resource and responsibility. Finally, chapter 3 examines documentary practices of holding agents of state power accountable for human rights violations that equate justice with criminal justice and liberatory listening with juridical listening. I ask how the jurification of audiences as arbiters of testimonial truth-claims reproduces the carceral relationships that compound anti-Black and anti-Palestinian violence and what it might mean to listen in ways that undo these relationships and disentangle justice from carceral punishment.

Listening has until recently figured in documentary debates mainly as an ethical obligation and as a metaphor for witnessing: a discourse focused on the formal strategies and activist uses of testimonial images and speech to expose wrongdoing, create awareness, and instigate action. This line of thinking was inaugurated by Shoshana Felman and Dori Laub's 1992 book, *Testimony: Crises of Witnessing in Literature, Psychoanalysis, and History*, which framed the act of listening to mediated testimonial claims as a necessary bulwark against unchecked state violence.[21] Michael Renov has argued, along these lines, that the testimonial turn in documentary cinema, journalism, and art that emerged alongside the late twentieth-century escalation of genocide, conflict, state violence, and trauma is uniquely capable of producing what Leshu Torchin calls "witnessing publics," that is, audiences who are hailed not in the Althusserian sense so much as in the Levinasian sense, as subjects who are "willing to listen" and therefore to take responsibility for the suffering of others.[22] But ethical calls to recognize the humanity of dehumanized others are, as I argued in *Immediations*, ideologically inscribed through and through. The documentary appeal to ethics over politics partakes of a particularly modern imaginary that Elaine Scarry and others have called "emergency thinking."[23] This appeal calls for a humanitarian rather than a political response, even as the urgency of that response suspends attention to documentary representations that actively define what constitutes a life worth saving and thus the contours of political imagination. In other words, documentary testimonies not only demand an ethic of receptivity or "listening in" but also cultivate what

Kate Lacey, gesturing toward something akin to Mowitt's "audit," calls attentive, anticipatory, and politicized dispositions of "listening out" that remake the world in their image.[24]

Four recent essay collections have taken up documentary's ethico-ideological hails from a sonic perspective. In 2017, Genevieve Yue and I put together a journal issue exploring how documentary forms have shaped what is recognized, politically, as "having a voice" and, concomitantly, listening publics that ratify those political meanings (Rangan and Yue, eds. "Documentary Audibilities," special issue of *Discourse*, 2017). We wished to displace the primacy of the visual in documentary studies, including the notion that sound is merely a rhetorical support to the image, employed in order to persuade audiences of the authenticity of what is being presented. Despite the prevalence of the "voice" metaphor, this intervention was limited, at the time, to one collection focusing on visual anthropology (Iversen, ed., *Beyond the Visual*, 2010) and another exploring the aesthetic specificity of music and sound in factual and realist genres such as the city film, newsreels, and indie music documentaries (Rogers, ed., *Music and Sound in Documentary Film*, 2014). "Documentary Audibilities" moves beyond this focus on cinematic subgenres to explore the destabilizing diversity of sound and vocal inflection opened up by the documentary encounter across a range of media forms and contexts of viewing and making. Contributors develop critical tools for attending to these disorienting, paralinguistic, or plurilingual sounds, amplifying, in the process, the value of documentary theory for understanding the stakes of "giving voice" across such wide-ranging media forms as collective filmmaking, experimental cinema, performance art, and data visualization (for instance, Irina Leimbacher argues that experimental filmmakers have developed strategies of noninstrumental or "haptic listening" that encourage documentary audiences to attend not only to the content of speech but also to the context and grain of the voice).[25] Two more volumes have since joined this conversation, focusing on how documentaries employ and subvert the affective potential of narrating, interviewed, or overheard voices (Honess Roe and Pramaggiore, eds., *Vocal Projections*, 2018), and the capacity of location sound recordings and compositional design to evoke feelings, which can in turn be leveraged toward various agendas, such as to promote, inform, or persuade (Cox and Corner, eds., *Soundings*, 2019).

The Documentary Audit draws on and builds out this burgeoning subfield of documentary sound and auditory culture studies. As I argue in my introduction to "Documentary Audibilities," documentary voices are not innate qualities or traits of social actors given a platform to speak out. They are *forms of audibility created by listening practices* that allow them to exist as a whisper, roar, or murmur—much as Gilles Deleuze argued, qua Foucault, that visibility is not a preexisting state or characteristic of an object that shows up under light but a form of luminosity "created by the light itself."[26] I was haunted then and remain haunted now by Trinh's insights from over thirty years ago. Like her contemporary Kaja Silverman, Trinh was ahead of her time in intuiting the role of cinematic conventions, specifically documentary conventions, in extending what the philosopher Mladen Dolar would much later name the Western metaphysical and linguistic imaginary of voice.[27] In this imaginary, also central to the documentary ethos, the speaker's voice is thought to be a guarantor of self-presence, consciousness, and truth that is compromised or disrupted by its own bodily materiality. An efflorescence of scholarship over the last two decades, dubbed the "sonic" turn in media and cultural studies—or the "auditory" turn among those who, like me, are interested in the cultural values that infuse sound and its reception—has sought to trace the metaphysical imaginary of voice across the domains of literature, radio, opera, popular music, and cinema, where the artificial distinction between a signifying, authorial voice and embodied nonreferential vocality is continually reproduced (in the form of binaries such as language v. music, human v. animal, able-bodied v. disabled, masculine v. feminine, cis v. trans, Western v. non-Western, and white v. Black) and continually challenged.

Documentary has until recently been poorly represented in these debates though it is absolutely critical to their elucidation. Documentary techniques of "giving voice," through vocal conventions such as voice-over, interview, conversation, and testimony offer crucial but overlooked insights into the mechanism whereby the second term in the binary, which is routinely framed as a deviation from the norm, is made sense of or *made audible* by the first. These techniques testify to documentary's role in the education and shaping of audition.[28] Conventions of documentary sound manifest what the xwélméxw scholar Dylan Robinson, referring to the way unmarked epistemic structures guide settler perception, calls "listening positionalities"—they model normative listening habits that powerfully screen apprehensions of what reality is and could be.[29] *Habit* refers to the largely unreflective or unconscious ways in which we each incorporate and enact the socially acquired, experientially shaped, and deeply embedded "patterns of thoughts, attitudes, practices, tastes, and preferences" that Pierre Bourdieu calls our "habitus." Lisbeth Lipari adds that each of us "habitually inhabits and performs ways of listening" (or not listening) shaped by our "listening habitus."[30]

The same is true of documentary. The voice of a documentary text ("how it is speaking to us and how it is organizing the materials it is presenting to us") performs *and* inflects socially acquired listening habits. Collectively, documentary films and media represent a valuable archive of otherwise ephemeral listening habits. Documentary techniques of organizing, marking, and discerning vocal data impart "formal and informal listening pedagogies" about the knowledge to be gleaned from voices.[31] They teach us how to listen and what to listen for. But they are equally capable of shaping counterpedagogies and counterhabits of "listening otherwise" that remain open, in Lipari's words, to what is difficult, different, or challenging to settled or verified paradigms.[32] Indeed, given its reputation for moral probity, documentary is a felicitous vehicle for teaching audiences to listen out of alignment with what Stoever calls "the listening ear."[33] We can learn to *listen with an accent*. To *listen in crip time*. To *listen like an abolitionist*. We can become accountable to the world that we deserve to inhabit—one that houses and sustains us in our dissonance, difference, and complexity.

The Documentary Audit argues, accordingly, that documentary listeners don't just receive and attend to the world; their listening practices actively filter, arrange, and build reality. But my focus departs from the predominant concerns of the documentary sound and auditory culture subfield, namely the aesthetic specificity of sound in documentary versus narrative fiction, the history of particular recording technologies such as the Nagra recorder, and the uses of sound design to move documentary audiences. I am more interested in *what documentary listeners do*. I am using *documentary* here in its adjectival form. In 2002, the documentary scholar John Corner argued that the term *documentary* is far more useful when used as an adjective than in the noun form that its early champions successfully popularized. "To ask 'is this a documentary project?' is more useful," he adds, "than to ask 'is this film a documentary?' with its inflection toward firm definitional criteria and the sense of something being more object than practice."[34] Corner's argument responded to the codification of documentary studies, the proliferation of documentary practices, and the growth of "discourses of facticity." Today, more than twenty years later, profound changes in media technologies, economies, and practices have further displaced documentary from its status as a noun, genre, and filmic object. These more conventional conceptions of documentary are now overshadowed by the use of documentary modes or forms in all aspects of public life—including medicine, legal proceedings, biometrics, advertising, warfare, and social media—as well as the commodification of documentary content in entertainment media and the art market. Corner's advocacy of the adjectival *documentary* has found new meaning under our current conditions, shifting our attention from the text to the material infrastructures, circulatory contexts, political economies, and social practices that fuel and are fueled by documentary investments.[35] Documentary listeners consolidate the material and immaterial infrastructure of social life; their activities exemplify what Josh Guilford and Toby Lee call the "world-making" capacity of documentary.[36]

My media archive accordingly follows the reverberations of the documentary audit across formal and geopolitical borders, into real and imagined courtrooms (chapter 3), the design of public infrastructures (chapter 2), and corporate communications protocols (chapter 1). Some of the contemporary and historical media I write about (feature documentaries and short films, audiovisual art installations) are documentary works in the more conventional sense, with recognizably factual aesthetic forms and modes of address shaped by the institutional contexts in which they are produced and by the exhibition spaces, viewing publics, and the networks of practitioners through which they circulate. To borrow Tess Takahashi's term, they are "marked" as documentary in that they "announce themselves as special events set apart from daily life."[37] But I also discuss "unmarked" documentary media that activate documentary expectations, attitudes of belief, and ethical comportments, even though they do not audibly or visibly announce their documentary status (such as Zoom meeting recordings, unedited cell phone videos shot during police encounters, and data visualizations used in forensic investigations), and "marked" documentary film and video works that incorporate "unmarked" documentary media as their raw materials. Like Takahashi, I am interested in the traffic between these two mutually reinforcing realms of documentary realism. In chapter 1, for instance, I discuss how instructional films produced by the British Crown's communications ministry popularized, validated, and verified the benevolent neutrality of a mode of listening that has migrated into corporate and juridical realms of communication that may not seem at first to have much to do with documentary. And in chapter 3, I consider, reciprocally, how the listening practices of Black communities gathered out of necessity in solidarity against the collective punishment of Black life exert pressure back on the verification practices of investigative agencies such as Forensic Architecture. This book is therefore addressed not only to documentary scholars or nonfiction film enthusiasts but to the far bigger audience of people who encounter, consume, produce, and recirculate "unmarked" documentary media in both professional and informal contexts. The resonances of their listening practices are more far reaching than the impact of any individual documentary film or the stylistic influence of any one auteur.

I have developed a vocabulary and method for studying documentary listening that attempts to think from a place of exteriority without resorting to what Rey Chow, my mentor and an enduring influence on my Foucauldian line of questioning, calls "transcendental guarantees."[38] As I have argued elsewhere, sound and listening do not by themselves constitute an alternative metaphysics or politics—listening can be just as effective a discriminatory practice as looking—even though the phenomenal impermanence, unboundedness, and fugitivity of sound poses a challenge to documentary claims to reality, or what Chow calls the indexical "thereness" associated with the image.[39] My close readings therefore pay attention to sound-image relations in order to outline the mechanisms whereby speech and sound are mined for their evidentiary value and to explain how documentary listenership can both reinforce and undermine visualist, object-centered epistemologies organized around measurement, certainty, and control. I think and write in fellowship with postcolonial, feminist, Black, disabled, Palestinian, and Indigenous scholars and makers of auditory and visual culture, framing their work not as any kind of ready fix for the problems of documentary realism but as cause for perpetual struggle against consensus reality. Foundational writings by documentary scholars such as Bill Nichols, Michael Renov, and Leshu Torchin and sound studies scholars such as Nina Sun Eidsheim, Lisbeth Lipari, and Mara Mills help to lay the groundwork for my discussions of documentary speech and listening, but I also engage interlocutors working in areas such as raciolinguistics, critical access studies, and forensic aesthetics in order to develop the interdisciplinary tools and methodologies needed to analyze documentary as a craft, a discourse, and a cultural form.

Beyond building bridges between documentary studies and sound studies, the book also expands the scope of scholarly subfields that I have helped develop or build out, such as interdisciplinary accent studies, disability media studies, and abolitionist visual media. Since I began writing this book, accent, disability, and carcerality have emerged from relative obscurity as significant topics in contemporary debates around listening, which remain critical to understanding how the documentary audit is involved in the adjudication of political and legal recognitions, the design of living environments, and the distribution of life chances. Accent is an understudied and rather poorly understood dimension of documentary sound. It represents the final, stubborn retreat of the tired documentary tactic whereby what is relational, comparative, and intersubjective ("an accent is happening" or "I perceive X's accent in a different way than Y does") is presented as positivist fact ("X speaks with an accent"). Leimbacher has noted, in an influential update to Trinh's 1991 essay, that conventional documentary forms invite an "acquisitive" and "inquisitive" listening desirous of knowledge and information and tend to neglect nonverbal aspects of voicing such as rhythm, intonation, accent, and gesture that are a "sonorous incarnation" of the social relations among speakers and listeners.[40] The "how" of what is said, in other words, interrupts the "what" to which documentary objectivity, with its emphasis on evidence, information, and facts, has historically laid claim.

The Anglophone documentary tradition has not neglected the embodied voice so much as it has leveraged a particular "way of speaking" (the colloquial definition of accent), specifically an "accentless" voice scrubbed of the phonological evidence of its social location, as a paragon of neutrality and as a narrational and organizing principle. The neutral coding of the commentator voice sustains a primary fantasy of documentary listening: that listeners can detect sonic facts without participating in their construction. Interdisciplinary accent studies, a field that I have worked to constitute at the nexus of raciolinguistics, auditory cultural studies, and postcolonial media studies, reveals that the documentary audit is never neutral: it functions as a "coloring ear" that marks, accentuates, and orders voices not just racially but in terms of social class, region, ethnicity, and other axes of difference.[41] But the accented stylings of documentary also yield a variety of critical tools that can be used to combat the weaponization of neutral listening against accented speakers in corporate and bureaucratic scenarios that range from the subtly coercive (call centers) to the overtly violent (border security and detention).

Just like the unseen "accentless" commentator, the hearing and seeing audience is another unannounced norm of the documentary audit. The axiom "show don't tell," which entered the documentary vocabulary alongside the vérité turn in the 1960s, valorized the purity of the film text as an aesthetic experience degraded by linguistic or sensory access features such as subtitles or captions. This was also a moment when the concept of documentary value crystallized around a transactional and extractive interpretation of "access" that conceives of documentary subjects as both legal liabilities and resources to be mined. Recently, access has emerged as the linchpin of a cultural shift driven by a vanguard of committed filmmakers of color fighting a corporate culture of predatory filmmaking that ransacks marginalized communities for stories.[42] "Accountability," an update to the older, more paternalistic concept of "responsibility" that emphasizes mutual respect, trust, and abiding commitment to the communities in question, is upheld in these conversations as a counterweight to the prevailing discourse of access as transaction or theft.[43]

The access activism of disability justice practitioners is a crucial but understudied precursor of these conversations. Crip-of-color makers, scholars, and activists have theorized access as a practice of collective care in ways that explode its litigious interpretation by documentarians as permission to enter, move within, and record people's everyday private environments. Access understood in this crip sense, as a *shared* resource, responsibility, and risk, functions as both a diagnostic and propositional tool when it comes to the acquisitive impulse of conventional documentary listening. To "crip" access is to understand how the conventional approach to access accommodations as an inconvenient afterthought takes a disproportionate toll on communities of color and disabled, poor, and immigrant people, shaping an experience of time characterized by waiting, setbacks, detours, and nonstarters—or what Ellen Samuels, following Alison Kafer, has elaborated as "crip time."[44] Treating access as a building block of narrative form offers new ways to see and listen through the camera. Crip time reorients the documentary audit away from the propertied logics of contracts, liability, and risk management and fosters a social vision grounded in the more difficult—but ultimately more rewarding—collective work of care and interdependence.

The exclusionary social relations maintained by documentary listening habits become all the harder to pry apart when the habits in question are predominantly understood as just and righteous. This is especially true of juridical listening, or the practice of "bearing witness" to testimonial claims in pursuit of oppressed truths—and by implication, in judgment of criminal wrongdoing—that was installed as the ethical bedrock of the documentary tradition following the Nuremberg trials. Over the last forty years, critical decades in the consolidation of documentary media that hail audiences as jurors deliberating on audiovisual evidence of human rights violations, unprecedented numbers of Black and brown people have also been forced into carceral and custodial systems, whether through imprisonment, detention, asylum, or other forms of humanitarian supervision. The coincidence of these phenomena demands that we investigate how the underlying assumptions of juridical listening—the adversarial dynamic of the legal trial, the politics of state-driven recognition, the evidentiary logic of forensic truth-claims, and the punitive interpretation of justice—have been accomplice to the proliferation of "carceral enclosures," understood as a discursive container both for physical spaces of containment and the representational logics and practices that sustain them.[45]

Approaching these bedrock assumptions from the perspective of those whose unfreedom is the basis of the freedoms of others allows us to reexamine the carceral complicities of documentary listening and, indeed, the very concept of human rights from an abolitionist perspective. Abolition, understood as a broad coalitional liberation movement that is anchored in the radical Black feminist tradition and invested in decolonial freedom struggles, offers a useful reorientation of the testimonial turn in documentary accountability. Documentary activists engaged with Palestinian and Black testimonies of anti-Palestinian and anti-Black violence contribute an abolitionist political and formal vocabulary of witnessing that, to invoke Tina Campt, refuses authoritative forms of visuality and audibility that are premised on their negation, in pursuit of transformative modes of justice that do not rely on the criminal legal system or create more violence.[46] If carcerality functions as a set of social and spatial relationships that structure and condition a variety of harms, only some of which are deemed "crimes," then remaking these relations, they show, requires documentary audiences to attend to fugitive modalities of evidence that appeal not to the state but to an abolitionist forum.

The chapters of this book are sequenced so that the reader's sense of the documentary audit builds in complexity as the book unfolds. Chapter 1, "Listening with an Accent," addresses documentary's role in supporting neutral listening habits that justify linguistic profiling and discrimination and its capacity to train audiences to listen with an accent—that is, to develop an awareness regarding one's listening vantage and the asymmetrical relational exchange among accented speaker and listeners that I call "accented interlistening." The objective listening vantage characteristic of the documentary audit emerged in the first sound documentaries sponsored by the General Post Office unit of the British Crown as part of an imperialist project of laying the infrastructure for modern telecommunications media. Pioneers of the "neutral" commentator voice, these films trained listeners to audit a hierarchy of accents from an abstract and ungrounded listening vantage, cultivating habits of neutral listening that resound well into the present. Contemporary corporate and juridical practices of monitoring and monetizing accent such as call center offshoring and asylum screening leverage the myths of "neutral accent" and "neutral listening" to relegate entire groups of people to the status of a linguistic underclass, with debilitating consequences, on the basis of how they are perceived to speak. But it is possible, I argue, as illustrated by documentarians working in these sites, to work against these habits to practice an *accented interlistening* that makes space for difference without denigrating it or subsuming it into sameness.

The GPO's lesser-known early films, including those considered "mere" PR spots or "primitive" cinematic experiments (including the musical comedy *Fairy of the Phone*, drama docs *Mony a Pickle* and *The Saving of Bill Blewitt*, and process films such as *6:30 Collection* and *Cable Ship*) offer fascinating evidence of how nascent documentary idioms, in conjunction with emerging telecommunications technologies, functioned as raciolinguistic pedagogies. My analyses of these films, informed by recently released materials from the British Film Institute and historical and contemporary analyses of their technological and linguistic milieus (education, elocution, print, radio, telephone) illustrate how the GPO films' accentuating style of marking regionally, ethnically, or socially coded speech taught audiences to locate their own verbal styles and those of others within a taxonomy of accents whose social status, desirability, and achievability were indicated by their audiovisual location and narrative function. I then turn to Sonali Gulati's *Nalini by Day, Nancy by Night* (2005) and Lawrence Abu Hamdan's *The Freedom of Speech Itself* (2012), drawing on ethnographies of business process outsourcing and border forensics to examine how the documentary audit has helped shape the corporate myth of the neutral accent exploited by call centers and the juridical myth of forensic listening mobilized in the linguistic profiling of asylum seekers. Gulati and Abu Hamdan work with and against obdurate documentary listening habits to cultivate in their audiences a mindfulness of the place from which one has been taught to listen and a willingness to listen otherwise, with an accent.

Where chapter 1 frames accented interlistening as a central tenet of documentary practices that acknowledge and valorize minoritarian epistemologies, chapter 2, "Listening in Crip Time," introduces "access intimacy" (a disability-informed practice of anticipating what others need in order to participate in society) as foundational to a transformative crip-of-color critique of documentary listening.[47] The chapter asks how ableism conditions documentary listening and outlines the transformative shift in values that documentarians can facilitate by listening in solidarity with the out-of-sync experiences of linear time and normative life stages that critical disability scholars have called "crip time." Access has been a keyword in documentary since the 1960s, but documentary discussions about access rarely acknowledge the role of disability activists in shaking up its meanings, norms, and possibilities. I amplify two episodes of that history, each of which illustrates a crip mode of documentary listening that reimagines basic assumptions about providing access, being in community, and negotiating consent. The first reveals how Aoi Shiba no Kai, an activist movement of people with mobility and speech disabilities in Japan, inspired Kobayashi Sachiko and Hara Kazuo to develop a crip documentary aesthetic of withholding access that forces listeners unaccustomed to disability-affected speech to listen, uncomfortably, in the mode of *crawling* rather than in the entitled "staring" mode that is often a default of documentary listening. The second examines efforts by contemporary American crip, queer, and crip-of-color film and video artists who recenter sensory access features such as captions and audio description as building blocks of documentary form, inviting what I call a *sideways listening* receptive to how access intimacy swells documentary meanings and horizons.

The two films that anchor this chapter, Hara and Kobayashi's first film, *Goodbye CP* (1972), and Jordan Lord's *Shared Resources* (2021), are not accessible to most audiences in their intended form. I amplify their commitments to redistributing access in an ableist mediascape by documenting their listening modes. My revisionist account of *Goodbye CP* situates it in the twinned contexts of the disability movement and emerging intersubjective and collaborative documentary approaches in Japan. Pulling from disability scholarship, film criticism, and autoethnographic accounts of film screenings, I reveal how the confrontational and intrusive aesthetic of wrested access attributed to Hara's filmmaking (reflected here in his refusal to subtitle disability-affected speech, which forces normate listeners to listen in acknowledgment of the asymmetry of access) was influenced by his disabled collaborators' protests against inaccessible public transport and segregated facilities. I situate Lord's embrace of open captions and audio description as an ethical and aesthetic principle as an inheritor of Kobayashi and Hara's crip documentary countertradition. I draw on conflicting accounts of access from film historians and disability justice activists to show how Lord repudiates the ableist disregard of sensory and linguistic access as burdensome additions that corrupt cinematic experience. By enlisting their disabled father's caregivers as audio describers, Lord offers access to a different dimension of the film than what unfurls in the foreground, transporting the listener through the detours that are a defining part of disability experience.

Chapter 3, "Listening Like an Abolitionist," pulls back to reexamine the post-Holocaust, trauma-informed discourse of witnessing that has fueled the jurification of documentary audiences as adjudicators of state and corporate crimes. I ask what it might mean, instead, to frame the documentary audit as a site of abolitionist struggle against the carceral state. Using the distinction that prison-abolitionist scholar-activists draw between reformist and nonreformist reforms (or reforms that tighten carceral dragnets and those that unravel them) as a heuristic, I parse two intertwined appeals to documentary listeners as arbiters of public truth that I see at work in an established mode of documentary accountability epitomized by the rise of watchdog media organizations such as B'Tselem (founded 1989) and WITNESS (1992) and, more recently, of research agencies such as Forensic Architecture (2010) that investigate and present proof of human rights violations on behalf of activists, NGOs, or victims of state and environmental violence in legal and public forums. I call these appeals *listening like a cop* and *listening like an abolitionist*. The chapter is structured around two projects that confront the political failures and betrayals of juridical listening in contexts where the law is founded on the violent negation of Palestinian and Black lives, respectively: first, the activist filmmaker Ra'anan Alexandrowicz's cinematic reckoning with Zionist repudiations of B'Tselem's efforts to document and expose violence against Palestinians residents by Israeli settlers and security forces in the occupied West Bank and, second, Forensic Architecture's collaboration with South Chicago–based media organization the Invisible Institute (henceforth FA and II) to investigate the killing of a Black man, Harith Augustus, by a white police officer in South Chicago.

In attending to the distinctive refusals of carceral justice animating these projects, this chapter teases out a minor strain of listening that constitutes an abolitionist documentary method and forum (recalling the Latin root of *forensics*, which refers to the art of public persuasion and debate). Alexandrowicz's *The Viewing Booth* (2019) is a tribunal on the efficacy of video documentation in nonviolent anti-occupation struggles in an era of disinformation and conflicting truth-claims. A meditation on a single viewer's skeptical response to Palestinian happenstance videos shot in the midst of IDF home raids and confrontations with settlers in Hebron, Alexandrowicz's film doubles as a portrait of his own nonadversarial listening, which unsettles both his interlocutor's defensive listening *and* the prosecutorial impulse of human rights witnessing in its refusal of the fiction of justice under apartheid law. FA and the II's investigation, *The Killing of Harith Augustus*, stages a reckoning with forensic forms of authority, knowledge, and display and the stakes of importing counterforensic strategies honed in the context of Israel's occupation of Palestine into the U.S. context, where forensics has distinctly racialized meanings and implications. FA's reformist appeal to audiences as a suspicious "neighborhood watch" listening for evidence of aberrant policing sits in tension with their efforts, in collaboration with II, to effect a transformative shift in how they ask audiences to listen, by seeking out and making audible what LaCharles Ward, describing testimonial evidence grounded in the daily experience of Black people, calls "Black evidence."[48] The final video of their six-video investigation hails listeners committed to looking out for Black life not as police or jurors but as members of an outlaw community of care.

The sound artist and scholar Lawrence Abu Hamdan writes, regarding an audio project that I discuss in chapter 1, that an accent is "a biography of migration, an irregular and itinerant concoction of contagiously accumulated voices."[49] I have often returned to this phrase, marveling at how it captures the commitments that have charted my course in this book. It is also a wonderful expression, in its evocation of irregularity, itinerance, contagion, and accumulation, of politics founded not in stable identity categories but in difficult and necessarily fraught practices of complicity, coalition, and solidarity. The projects that yield the insights and methods of this book are grounded in solidarity politics. Solidarity offers a more capacious and radical political model for documentary than empathy, which pivots on singular stories and individual voices, because solidarity, as my frequent collaborator, the filmmaker and prison abolitionist Brett Story puts it, "takes as its prerequisite not just recognition of oneself in another self, but a view, however achieved, onto shared conditions and common cause."[50] My appreciation for this view has accumulated over several multiyear collaborations and conversations: a research and pedagogy project with Ragini Tharoor Srinivasan, Akshya

Saxena, and Pavitra Sundar that included a conference, collaboratively developed syllabi, and an anthology, *Thinking with an Accent*; an extended residency that allowed me to workshop my research on documentary and disability in community with resident scholars at NYU's Center for Disability Studies, including its cofounders, Mara Mills and Faye Ginsburg, my fellow visitors Laura Mauldin, Alexis Mitchell, and Yan Grenier, and my trusted interlocutor, Neta Alexander; and a coauthored book on abolitionist documentary with Story, which helped me to develop this book's final chapter over the course of an ongoing exchange with Laliv Melamed, Ra'anan Alexandrowicz, and Vinzenz Hediger around the collapse of public trust in documentary. These exchanges, especially with Melamed, have profoundly shaped my thinking around documentary listening and convinced me that there can be no accent justice (the initial impulse for this project) without disability justice and decarceral justice, both broad-based movements whose ambitions are not limited to any one interest group. The chapters of this book are bound by my effort to develop a coalitional politics of documentary listening that dispenses with the preconceptions of listening *for* or listening *to* in favor of listening *with*, listening *in*, and listening *like*. Each of these prepositions communicates a disposition of humility and the likelihood that the positionality from which one listens is partial, incomplete, and flawed, and that the activity of listening is subtended by an oblivion only revealed in the company of others.

1

LISTENING WITH AN ACCENT

The Myth of Neutral Listening

In September 2020, a white university professor's "fake accent" was trending on social media. Jessica Krug, a Jewish, suburban Kansas-born history professor at George Washington University, revealed, to widespread condemnation, that she had falsely claimed a range of immigrant and working-class Black ethnic identities throughout her academic career. Many pointed to a Zoom recording of Krug speaking at a New York City Council hearing in an unconvincing approximation of a Black Boriqua accent as conclusive if belated evidence of her deception (see fig. 1.1).[1] YouTube commenters have since panned Krug's accent ("fake"; "awful"; "horrible"; "inconsistent"; "drifting"), comparing it to media caricatures ("Dee playing Martina Martinez in Always Sunny"; "like Prison Mike on the Office") and pointing out her "tells" ("she ain't got no lips"; "I am hearing mid-west Kansas flat nasally 'a'"; "the accent drops on certain words"; "the NY accent is unmistakable"). One commenter, identifying herself as Afro-Borinqueña from the Bronx, says she is "thoroughly offended that anyone believed this perpetrator was who she claimed to be."[2]

Responses such as these offer less evidence of Krug's made-up accent than of a listening habit that is exceedingly common but rarely acknowledged in documentary circles. *Neutral listening* inhabits an

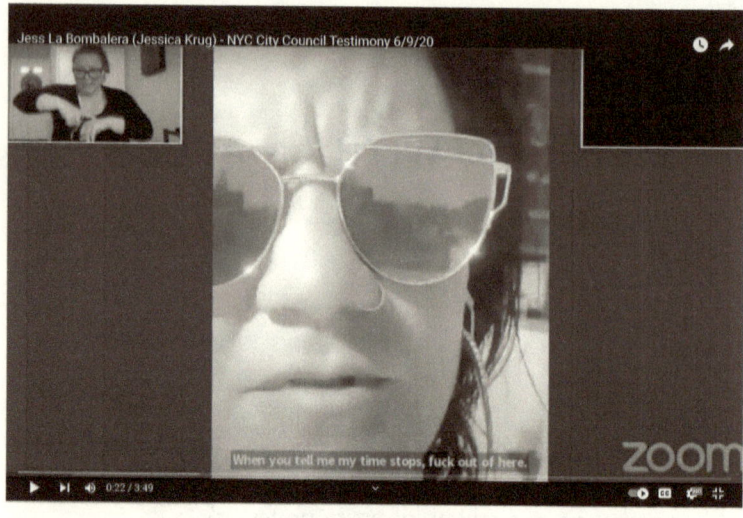

FIGURE 1.1 Screenshot of Jessica Krug offering testimony over Zoom as "Jess La Bombalera."

abstract and ungrounded listening vantage—an auditory nonplace that I will frame as the locus of the documentary audit. This chapter traces the emergence of this listening habit and its powerful resonances. Conventional documentary forms unwittingly model the act of auditing (detecting, verifying, naming, marking, and classifying) accented speech and thereby invite audiences to listen *for* an accent (as in, "she has a foreign/Indian/fake/thick/posh accent"). Neutral listening conjures the fantasy of an ear that is nowhere and everywhere: a projection or ideal of an abstract listening vantage that is formed and sustained out of the autonomous activity of listening.[3] The practice of auditing accented speech, or *listening for an accent*, sustains this fantasy of an autonomous, "neutral" listening body that can detect an accent without participating in its construction. Makers and consumers of all kinds of documentary media, from feature films to cell phone videos, routinely and casually audit accented speech (including their own), holding what they hear at a remove, as did those who viewed and commented on Krug's teleconference recording.

This chapter excavates the role of documentary forms in supporting as well as dispelling the myth of neutral listening. I trace the imperial origins of this listening habit in educational and promotional films that introduced documentary conventions for auditing accented speech in the process of familiarizing audiences with telecommunications infrastructures operated by the British Crown. I then turn to the postcolonial afterlives of these listening conventions in corporate and juridical telecommunications that are not explicitly "marked" as documentary but that nonetheless activate what I call the documentary audit. Along the way, I analyze works by documentary artists that amplify and confront the implications of this listening vantage, even as they are complicit in its construction. In so doing, I argue that documentary forms have taught listeners to audit a hierarchy of accents, but they are also being tactically harnessed to interrupt auditory discrimination—to train audiences to listen *with*, as opposed to *for*, an accent.[4] The delusion that listening can be accent-neutral is more commonplace than Krug's deception and more insidiously effective in entrenching social hierarchies based on race and class. These delusions are borne out in the assumptions made by Krug's adjudicators regarding accented speech, which I will dismantle over the course of this chapter:

1. An accent is something one "has" or possesses, as opposed to something that happens between people.
2. Only some people have an accent because accents emerge from the speaker, as opposed to the listener.
3. "Genuine" (consistent, truthful, authentic) accents can be told apart from "fake" (inconsistent, drifting, false, appropriated) accents, and the distinctions between the two are objective rather than deeply subjective and stark instead of muddy.

These assumptions, rooted in a powerful belief that the human voice is essential or innate rather than enculturated, dialogical, and evolving, shape a somewhat contradictory attitude to testimonial speech that is evident in the Zoom video's reception.[5] Krug's commenters are made aware of the performative context of her testimony, which was delivered, as Krug complains, to an audience dominated by white speakers. But they still judge Krug's accent for being disingenuous, and this judgment is predicated on the documentary frame, which allows them to forget their own listening. Like Zoom's default "active speaker view" setting, which frames the speaker and minimizes the presence of listeners, those who watched Krug on video also edited out the fact of their own listening by default, as well as the mediating presence of listeners (barring the ASL interpreter, who is primarily perceived by hearing audiences as a performer rather than a listener-speaker) participating in the public hearing.

In these ways, then, Krug's audience exhibits a *documentary comportment*: an unconscious set of assumptions and expectations that shapes their sense that a film or video is about reality, about real people, and that it will tell stories about what actually happened.[6] Their disavowal of their own status as an audience shapes their expectation that Krug will both represent herself truthfully and "act naturally," that is, conduct herself without self-consciousness about the presence of the camera and, by implication, an audience. As a general rule, documentary audiences rely on formal and contextual cues that signal to them what mode of performance they are witnessing—one that acknowledges or does not acknowledge the camera—and therefore the expectations they should bring to it.[7] Krug's performance reveals something about the expectations that are applied to testimonial speech in contexts that are not explicitly marked as presentational or *for* an audience: that it should sound natural and not phony, stagey, or untrue, especially in a way that reminds audiences of their own audition.[8] I would even wager—though this claim exceeds the proof that this chapter can provide—that although documentary audiences have come to expect a certain reflexivity from documentary images, whose claims to authenticity have steadily eroded under the pressure of a half century of critiques of objectivity, as a general rule, they do not enjoy being reminded of their own audition. Krug's "bad" accent breaks this rule. It brings forth suppressed anxieties regarding the artifactuality of accents even under circumstances that do not appear to be mediated.

Accents may seem to originate in the speaker, but they are, in fact, a product of listening. Linguists regard accent as a geographically and socially grounded manner of speaking. In Rosina Lippi-Green's much-cited definition, *accent* is a phonological index of identity or the sonic evidence of the speaker's social or linguistic history that lingers in their "way of speaking."[9] This would suggest that there is no such thing as a voice without an accent, but in colloquial exchange, not all speakers are considered accented. As Nina Sun Eidsheim has observed, "Only some accents are *accented* in their reception, to invoke an alternate meaning of accent: *emphasized*. Within a broader linguistic context, *accent* is defined as a 'distinct mode of pronouncing a language'; it is therefore something every speaker displays. But the colloquial use of the word suggests that only some speak *with an accent*, and some even with a *strong accent*. In other words, not all accents are accented. The assessment that accentuates some accents is added in the process of listening."[10] What is identified, often pejoratively, as the accented voice of the other always emerges through relations of perception and, specifically, as the result of an *accentuating* mode of assessment—what Eidsheim calls "accented listening," or a listening that accents.[11] Both listeners whose speaking styles have been sonically coded as "standard" and those whose voices have been marked in advance as "accented" speak *and* listen (or "interlisten," to borrow a term from the critical listening studies scholar Lisbeth Lipari) from an embodied and situated locus that colors and genders—and by implication, narrows and inflects—their expression and perception.[12] Lipari, building on the work of Pierre Bourdieu, writes that this embodied locus is thickened by the accumulated cultural, social, and personal experiences that shape the place from which each of us listens, or what she calls a "listening habitus."[13] The act of performing an audit or a self-audit makes the listener believe that they can distance themselves from their listening habitus and inhabit a neutral listening position. Just like speaking, listening is also accented, and the process of listening is shaped by a lifelong accretion of accented speaking-listening-interpreting practices, or what I, building on Lipari's work, term "accented interlistening."[14] The very notion that a listener can code and parse what they hear as a taxonomy of accents disavows the fact of accented interlistening.

Documentary accents are also the product of a prior listening. The "voice" of a documentary—Bill Nichols's term for the rhetorically diverse ways in which every documentary film conveys its distinct social point of view—inevitably involves transactions of authority among accented voices, which is to say, geographically and socially grounded speaking voices.[15] To extend Nichols's metaphor, every documentary film speaks with an accent, and that speaking position also represents an accented listening positionality. Consequently, documentary forms obfuscate their potentially transformative role, and that of the audience, in the negotiations of power involved in accented interlistening when they neutralize the role of accent in the way they speak and represent the voices of others. Not all of these negotiations are well understood or represented in documentary scholarship. For instance, it is by now well established that the conventions of documentary sound reinforce the listening habit that Michel Chion calls "vococentrism," or the attunement to a speaking voice as the apex of a soundscape, and that voices that address audiences directly tend to command authority over indirect and overheard voices, usually in that order.[16] Less well understood, however, is how documentary filmmakers construct hierarchies of accent when they represent socially grounded speech using vocal conventions such as expository narration, the filmed interview, or the observed conversation. Here, theory lags behind practice.

LISTENING WITH AN ACCENT   33

This chapter explores the role that documentary forms and practices play in standardizing accented modes of speaking and listening. My purview therefore differs from Hamid Naficy's account of an "accented cinema," which employs "accent" as a metaphor for the textual and stylistic features of mainly fictional and narrative films produced under conditions of linguistic and geographic displacement.[17] I am concerned, rather, with how the documentary canon has developed and lent credence to a whole arsenal of techniques for marking or accentuating the difference of certain accents (those of speakers marshaled as evidence) and masking or neutralizing the particularity of others (those of listeners who report on the sayings of other). I show how these techniques have been absorbed into corporate and bureaucratic screening operations—especially those involved in training people or machines—that activate the documentary audit even though they do not announce their formal status as documentary. In the following section, I show how some of the first sound documentaries sponsored by the British Crown pioneered techniques of accentuation and accent neutralization as part of an imperialist project of laying the infrastructure for modern telecommunications media. During the 1930s, films produced by the General Post Office (GPO) for the purpose of marketing its national postal, telephone, and telegraph services introduced speaking and listening conventions that have since become the common tongue of Anglophone documentary: namely, "neutral" or "accentless" commentary and an audiovisual hierarchy of regional and ethnic accents (or what Eidsheim terms "accented accents"). I illustrate, through a brief survey of key films, how these conventions constructed the "placeless" listening vantage that I call the locus of the documentary audit. I frame the formal system developed in these films as a quasi-institutionalized practice of accent training that has become a banal, even unremarkable aspect of the documentary lexicon. In its invitation to audiences, regardless of their own situated embodiment, to "place" their own speaking styles and those of others within a precoded taxonomy of accents, this system enacts what linguists call a raciolinguistic pedagogy—a pedagogy that uses language to normalize racism.

The documentary audit formed in the GPO's early films continues to resonate today in corporate and bureaucratic telecommunications procedures that leverage socially normalized forms of accentism, or discriminatory attitudes toward nonstandard and nonnative modes of speaking, writing, and communication, especially those of plurilingual postcolonial subjects. The last twenty years, key decades in an era shaped by "Anglobalization," forced migration, and diaspora, have witnessed the rise of significant industries, including offshore call centers and asylum screening, that traffic in projects of accent detection, modification, commodification, and evaluation. Perhaps unsurprisingly, documentarians interested in the human rights implications of accent monitoring and monetization have been drawn to sites such as transnational call centers, whose workers are often required to undergo "accent neutralization" in order to make telemarketing calls or assist overseas customers with online transactions. Others have turned their attention to the forensic accent-screening procedures employed by border control authorities or subcontracted private firms in the UK, Australia, Canada, and a number of EU member states in order to determine the nationality of undocumented or "suspicious" asylum seekers and therefore the legitimacy of their asylum claims.

I have chosen to focus on two of these works, by Sonali Gulati and Lawrence Abu Hamdan, because their symptomatic yet revelatory uses of documentary conventions peel back neutral listening habits that might otherwise remain imperceptible—habits that documentary traditions have helped to justify and that documentarians may yet help to undo. Gulati's short film *Nalini by Day, Nancy by Night* (2005) and Abu Hamdan's audio documentary *The Freedom of Speech Itself* (2012) explore, respectively, remote exchanges among New Delhi–based call center agents and their American clients, and forensic speech analysts located mainly in Sweden and asylum seekers fleeing settler violence and conflict in Palestine and Syria. Moreover, each work represents a larger genre or oeuvre. Gulati's is one of several call-center documentaries from the early 2000s that investigate the then-nascent business process outsourcing (BPO) industry in India. Abu Hamdan, an audio-based artist and researcher, has produced a number of essays, videos, and artworks on the linguistic profiling of asylum seekers via forensic accent analysis.

My analysis of these works brings critical vocabularies from the adjacent interdisciplines of raciolinguistics, forensic aesthetics, and postcolonial sound studies—a necessity for studying such a disciplinarily restless concept as accent—into the documentary fold. My purpose in doing so is twofold: First, through my focus on documentary listening, I demonstrate how documentary studies can be a valuable interlocutor for accent studies. An interdisciplinary field that I have helped to constitute, accent studies respecifies accent as an *object* of inquiry, enabling us to understand accent not just as an utterance but also as a perceptual and interpretive mode; as a *method* of analysis that does not listen "for" so much as "with" an accent, to paraphrase and slightly alter the emphasis of Trinh T. Minh-ha's decolonial attitude of "speaking nearby"; and as a *practice* that embraces accent as a minoritarian skill and expertise rather than a stigmatized identity.[18] Second, I view this chapter as a methodological illustration of what it means to engage in accented thought as a documentary scholar. To think with an accent is to affirm ways of knowing rooted in linguistic experiences of migration, exile, and displacement.[19] It is to practice a labile mode of scholarship that moves, as my coauthors and I have written in a book introducing this method, across "media forms, cultural industries, interpretive practices, disciplinary frameworks, and scales of analyses."[20] The elusiveness of accented listening habits to any single mode of knowing demands a research approach that attends at once to documentary infrastructures, bureaucracies, representations, and operations. These are the twinned tenets of *listening with an accent*.

THE ORIGINS OF THE DOCUMENTARY AUDIT

The cinematic output of the General Post Office film unit (1933–1940) has been canonized largely for its modernist contributions to documentary sound. Produced by John Grierson and his more avant-garde-inclined successor Alberto Cavalcanti with the unit's first mobile sound-recording equipment, films such as *Coal Face* (1935) and *Night Mail* (1936) wove lyrical soundtracks from the mechanical and social rhythms of technological modernity.[21] But the GPO film unit also produced a number of less well-regarded promotional films whose experiments with still-emerging documentary conventions and idioms might have fallen outside Grierson's own high-minded definition of documentary films as being intentionally authored, altruistic, and socially concerned.[22] These films—among the first to acquaint Anglophone audiences with the vocal conventions that have since come to define documentary, including voiceover commentary, recorded speech, and overheard conversations—are worth revisiting for their role in consolidating the documentary audit with institutionally ratified raciolinguistic norms.

Audit as noun and verb offers a useful way of thinking about the listening vantage offered by documentary films. As discussed in the introduction, the word has two common colloquial uses: In its noun form, an *audit* refers to "rituals of verification" that originated in the medieval practice of checking financial accounts by reading ledger entries out loud but which now function more generally to describe forms of administrative oversight, evaluation, or measurement, especially those undertaken internally, to ensure public trust in governmental or corporate institutions;[23] in its verb form, *auditing* refers to an informal mode of attendance in a college course in which the student is responsible for their own learning. Both meanings imply audition and audience, terms with which *audit* shares its etymology; together, they indicate how listening can function as a means of monitoring others as well as oneself. Taking into account its twinned implications of oversight and discipline, the sound studies scholar John Mowitt defines *audit* (noun) as an analog of "gaze" in the sonic domain: a term that roughly designates "that which exceeds and conditions hearing and organizes the field of the audible."²⁴ Mowitt further describes audit as a "hearing," or a mode of perception that has a primordial tie with aesthetics, or "the distribution of the sensible."²⁵ Here, Mowitt means that aesthetic forms introduce thoroughly ideological, though sometimes unconscious, perceptual distinctions, hierarchies, or distributions into the conceptual domain of sound. These learned perceptual distinctions can assume the status of neutrality, conditioning as universal listening habits those which are socially grounded and culturally particular. Mowitt also cautions that hearing does not operate in the same manner as vision; we cannot speak of a "point of audition" as we might speak of a point of view because sound cannot be "framed" in the manner of an object. One of the signal achievements of the documentary tradition has been its construction of precisely such a phantasmatic listening vantage—a hearing or mode of perception, in Mowitt's words—one from which sonic events can be represented and regarded with a perceived sense of objective detachment.

The GPO unit's early films offer a glimpse into the construction of such an objective or neutral listening vantage as the locus of the documentary audit. In the interwar period, before its nation-building capacities were reharnessed by the war effort, the GPO, Britain's largest employer at the time, and a leader in establishing the infrastructure for modern telecommunications, was also in the business of producing films that sought to reunite the nation by teaching audiences how to speak and listen "correctly." Grierson ran the unit he founded as an informal film school. He consolidated documentary's educational value by marketing GPO films to schools, community groups, trade unions, political parties, and cooperative movements (to the tune of up to five million viewers annually, per some reports); these remained key demographics even after he left the GPO in 1937.²⁶ Some of these films explicitly address the protocols and etiquette of the telephone, telegraph, and postal services. Others communicate the opportunities for social mobility afforded by these new technologies of self-presentation and address. Taken as a group, they offer fascinating evidence of how nascent documentary idioms intersected with emerging technologies central to modern urban planning to make a large, complex, and irregular population—one that was still recovering from war devastation and displacement—graspable from a synoptic vantage.²⁷

The GPO films, of which only a handful have been taken seriously following the antirealist turn in documentary studies in the 1970s, are overdue consideration for their role in honing an audiovisual vernacular that we might regard as "the standard documentary accent."²⁸ The British Film Institute (BFI), responsible for much of what has been preserved, archived, and published about this period, describes many GPO films as having little significance or impact other than as PR spots for the GPO or fledgling experiments with the cinematic idioms of comedy, fantasy, musical, animation, and actuality prior to their industrial segregation. *Night Mail*'s relative formal ambition, we are told, outshines other commentary-driven Griersonian process films ("two-reelers") describing the mechanisms and services of the Post Office, including *Cable Ship* (1933), *Air Post* (1934), and *6:30 Collection* (1934).²⁹ Comic caper *Pett and Pott* (1934) and musical fantasy *The Fairy of the Phone* (1936) are deemed oddball attempts to connect with the public, and Cavalcanti's "drama documentaries," *The Saving of Bill Blewitt* (1936), *A Job in a Million* (1937), and *Mony a Pickle* (1938), are considered less accomplished precursors of the unit's most commercially successful merger of real locales, nonprofessional actors, and narrative scripting than *The North Sea* (1938).

These seemingly trifling films take on a more complex set of meanings if we approach them as efforts by a cohort of white filmmakers (mostly middle-class, Cambridge-educated men) to represent ethnic minorities (Scots, Sinhalese) and working-class people (coalminers, fishermen, postmen, slum-dwellers, shipbuilders) whose voices were seldom featured in mainstream fiction cinema at the time except as humorous punchlines.[30] These encounters coalesce in vocal idioms that function as informal public pedagogical exercises in neutral listening from a surveillant perspective that allows the auditor to survey, observe, and evaluate accents as objective social facts. Accent is an understudied linchpin of these vocal idioms, which resolve the encounter of working-class people with media infrastructures by arranging a diverse range of colloquialisms in a taxonomical array. We can see in them the emergence of an audit that turns unruly and illegible languaging practices into measurable social facts that can be described, compared, and aggregated. These early sound documentaries modeled ways of auditing socially validated accent hierarchies; they standardized vocal conventions whose impacts continue to reverberate, as the remainder of this chapter will show, well into the postcolonial present.

As a producer and distributor of educational films, the GPO film unit joined the modern industries of education, elocution, print, and radio in circulating and exporting a supralocal accent as a national-imperial norm and ideal. This geographically "placeless" accent, referred to by contemporary linguists as Received Pronunciation (RP), was employed as the phonetic basis of instruction in elite English universities and publicized through elocution manuals. By the late nineteenth century, RP was synonymous with upward class mobility. Modes of pronunciation that effaced the geographic origins of the speaker came to be associated with "good breeding"; conversely, the presence of an "accent," or the undesirable presence in speech of regional or social marking, indicated "inferior breeding or upbringing."[31] Other enregistered forms (speech varieties regarding whose social meanings there is cultural awareness among a given population), including dialects such as Cockney and Scots that indicate the speaker's region or class identity, and what linguists call an "L2" accent (the audible presence of native language phonology in English) were deemed deviations or distortions of an accepted norm requiring the mediation of an "accentless" interpreter class.[32]

RP is also colloquially known as "BBC English." RP's canonization as the voice of the British Broadcasting Corporation was, as Tom McEnany notes, a marriage of social and technological standards, namely the Oxbridge voice (Cambridge and Oxford graduates trained in RP dominated the BBC's national and international broadcasting from the early to mid-1930s) and the radio voice (the technical requirements of early sound reproduction mandated a neutral or "pure" voice devoid of spatial resonance to minimize distortions that would interfere with its "presence").[33] RP/BBC English served as an important medium of British imperialism both in the colonies and across the metropole. Its idealization as accentless is a classic example of what Jonathan Rosa and Nelson Flores call a "raciolinguistic ideology": a mode of representation that constructs an ethnic, racial, or social underclass as linguistically deviant or deficient in comparison with a privileged class whose vocal standards and speaking practices (for instance, scrubbing the regional or social "tells" from one's speech patterns) are upheld as a normative benchmark against which those of others are measured.[34] Steeped in European colonialist attitudes regarding the racial inferiority of colonized people and their language practices, these ideologies represent and reproduce a racialized mode of perception that has historically been embodied and modeled by white listening subjects.[35] The BBC's imagined audience, both within Britain and overseas, was similarly monolithic, despite its actual geographic and linguistic heterogeneity.[36]

Stuart Legg's *BBC: The Voice of Britain* (1935) is perhaps the most overt example of the GPO's contributions to "raising social standards [through] speech standards," to quote the BBC's explicit goal in institutionalizing national radio broadcasting in 1923.[37] A sweeping survey of the BBC's headquarters, staff, performers, programs, and star broadcasters, the film (purportedly the unit's most expensive) is a veritable endorsement of what Frances Dyson calls the "radio voice": factual, informative, newsworthy speech whose clarity, articulateness, and eloquence (from professional training and studio recording) emanates as though unencumbered by the body, from the mind's chamber itself.[38] If this agenda did not line up with the GPO's in principle, it did in practice. GPO filmmakers (see fig. 1.2), in fact, hoped to avoid the commercial and elite associations of professional commentary in pursuit of the "intimacy and authenticity" that Grierson associated with the unalienated idioms, accents, and colloquialisms of workers.[39] But this pursuit was frequently thwarted, sometimes by sponsors concerned with the practicality of reaching multiple audiences (for instance, Gaumont-British Instructional, the theatrical distributor of Paul Rotha's 1935 film *Shipyard* replaced commentary voiced by a shipbuilder from the Cumbrian town of Barrow with narration by the in-house newsreader E. V. H. Emmett) and at other times by the filmmakers' own parsimony in narrating their own films and those of others in the unit.[40]

That RP—widely perceived today as a markedly British and pretentious manner of speaking—was ever regarded as placeless or neutral speaks volumes about changing historical perceptions of accent and the persuasive power of hegemonic listening practices. What is important to note is that the GPO films participated in constructing these hegemonic listening practices, for which Jennifer Lynn Stoever has coined the term "the listening ear," and, furthermore, that they consolidated the social meanings of different varieties of speech by inserting them into what has, through repetition, become a conventional documentary idiom.[41] Abstract narratorial functions (analyzing data; providing spatiotemporal orientation, historical and political context, or psychological insight; explaining complex ideas; interpreting the significance of events depicted) are undertaken by unseen "accentless" commentators while on-screen "accented" speakers serve concrete demonstrative or illustrative functions (see fig. 1.3). This translates to an *accentuating* style in which the commentator (almost always white, masculine-presenting, and speaking in RP from a vantage that is positioned as neutral precisely because it is unmarked) points out and accentuates (highlights, stresses, or emphasizes the informational value of) speech that is regionally, ethnically, or socially marked.

FIGURE 1.2 Portraits of the GPO filmmakers Edgar Anstey, John Grierson, Harry Watt, Alberto Cavalcanti, Stuart Legg, and Basil Wright.
© GPO / Courtesy of the BFI National Archive.

FIGURE 1.3 Six screenshots depicting images of accented speakers from the following GPO films: (a) *Coal Face*, (b) *On the Fishing Banks of Skye*, (c) *Song of Ceylon*, (d) *Cable Ship*, (e) *Mony a Pickle*, and (f) *Six Thirty Collection*.

All photos are copyright GPO and courtesy of the BFI National Archive.
Images (a) and (b) © 1935; (c) and (f) © 1934, (d) © 1933; and (e) © 1938.

The act of identifying and marking accented speech takes on varied functions and inflections in the GPO's process films, comedies, and drama documentaries. Nearly all of the early GPO films offer instructions about modern telecommunications, but these lessons about emerging media double as raciolinguistic lessons. Furthermore, they encode a *raciolinguistic system* that has persisted in documentary form, which has become so naturalized that it almost always goes unremarked. Here, we listen as this system is being constructed. The accentuating style of these films teaches characters within the diegesis how to eliminate verbal barriers to smooth communication and, thereby, social mobility, and audiences beyond the diegesis how to inhabit an imperious listening position that is nonetheless coded as neutral and unaccented. As I show below, the GPO films' raciolinguistic pedagogies shape a taxonomy of accents, inviting audiences to audit their own verbal styles and those of others by locating them on a geosocial grid mapped in audiovisual and narrative terms.

To illustrate how the GPO films accomplished this astonishing documentary project of social legibility, I have compiled a number of examples. In the following illustrations, drawn from the films *6:30 Collection, Cable Ship, Song of Ceylon, The Saving of Bill Blewitt, Mony a Pickle, The Fairy of the Phone, A Job in a Million,* and *Pett and Pott,* I note key binary distinctions that serve as axes for plotting and classifying accented speakers: Sensation v. Information; Witness v. Anchor; Regional v. Global; and Amateur v. Professional. In each pair, accented accents function as the first term and "accentless" accents as the second. Together they demonstrate how these early instructional films segregated the population by class and function by embedding raciolinguistic lessons in documentary form.

Sensation v. Information

In perhaps the first film to use recorded speech, *6:30 Collection* produces a working-class atmosphere from the muffled and indistinct speech of post office sorters distinct in tone and sound quality from the studio-recorded, closely miked, and crisply articulated RP of the commentary, which occupies the sonic foreground even as it emanates from off-screen.[42] The narrator of *Cable Ship* similarly slices through the first sounds we hear—the atmospheric crackle of static, and the voices of women switchboard operators announcing the names of global cities in regional accents: "Birmingham, Berlin, Casablanca, Barcelona"—to explain the goings-on at the telephone exchange. Colonized Sinhalese people are given sonic treatment comparable to the aforementioned manual laborers and low-ranking employees in *Song of Ceylon*. In her analysis of films produced by Gaumont-British Instructional about Indian towns under colonial rule in the late 1930s, Priya Jaikumar observes a semiotic relay between abstract framing discourses (diagrammatic maps, ethnographic images enumerating vocational or ethnic types) and actuality footage (of locations and crowds) that registers affective and sensual detail in excess of these frames.[43] A similar sonic dynamic can be observed in *Song of Ceylon* and other early GPO films. Shot in pre-Independence Sri Lanka and cosponsored by the Empire Tea Marketing Board, *Song of Ceylon* depicts Buddhist pilgrims and peasants as a sensual soundscape (ceremonial gongs, drums, cymbals, and chanting) made sense of by a British narrator who, at one point, represents the commodity value of these sonic transactions as a data log of sales numbers relayed in telegraphs sent home to England by East India Company traders.

Witness v. Anchor

Where films such as *Song of Ceylon* sought to bring distant lands closer, *Cable Ship* seeks to make undersea telecommunications infrastructures graspable.[44] The film's narrative scenario (repairing a faulty undersea cable that interrupts the work of the telephone exchange) has an auditory parallel in a relay of voices that maintains a smooth flow of information, setting the stage for a future broadcast standard.

The off-screen commentator serves as a stabilizing presence, an anchor providing an overview of the scenario before introducing the cable foreman. The foreman describes the fault in the cable and, in turn, introduces the joinder, who identifies himself on screen ("that's me on the left") before showing and describing the process of soldering the cable. The foreman and joinder, both of whom function as embodied witnesses from the setting describing their own experience, occasionally stumble over their prepared script. Evidently recorded in studio and later synchronized to the action, their somewhat stiff and overly formal delivery betrays their discomfort with mediated public speaking relative to the off-screen commentator. It also previews the awkward vernacular testimonial performances of slum housing tenants in codirector Edgar Anstey's *Housing Problems* (released a year later), whose on-the-ground accounts are similarly anchored and bookended by off-screen RP narration.[45]

Regional v. Global

Drama documentaries such as *The Saving of Bill Blewitt* and *Mony a Pickle* (from the Scots colloquialism "mony a pickle maks a puckle" or "lots of little things make a big thing") advertised GPO services like savings accounts to vernacular audiences. The former casts Cornish villagers, including the real-life postman Bill Blewitt, who plays a fisherman, as versions of themselves, while *Mony a Pickle* features a commentator speaking in a broad Scottish brogue and protagonists whose speech is peppered with other widely recognized Scots phrases ("ye ken," "braw"). But these films also stage regional vernaculars as an obstacle to participation in the modern economy. In one scene from *Mony a Pickle*, a Scotsman repeatedly suffers mispronunciations of his surname ("MacLachlan") by English employees at the bank until, finally, he encounters a Scottish clerk who pronounces his name perfectly. If this confirms the GPO's friendliness to regional differences, other films, such as *The Fairy of the Phone* (see the following section), clarify that such inclusion is contingent on the adoption by GPO customers of English phrases that function as a national and even global vernacular.[46]

Amateur v. Professional

In *The Fairy of the Phone* and *A Job in a Million*, telephone operators and postal employees function as etiquette and life coaches ushering GPO users into the professional classes. The eponymous protagonist of *The Fairy of the Phone*, an impeccably well-spoken and -attired blonde, earns her status as narrator by demonstrating her technological competence. Tiptoeing across telephone wires to magically appear in homes and places of business (see fig. 1.4), the fairy trains a variety of inept, gauche, and downright rude subscribers in proper telecommunications protocols ("Answer the telephone call promptly!"; "Don't just say hello, announce your identity"; "Speak clearly and directly into the transmitter"). Mara Mills has observed that the emergence of telephone, radio, and microphone technologies amplified and isolated the human voice, turning it into an object of scientific scrutiny; the fairy's instructions illustrate how documentary forms were enjoined in this project.[47] Like *Pett and Pott*, whose tale of two families equates telephone use with domestic and marital bliss, *The Fairy of the Phone* invokes the "telephone exchange girl" as an ideal of social and professional mobility: the film ends with a chorus line of coiffed blonde women singing "Get yourself a phone!" Professional growth is also the theme of *A Job in a Million*, directed by Evelyn Spice, one of the few women directors to achieve a measure of recognition within the British documentary movement.[48] An "underheight" Cockney messenger boy trainee (see fig. 1.5) matures under the kindly tutelage of postmasters, who, speaking a paralect of RP, communicate a coded message to all the young trainees: "Some of you will become postmen,

FIGURE 1.4 A pair of screenshots from *The Fairy of the Phone* depicting the titular character walking on telephone wires and into the home of a telephone user. © 1936 GPO / Courtesy of the BFI Archive.

FIGURE 1.5 Screenshot from *A Job in a Million* depicting the protagonist, a young "underheight" boy. © 1937 GPO / Courtesy of the BFI Archive.

sorters, clerks, [and] some will climb higher and reach executive posts." Professional ambition, here, is equated with the vocal standards of a privileged class.

The GPO's early films modeled racialized standards of speaking. Perhaps as importantly, they also modeled racialized habits of listening. They acquainted one of the first generations of documentary audiences with a class system of accents (those who explain and those who exemplify; those who instruct and those who learn; those who interpret and those who inform; those who give voice and those who make noise) whose social status, desirability, and achievability were indicated by their audiovisual location and narrative function. Commentary sits atop this emerging documentary architecture, assuming a privileged and synoptic stance. Commentary in the GPO films models both an abstract, "placeless" audit and a disembodied, neutral mode of auditing speech in accordance with imperial norms and bureaucratic and technological protocols. The commentator, usually unseen, assumes the function, explicitly or implicitly, of modeling elocutionary standards associated with white, college-educated, Anglophone masculinity, while evaluating, sorting, and interpreting aberrant, divergent, or irregular accents. This taxonomic impulse is not at odds with the "calmly moderate yet committed," "sober," "neutral," and "open-ended" commentary for which GPO films were known so much as it is symptomatic of the status of such commentary as a listening ear convinced of its own benevolent neutrality.[49] This self-effacing accent was better suited to the GPO's brand than other, more performative, supralocal accents associated with the educated English upper classes in the early decades of the twentieth century, including the overblown *March of Time* accent (which has been called stentorian, didactic, and authoritarian) or the affected, carefully articulated, posh accent that Mills names "the queer plummy voice."[50] GPO filmmakers believed that they were giving voice to the Empire's vocal diversity, even as imperial accentual hierarchies resounded in the sound design of their films.

The post office, the radio studio, and the telephone exchange were among the imperial sites that conditioned the emergence of the documentary audit, and now, in order to trace its postcolonial itineraries, I turn to the offshore call center and border forensics. The GPO's early films gave audiovisual expression to raciolinguistic ideologies, and these expressive conventions have, in turn, lent support to institutionalized practices of accentless speaking and neutral listening that do not represent a preexisting reality so much as they call it into being. Understanding the relationship between films produced by the British Crown's de facto communications ministry and contemporary corporate and juridical telecommunications requires a mode of analysis that moves fluidly between the realm of documentary representations and that of documentary operations. Operative images and sounds, to invoke an early and influential text by Harun Farocki, refer to images and sounds that are "made neither to entertain nor inform"; they "do not represent an object, but rather are part of an operation."[51] My argument is that documentary listening habits have been embedded into "societal operations" of auditing (tracking, measuring, verifying) accented speech that do not necessarily resemble their industrial predecessors.[52] These operations may not seem at first glance to be meaningfully connected to documentary aesthetics, but this connection is precisely what I aim to elucidate. "Operations," as the documentary scholar Laliv Melamed has observed, "entail representation."[53] In the sections to follow, I frame the "call center voice" and forensic listening as raciolinguistic operations that habituate speaking and listening bodies to the documentary audit in the course of disciplinary routines in the domains, respectively, of customer support and telemarketing, and border security and bureaucracy.

My case studies—Gulati's *Nalini by Day, Nancy by Night* and Abu Hamdan's *The Freedom of Speech Itself*—are especially helpful to think with because they simultaneously enact and confront routinized operations of auditing accented speech that circulate across institutional sites and uses as a discursive by-product of the documentary audit. Gulati and Abu Hamdan contribute to the evolution of the multilingual film style associated with exilic and diasporic filmmaking that Naficy calls "accented cinema," but just as urgently their work explains why documentary practitioners have a stake in and a responsibility to intervene in practices of accent neutralization and forensic listening.[54] They train a new generation of audiences to hear the thoroughly naturalized but nonetheless artful ways in which documentarians speak and listen with an accent, and they cultivate an awareness of the often-imperceptible dialogic relay among accented speakers and listeners that I call "accented interlistening." My reading of *Nalini by Day, Nancy by Night* attends to how Gulati encourages me to harness my own accented listening to hear the true locus of the documentary audit. I find in *The Freedom of Speech Itself* an invitation to a genuinely relational interlistening practice that acknowledges difference in its multiplicity and mutuality without denigrating it or subsuming it into sameness.

AUDITING THE CALL CENTER DOCUMENTARY

Gulati begins *Nalini by Day, Nancy by Night* with an anecdote explaining why she was compelled to make this short film. Having grown accustomed to hearing her name mangled by American telemarketers ("Sonali Gelato," "Somalia Gelatin"), she was caught off guard when she received a telephone call offering her a Visa Platinum card and the agent pronounced her name "as perfectly as people back home," even though she introduced herself as "Nancy Smith." Gulati would learn, by engaging her unseen interlocutor in conversation, that her given name was Nalini, and that she was calling Gulati in Philadelphia from a call center in New Delhi, India, where Gulati had grown up. Gulati's accented ear places Nalini's accent despite the agent's (failed) attempt to disguise her geographic and social location.

Gulati's is one of several documentary films produced in the early 2000s that go behind the scenes of the call center industry in India to expose the vocal norms in which call center agents are trained. India has a high concentration of English speakers, a colonial legacy that has made it an attractive location for U.S.-based multinational corporations looking to cheaply outsource their business processes. However, the call center industry deems the breakthrough phonology of regional languages in spoken English (colloquially referred to as the "Indian accent") to be an impediment to intelligibility and, thus, to call center optimization—one that it has attempted to minimize by stressing a "neutral" accent that is at once "global" and "standard" English.[55] Indeed, the relative "neutrality" or "lightness" of the Filipino accent relative to the Indian accent has been cited as a key reason why the Philippines surpassed India by 2011 as the "call center capital of the world," despite having only a fraction of India's productive capacity.[56]

In its inception in the late 1990s, the call center industry in India operated under a cloak of secrecy because American and multinational corporations feared backlash for outsourcing their customer-facing business processes. "Agents were instructed," one landmark ethnographic study notes, "to act as if they were stationed in the United States: they were required to take pseudonyms, speak with American accents, and deny their geographical and social locations as Indians."[57] Although this pretense has since been dropped, the practice of accent neutralization still permeates the Indian call center industry. This practice, alleged to minimize aural and cultural dissonance for English-speaking customers in the United States, as well as in the UK, Canada, and Australia, takes the form of rigorous voice training and cultural competency programs that can last anywhere from two to eight weeks, covering everything from informal expressions ("dude," "jerk," "nuts," and "bollocks") and culturally specific references (sports metaphors ["cover all the bases"; "drop the ball"] and street designations [road, court, and boulevard]) to workplace mores and affects, laws and regulations, and repeat viewings of popular TV programs such as *Friends* for the purpose of learning the cultural contexts for styles of speech.[58] While many aspects of customer support have been automated in recent years through the use of AI-powered conversational chatbots, the "problem" of accent remains at the bleeding edge of call center optimization. Phone calls between customers and call center agents are subject to constant audio monitoring in order to supply datasets for machine-learning systems that extract and analyze the emotional content of acoustic and voice signals to provide real-time feedback to agents on how to optimize their vocal performance.[59] As of 2021, a Silicon Valley start-up, Sanas, has begun marketing an app that uses AI to modify the accents of call center agents in real time.[60]

Accent neutralization (sometimes referred to as accent modification or accent reduction) constructs the problem it sets itself up to solve. A largely unregulated pseudoscience based on faulty premises (that the way one speaks is a static thing that can be trimmed away) and unproven claims (that lingual habits acquired over decades can be relinquished or replaced within weeks), accent neutralization functions, as Vijay A. Ramjattan has argued, as a corporate raciolinguistic pedagogy.[61] If the GPO films taught an implicitly racialized and classed hierarchy of English accents and audiences, the call center industry makes explicit and exploits this hierarchy by training Indian agents *and* their overseas customers to hear regionally marked Indian accents as flawed and in need of correction. Many call center trainees are middle- or lower-middle-class migrants from second-tier Indian cities and towns. Trainee agents are taught to perform a globalized class identity by adopting Anglicized pseudonyms, "switching off" local and regional linguistic habits, and imitating common features of speech that persist, to degrees, in "preferred" English accents (American, British, Australian, and Canadian).[62]

The resulting "neutral accent," argues A. Aneesh, the author of an ethnography of call centers in New Delhi, does not allude to a preexisting reality so much as it performatively invokes—or at least attempts to invoke—a certain placelessness.[63] The deception, as anyone familiar with Indian accents can testify, is not always successful. In fact, linguists claim that success is impossible. In her classic study of linguistic discrimination, *English with an Accent*, Lippi-Green argues that the demand that anyone "lose" their native phonology is akin to demanding that they change the color of their skin.[64] The postcolonial literary scholar Rey Chow extends this analogy, attributing the uncanny effect of the "call center accent" to its "double disfigurement (a defective correction of something already deemed defective)."[65] She elaborates, "The upbeat, Americanized tones of voice required of these agents . . . are unattained and unattainable skin tones, bearing in this case an audible record of being cut (into)—of being racialized by language and languaged by race."[66] I would add that the auditory nonplace of neutral listening is equally unattainable, equally cut into, by raciolinguistic ideology. The call center accent performatively invokes a neutral listener who doesn't exist except as a projection.[67] Accent neutralization and neutral listening are partners in constructing the abstract, placeless voice whose linguistic capital is exploited by both transnational call centers and documentary convention.

Gulati's detection of Nalini's accent serves as a point of narrative intrigue that structures her cinematic quest to "unmask" Nalini's placeless acousmatic phone voice by localizing it in a "real" face, body, and story—that is, to give her back her voice by restoring her identity. *Diverted to Delhi* (dir. Greg Stitt, 2002), *Bombay Calling* (dir. Samir Mallal and Ben Addelman, 2006), and *John and Jane* (dir. Ashim Ahluwalia, 2005) share this humanitarian impulse of "giving a voice," which takes the form, in this context, of "giving an image" to the faceless, nameless call center agents obliged to communicate using pseudonyms and altered voices. These films use a range of strategies, including satire and reenactment, to amplify the alienating indignities endured by call center agents. In contrast to the other films, which are fairly conventional documentaries shot on video, Ahluwalia's is shot on 35 mm film and includes documentary material originally shot on video that was subsequently reenacted and reshot on film, producing an observational effect that is estranging and uncanny, much like the call center voice itself. But it is Gulati's film that stands out to me, for its exemplary demonstration of the estranging effects of thoroughly conventional documentary representations of accented speech. In principle and ethos, Gulati works *against* the raciolinguistic ideology that constructs the Indian accent as flawed, but formally, her film tells a different and more complex story that is as much about the call center voice as it is about the documentary audit.

One scene in particular manifests in content and form the internalization of this audit as a formal hierarchy—one in which a "neutral accent," however chimerical, is deemed indispensable both for professional advancement and for climbing the ladder of documentary speech. Turning now to this scene, I posit the following: Much like the call center voice, the audit of a documentary film only becomes perceptible when an embodied, accented ear picks up on its subterfuge.[68] The scene in question takes place midway through Gulati's film and features an excerpt from a failed job interview. We learn at the scene's outset from Gulati's voice-over commentary that it is the candidate's fifth attempt at procuring a job as a call center agent, and we learn at its conclusion that he has failed the interview yet again because of his "heavy" North Indian accent (see fig. 1.6). The recruiter, a young Indian woman who speaks English fluently but whose accent is harder to place, remarks to Gulati, who is behind the camera, that the candidate's pronunciation is "nowhere."

I'd like to draw attention to two observations regarding this scene that have to do with the documentary representation of accented speech—specifically, the manner in which Gulati's film audits the job interview, itself an audition of sorts. The first, which is readily apparent, concerns the way the candidate's accented English is heard and judged by himself and the recruiter as lacking. The second hides in plain sight: I am intrigued by how this structure of self-consciousness manifests in Gulati's film in the form of textual signs or conventions (voice-over commentary, subtitles, and captions), which shape a hierarchy of accented voices based on their proximity to an unspoken yet palpable norm. This vocal hierarchy testifies to the power and persistence of the documentary audit.

To allow close attention to these audiovisual choices alongside the word choices of the three subjects, I have made note of both in the following transcript of the interview scene. The interview takes place in English, and both of the speakers are subtitled, while Gulati's off-screen voice-over is not subtitled. As Gulati has explained, there were technical reasons for these decisions: She was not able to use lavalier microphones on most of the people she interviewed since the call center was concerned that these sensitive microphones would pick up the voices of customers through the agents' headsets. In this particular scene, since there were people speaking loudly in the adjacent room,

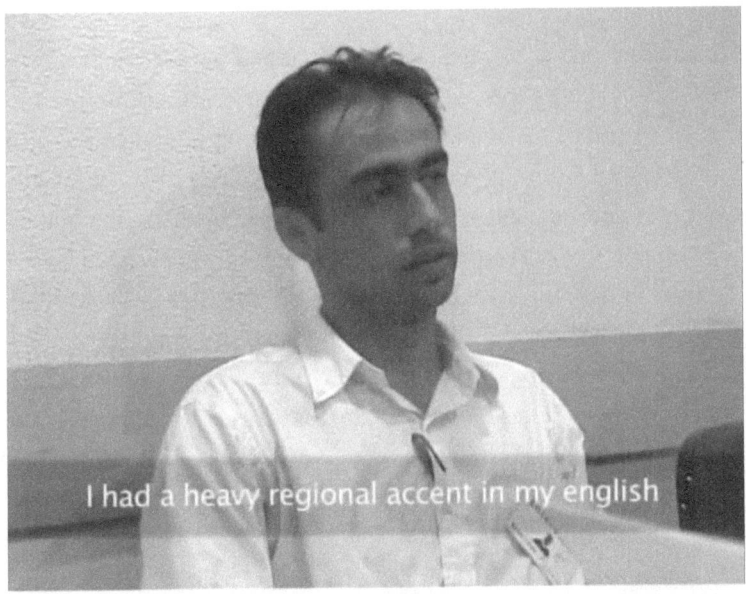
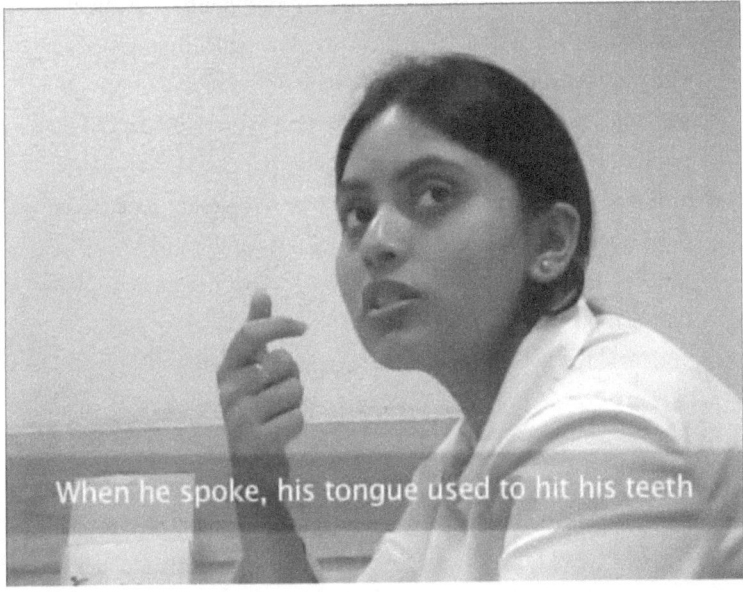

FIGURE 1.6 A pair of screenshots from *Nalini by Day, Nancy by Night* depicting the job candidate and recruiter. Courtesy of the artist.

Gulati relied on her in-camera microphone and subtitled both speakers. Gulati includes this scene in her film despite its technical shortcomings because the candidate's mention during his interview of a film, *Face/Off*, whose plot involves John Travolta and Nicolas Cage swapping identities, was a "documentary gold moment" in the context of her film about call center employees taking on whitewashed personas. Gulati has also shared that she initially subtitled her voice-over as well, but she was advised by one of her thesis committee members at Temple University, where she was an MFA candidate at the time, to remove the subtitles as "[her] audio was very clear and the film was getting to be quite text heavy."[69]

GULATI *(off-screen voice-over heard over street scenes of New Delhi shot at night—no subtitles)*: It hasn't taken me long to realize that call center jobs are indeed the most sought-after jobs in urban middle-class India today. I've learned that there are three million people scrambling to land a prestigious job as a telemarketer. I even met with a structural engineer who's desperately trying to get a job at a call center. This is his fifth attempt at a job interview.

CANDIDATE *(framed in medium shot—subtitled throughout)*: Spectramind, I was up in fourth round, fourth round I was out.

RECRUITER *(off-screen—subtitled throughout)*: What went wrong? What do you think must have gone wrong in Spectramind?

CANDIDATE: I had a heavy regional accent in my English.

RECRUITER *(off-screen)*: What kind of a regional accent are you talking about?

CANDIDATE: North Indian accent. . . . Then I tried copying National Geographic's channel. Whatever they spoke, I tried it. I bought a tape recorder. I spoke, I heard what my voice looks like. I tried to improve on it. *Image cuts to medium profile shot of interviewer.* I have a friend. She's working at EXL (subtitled as "EXL [call center]"). She helps me a lot in it. *Image cuts back to candidate.*

LISTENING WITH AN ACCENT 59

RECRUITER *(off-screen)*: Okay. . . . Which was the last movie that you saw?

CANDIDATE: Last movie was *Face/Off.* Just 2 days before I saw it. I had seen it before, in between I saw it.

RECRUITER *(off-screen)*: Two days before where?

CANDIDATE: On the TV, yesterday night I think it was . . .

RECRUITER *(off-screen)*: Can you describe it?

CANDIDATE: Okay.

RECRUITER *(off-screen)*: Narrate the movie to me.

CANDIDATE: In that movie there are two main characters, Nicolas Cage and John Travolta. Nicolas Ca . . . sorry John Travolta, he's a cop, and this Nicolas Cage, he's a criminal. What he does . . . he makes arrangements with his friends, captures the other fellow, takes him to the hospital, they change their faces. All the other assistants . . .

RECRUITER *(interrupts from off-screen)*: Change their faces?

CANDIDATE: Yes.

RECRUITER *(off-screen)*: How do they do that?

CANDIDATE: Some medical technology. He feeds them and changes it.

RECRUITER *(off-screen)*: Mm hmm.

CANDIDATE: Then what happens after that, all his assistants, he kills them. So now there are only two people who know. Nicolas Cage and John Travolta, which is the real one?

RECRUITER *(off-screen)*: Right, thank you.

RECRUITER *(gets up, leaves the room)*: Welcome. Image cuts back to recruiter.

RECRUITER *(to an unseen interlocutor, possibly Gulati—subtitled as "When he spoke, his tongue used to hit his teeth. He had a lisp and he was stammering in between")*: To . . . it was like, he had a lisp also, *jab woh bolta tha to* his tongue used to hit his teeth. "Duh-duh" . . . *jab main . . . voh . . . lisp aa jaata hai na.* . . . Then he was stammering also *beech beech mein.* Then he said, "I don't want to be a follower, I want to be a leader," *To* . . . pronunciation was, like, nowhere. Next candidate.

This scene frames the candidate's accent as deficient—the recruiter announces that his pronunciation was "nowhere"—even as Gulati attempts to lend an accented ear to his predicament. The implication is that this arguably overqualified candidate is "going nowhere" because the audible geographic particularity of his speech portends limited social mobility. If he wants to "go somewhere" in life, that is, if he desires economic and geographic mobility, however illusory or virtual that mobility might be, he must be able to scrub, mask, or disguise his identity—not his face, as one might surmise from his rather ingenious plot summary of the film *Face/Off* but the audible vocal markers that "place" his voice in a location associated with underdevelopment. But the candidate's larynx, teeth, tongue, and neural wiring are so stubbornly molded by his inhabitation of a North Indian dialect that his accented English utterances tether him to a local identity that he cannot escape or efface. A parochial accent that is too stuck in place, too "place-full," becomes a class signifier—a poor cousin of the cosmopolitan globe-trotting accent that is placeless or "nowhere."

The scene also employs vocal conventions that position the three speakers (Gulati, the recruiter, and the candidate) at various rungs along a formal hierarchy of accents whose classificatory logic (sensation v. information, witness v. anchor, regional v. national-global, and amateur v. professional) evinces the abiding influence of the GPO's accentuating style. Gulati's expository first-person voice-over, which is in direct and seemingly unmediated conversation with the audience, is at the apex of the hierarchy. Gulati's speech is not anchored in text, even though it is not unaccented. Her American-influenced lexical stresses and drawling vocal delivery intimate her expatriate status as a film student in Philadelphia (a piece of information Gulati volunteers early on in the film) even as its melodious up-down intonations and rounded vowel sounds, evidence of a British English-medium education, respectively hint at her South Asian nationality and middle to upper-middle-class status.

In contrast, every word uttered by the job candidate is subtitled, lassoing our gaze to the content of his words lest we be distracted by his "erroneous" syntax and pronunciation (he rolls his Ds and Rs and strings words together). Gulati's decision to subtitle the candidate's accented English may have been technical (his voice did not meet the technical standards for intelligibility), but because his pronunciation is also being judged in the interview for intelligibility, the subtitles have the aesthetic effect of confirming the recruiter's judgment that the candidate's pronunciation is "nowhere." His accented English indicates the audible influence of his native North Indian dialect on his manner of speaking English (I could not tell you which; my own auditory trajectory, which resembles Gulati's but began in an English and Tamil-speaking family in Mumbai, means that I can only zoom in to the general region and not street-view level, to use the vocabulary popularized by Google Maps). Subtitling his speech serves the function not of translating a foreign language but of transcribing a nonstandard accent. There is, to my knowledge, no industry-wide terminology for describing this quite common practice, which is another way of saying "it goes without saying." These are not quite subtitles (which only translate speech sounds) and not quite captions (which make speech and nonspeech sounds accessible to deaf or hard-of-hearing viewers).[70] Streamers, movie theaters, and broadcasters in the United States typically employ subtitles as a default setting, as opposed to a customizable option, only for "foreign language" (meaning non-English) films. Closed captions have become a near-ubiquitous option on digital screens thanks to recent legal mandates, but they are employed as a default option only in contexts that create temporary or "situational disabilities" for hearing audiences (for instance, on content broadcast in noisy airport lounges or in TikTok videos designed to be viewed silently).[71]

These burned-in and transcribed "open subtitles" function in a manner similar to open captions—they provide sensory as opposed to linguistic access—with the difference being that they are limited to only *some* speech sounds. There is a lot more to be said here about linguistic and sensory access, but I have saved that discussion for chapter 2, "Listening in Crip Time." For now, I will note that the selective use of "open subtitles" to transcribe nonstandard accented speech indicates that a particular listening ear is being accommodated as though it were a universal or default setting. This accommodation justifies the raciolinguistic ideology of neutral listening: Like the neutral accent, the open subtitle masks the accented nature of listening by coding the listening ear of its ideal auditor as an accent-neutral norm. The auditor hailed by Gulati's film is the same ideal auditor that the call center industry hails by training agents in a "neutral accent." I know this is not my ear the same way Gulati knew she was not the intended addressee of Nalini/Nancy's sales pitch, and in the same way, too, that the Afro-Borinqueña commentator who verified Jessica Krug's Black Boriqua accent as being fake knew that she was not the target of Krug's deception.[72] We all pay attention to the medium rather than the message of what is being communicated. Here, another powerful interpellation works in place of the failed one: Like Gulati, I am hailed not as a "someone" from "nowhere" but as a "no one" from "somewhere." I feel my accent in my ear.

The recruiter's voice is harder to place. This may well be because she speaks in the "neutral call center accent" that mimics a mixed set of features of British, American, Australian, and Canadian English and is thus aspirationally "placeless," even as she criticizes the candidate's voice as a "nowhere" voice. Her words are anchored in text as well, but as Gulati has explained, the motivation for this choice was technical. Beyond not being miked, she is off-screen for much of the exchange, and viewers cannot follow her moving lips. When she finally appears on-screen, the function of this text changes from transcription to translation since she switches between Hindi and English when addressing Gulati, relaxing the contrived norms of the interview and acknowledging Gulati's bilingualism as well as their membership in a shared linguistic class that does not include the job candidate: a class capable of "masking" its origins. Even though we lose some of the content of what the recruiter says in translation (Gulati was rushing to subtitle the film and missed her last sentence), the suggestion is that her words do not require textual transcription since the *sound* of her voice, unlike that of the candidate, approaches the aspirational linguistic norm of a neutral, placeless accent that can "go anywhere."[73] That Gulati has achieved this global standard of cosmopolitanism by emigrating to the United States (an experience beyond the reach of most call center agents in India) is confirmed at the end of her trip to New Delhi, when she is offered a job as a voice and accent trainer at a call center.[74]

How should we think of these textual signs or audiovisual conventions: Gulati's off-screen commentary, the subtitled speech of the recruiter, and the "open subtitled" or captioned speech of the candidate? Are they perfectly ordinary and unremarkable conventions, just the marks of an accented film? Or are they techniques of accent neutralization: a cloak or disguise that simultaneously masks the accented basis of some voices and marks or accentuates the otherness of others? To me, they are both. They are unremarkable and conventional only to the extent that they camouflage the film's audit, that is, its mode of listening in conformity with unspoken raciolinguistic norms. It takes an accented ear to detect this subterfuge. Watching this scene, I am reminded of Gulati's accidental misinterpellation by the "correct" pronunciation of her name. Just as Gulati misrecognizes herself in Nalini/Nancy as a member of an increasingly placeless linguistic community that is both nowhere and everywhere, I am constructively mistargeted by the accentuating style of Gulati's film. Gulati's doubling of the candidate's self-consciousness at the level of documentary form points me not to the accented speech of the job candidate but to my own accented listening. And perhaps as importantly, it points out how documentary conventions and corporate raciolinguistic operations function as mutually reinforcing supports and coconspirators in

Asserting the accentedness of listening amid the forces that deny its existence has never been more urgent. Gulati takes aim at the professional myth of the neutral accent and demonstrates, using her own accented tongue and ear, how documentary forms fail (often in unintended and telling ways) to disguise their accentuating marks and neutralizing masks. Lawrence Abu Hamdan, an audio investigator and artist, sets his sights on the equally specious juridical myth of neutral listening, one that is mobilized by immigration authorities in the linguistic profiling of asylum seekers. Like Gulati, Abu Hamdan argues his case using documentary means. My analysis of his audio documentary *The Freedom of Speech Itself* explores how the acquisitive and inquisitive logic of documentary listening is complicit in the emergence of what he terms "forensic listening" and how he works against this logic to cultivate an ethic of accented interlistening.

INTERLISTENING TO FORENSIC ACCENT ANALYSIS

Can a voice be frisked to determine the "true" origin of its accent? Abu Hamdan's early work revolves around this question. His practice represents an emergent strain of multimodal investigative research that assumes a range of documentary forms (critical essays, essayistic films, video installations, and forensic reports), sometimes designed for display in art venues and other times for use as evidence in asylum and immigration trials or within human rights advocacy campaigns. Abu Hamdan's early works uncover intensified attacks on free speech in late-twentieth-century juridical practice stemming from the reliance on a variant of neutral listening that he calls "forensic listening." Forensic listening has found its widest application in the linguistic profiling of asylum seekers via forensic speech analysis, also known as language analysis for the determination of origin (LADO) or, colloquially, "the accent test." In his pathbreaking work on linguistic profiling, John Baugh has argued that making racial assessments on the basis of auditory cues is tantamount to using visual cues for racial profiling.[75] While accent is not reducible to race or place, LADO reduces accent to a passport or proof of citizenship and uses it to assess not only whether or not the speaker is from where they say they are but also where the speaker should be allowed to go.[76]

LADO has been practiced or commissioned by immigration authorities across Europe and in Australia and Canada since the early 2000s in response to the perceived problem of growing numbers of asylum seekers without identification papers.[77] Driven by what Michelle Pfeifer calls a racialized "hermeneutics of suspicion" toward people whose identity papers have been abandoned, lost, stolen, or confiscated in the course of fleeing persecution and conflict, LADO purports to differentiate between "fake" (or undeserving) and "real" (or deserving) asylum claims by forensically analyzing the asylum seeker's voice, dialect, and accent to determine their place of origin.[78] Abu Hamdan argues that forensic listening is a perversion of the freedom of speech: Refugees are incited to speak in a manner designed to be comprehensible to their interlocutor for which they are then held culpable and criminalized.[79] LADO extracts accent-as-information from the relational scene of interlistening taking place among accented speakers and interpreters; it listens *for* an accent rather than listening *with* an accent. Abu Hamdan's *The Freedom of Speech Itself* suggests that documentary listening frequently partakes of the same extractive logic. My reading of this work attends to how the formal logic of the documentary interview—one that Abu Hamdan both employs and critiques—lends support to the juridical operations of forensic listening in obfuscating the fact of "accented interlistening."

Although LADO was not developed by linguists, it derives its legitimacy from the science of forensic linguistics. Forensic linguists study the molecular constitution of individual phonemes to glean information about the conditions of production (including recording conditions) and details such as the age, health, and ethnicity of a voice and the geographic origin of its accent. However, forensic linguists and phoneticians widely acknowledge that voices cannot be studied outside the social, cultural, political, and technical contexts that mediate their production, whereas LADO—in a move critiqued by immigration lawyers and activists as well as linguists—treats the voice as an object that can be separated from the specific discursive encounter of speaker and listener and examined as evidence.[80] In this regard LADO both exemplifies and exploits what Thomas Keenan and Eyal Weizman have called the "forensic turn" in law and popular culture, which I discuss in greater length in this book's final chapter, "Listening Like an Abolitionist." Keenan and Weizman trace this tendency to the mid-1960s, when scientists began to appear in human rights cases as expert witnesses testifying on behalf of materials such as human bones, traces, or remains.[81] Derived from *forensis*, the Latin term for "pertaining to the *forum*" (the place where the results of an investigation are presented and contested), forensics refers to the legal art of making persuasive interpretive claims on behalf of objects (e.g., handwriting, fingerprints, dental records, clothing, photographs or filmed footage of arrests, confessions, or crime scenes) admitted as evidence in courts of law.[82] LADO weaponizes prosopopoeia, or the art of "giving voice" to inanimate materials. It exhorts asylum speakers to speak but strips them of interpretive authority, turning their subjective testimony into an inert object on whose behalf pseudoscientific claims can be made.

LADO's evolution tells a fascinating story of how discriminatory attitudes become encoded in media protocols, which then spawn mutations of those attitudes. Procedures differ by country, with language analysis variously managed in-house by state-run departments, commissioned from independent experts, or subcontracted to private firms (Sprakab and Verified, both Swedish companies, have established themselves as market leaders). For instance, the UK collects a speech sample from asylum seekers during a twenty- to thirty-minute interview conducted over the telephone or the internet by subcontracted analysts. These analysts—sometimes former refugees themselves, and typically native speakers of the applicant's preferred language who have no formal training in linguistics—are tasked with assessing whether the asylum seeker's accent corresponds with the typical features of speech in their claimed place of origin, based on recordings of the interviews. These assessments are then reworked by linguists and turned into forensic reports for use in court during deportation hearings. Other countries, such as Norway, have replaced the interview with a procedure deemed more efficient and objective: an audio recording of a fifteen-minute monologue by the asylum seeker (with little concern for how the incitement to speak and the recording device shapes the speaker's response).[83] As of 2016, Germany's central immigration agency has further streamlined the LADO procedure by developing voice biometric software that claims to pinpoint the asylum seeker's place of origin based on recorded speech samples averaging a little under thirty seconds.[84] A circular logic is at work here: To legitimize raciolinguistic ideologies as "objective," humans strive to listen like machines, and now machine-listening in the form of algorithmically encoded raciolinguistic ideologies is replacing human listeners.

LADO's endorsement of objective listening is symptomatic of the forensic revival of objectivity, an epistemological stance with aspirations to neutral knowledge that "bears no trace of the knower."[85] Abu Hamdan takes explicit aim at the purported objectivity of juridical listening, but his audio documentary *The Freedom of Speech Itself* (see fig. 1.7) also brings into unexpected focus the vestiges of objectivity that inhere in conventional habits of documentary listening. Abu Hamdan introduces his thirty-four-minute work—a formally playful essayistic composition combining commentary, reenacted interviews, and testimony from asylum seekers, forensic linguists, immigration lawyers, and UK border officers—as "a documentary about the politics of listening."[86] Given its metareflection on form, I would add that this work functions as an audit of—or hearing on—the politics of

FIGURE 1.7 Installation view of *The Freedom of Speech Itself* from *Aural Contract: The Freedom of Speech Itself*, Lawrence Abu Hamdan, 2012, The Showroom, London. © Lawrence Abu Hamdan. Photo Rachel Dowel. Courtesy of the artist.

conventional documentary listening and its complicity with forensic modes of juridical listening. In documentary conversations today, the stance of the neutral observer is largely regarded as a naive relic from the early, heady days of direct cinema. In the early 1960s, filmmakers such as Robert Drew advocated an observational approach to filmmaking that involved "being as unobtrusive as possible"—one that film theorists quickly dismissed for its guileless attachments to the unmediated pursuit of "honesty, intimacy, and above all, objectivity."[87] But documentary attachments to neutrality and objectivity are harder to shake when it comes to listening. This is especially true of works that activate documentary expectations—including Abu Hamdan's own—by appealing to their listeners as jurors auditing the veracity of testimonial speech to which their access is nonetheless mediated by persuasive formal and rhetorical claims.

Abu Hamdan's concerns regarding forensic listening are paralleled by those of documentary scholars who argue that the presentation of filmed interview testimony as evidence supporting the filmmaker's argument solicits what Irina Leimbacher calls an "inquisitive and acquisitive listening" that privileges the content rather than the context of what is said.[88] Makers of conventional nonfiction films, Leimbacher notes, routinely extract, chop, reassemble, and decontextualize recorded speech to shape a message or prove a point. This is exceedingly common in the presentation of filmed interview footage, where the presence of the interviewer (and thus the scene of listening) is deliberately removed to create the impression of unprompted spontaneity on the part of the interviewee. Such extractive treatment of documentary speech lends inadvertent support to the juridical use of recorded testimony, or what the legal scholar Jessica Silbey calls "evidence *verité*": filmed footage of arrests, confessions, and crime scenes routinely admitted in U.S. courts of law as the best evidence of what happened, especially of disputed past events.[89] The problem with using such materials in an evidentiary capacity, as Stella Bruzzi has argued regarding true crime documentary, is that documentary audiences and juries are largely untrained in the science of situating these materials in relational, medial, and institutional context.[90] This makes the persuasive arts practiced by trial lawyers, or what Keenan and Weizman call "forensic aesthetics"—an aesthetic that is increasingly common among documentarians such as Abu Hamdan, who are engaged in investigative work that moves between artistic and legal forums—both powerful and dangerous.

The LADO protocol, skewered in Abu Hamdan's audio documentary, treats accented speech as evidence verité. That is to say, LADO regards accented speech as material evidence, independent of the mediated encounter among asylum seekers and the nonspecialist analysts tasked with assessing the origin of the asylum seeker's accent on the basis of recorded speech that is produced for an accented listener. *The Freedom of Speech Itself* revolves around the case of Mohammed, one among countless asylum seekers who was marked for wrongful deportation on the basis of LADO, in this instance, as a result of how he pronounced the Arabic word for "tomato." Abu Hamdan invokes the LADO protocol in his narration and analysis of Mohammed's experience. The click of a tape recorder materializes the mediating presence of an auditor, followed by Abu Hamdan's own ambiguously accented voice asking Mohammed the types of questions that Mohammed might have been asked by his interviewer: "Where are you from?" "Can you speak Arabic?"

Abu Hamdan soon transitions to questions about Mohammed's experiences with LADO. Mohammed responds, alternating between English and Arabic, that he came to the UK from the city of Jenin in the West Bank of Palestine. He was apprehended and detained by police and forced to undergo accent analysis to prove his origins after UK immigration authorities lost his Palestinian identity card. He was then asked to speak to an interviewer in Sweden who sounded, to Mohammed, like an Iraqi Kurd. The interviewer spoke an extremely formal version of Arabic so different from Mohammed's dialect that Mohammed had to shift his manner of speech and pronunciation in order to be understood by his interviewer. At the end of the twenty-minute interview, Mohammed's interviewee concluded that the way Mohammad pronounced the word for tomato ("banadora," which the interviewer deemed more typical of Syria, instead of "bandora," as Palestianians might be expected to pronounce it) proved Mohammed's Syrian origin, even though the Palestinian city of Jenin is located a mere twenty-two kilometers from the Syrian border.

The Freedom of Speech Itself may mount a blistering critique of LADO's "auditory patdown" of asylum seekers, but it also demonstrates how documentary constructions are complicit in this very maneuver. Abu Hamdan's editing relies on the extractive strategy Leimbacher names even as he deploys documentary's rhetorical arsenal against LADO. Mohammed's testimony is shrouded in layers of "expert" interpretation, including translation from an interpreter who interjects when Mohammad speaks in Arabic, and critical commentary from forensic linguists and sociolinguists. These professionals both provide valuable insight into the various forms of prejudice built into LADO *and* inevitably replicate its forensic privileging of the testimonial agency of the expert witness "making sense of things." We learn that interviewers are usually located in a different country than the asylum seeker; that they usually have no first-hand knowledge of the linguistic cultures or regional landmarks about which they quiz asylum seekers; that they make their assessments without the crucial visual cues that body language and gesture can provide; that interviews can be as brief as fourteen minutes; and that their reports offer opinion in the guise of certainty. We learn, to paraphrase Emily Apter's reading of Abu Hamdan's work, that LADO treats the subjective impressions of lay listeners as objective proof of the difference between those who get to enjoy the liberties and privileges of citizenship and others who are marked for "misattributed citizenship, internment in holding pens, imprisonment, and deportation."[91]

At the midway point, Abu Hamdan inserts a sequence that turns the tables on his own counterdeployment of documentary prosopopoeia against LADO. The sequence upsets the power dynamic between interviewer and interviewee that shapes both forensic and documentary listening. Coming close on the heels of the interview with Mohammed, the sequence features a playful interview with the London-based translator who interprets Mohammed's Arabic speech for Abu Hamdan's audio documentary.[92] As the wryly digressive exchange between Abu Hamdan and the translator unfolds, the answer to the seemingly simple question "Where are you from?" deviates from and is overdetermined by Abu Hamdan's accented auditory expectations:

LAH: So, where are you from?
TRANSLATOR: What do you mean, I'm from Hackney.
LAH: Yeah, Hackney, but . . . you're Danish, aren't you?

TRANSLATOR: No, I'm Palestinian. Well, I grew up in Denmark.
LAH: I see, so you're from where in Palestine?
TRANSLATOR: I'm not from Palestine.
LAH: So, where are you from?
TRANSLATOR: Well, we're Palestinians from a refugee camp in Lebanon, Al-Hilweh.
LAH: Ah OK, so you were born in Lebanon?
TRANSLATOR: No, I was born in Dubai.
LAH: OK. So how come you have an American accent?
TRANSLATOR: What do you mean?
LAH: Well, you have this like American twang to your English.
TRANSLATOR: Oh it's just . . . you know . . . Eddie Murphy and, uh, Stallone and all these guys, y'know?
LAH: So you're from Hollywood?
TRANSLATOR: Nah, nah, I'm from Hackney.

Abu Hamdan intends this exchange to demonstrate, contra LADO, that an accent is not an object but a relational process. The cascade of humorous misrecognitions recalls a scene in Gulati's film where a call center employee says she was asked to watch *The Sound of Music*—a film set in Austria featuring a mostly American cast—to learn the British accent. Accent's relationality makes it fundamentally deceptive as a marker of identity, which is, of course, itself an ongoing performance. Not only are accents borrowed, syncretic, and constantly in formation, they also rely on the situated and provisional knowledges of listeners, also constantly in formation, for their meaning. Abu Hamdan reflects, "The instability of an accent, its borrowed and hybridized phonetic form, is testament not to someone's origins but only to an unstable and migratory lifestyle, which is of course common among those fleeing from conflict and seeking asylum, often spending years getting to the target country and living in diversely populated camps along the way."[93] The wandering accents of refugees are evidence not of their fakery but of the roadblocks and detours thrown up by securitized borders. Even though he attempts at first to pin down his interlocutor's accent, Abu Hamdan's queries eventually reveal that his listening, too, may be accented by complex colonial and medial itineraries.

Indeed, this brief sequence illustrates that a listening habitus is not a single or stable location but something that grows, accrues, and moves over time. As Pavitra Sundar puts it, "The temporality of listening . . . spans past and present—and, I argue, the future. How one listens is a function of the gradual accretion of listening habits that becomes one's habitus."[94] Lipari argues that this resonant temporality is a feature of interlistening, or the entanglement of listening, speaking, and thinking, which are often wrongly understood as independent and temporally distinct processes. "The idea of interlistening," she explains, "thus aims to describe how listening itself is a form of speaking that resonates with echoes of everything we have ever heard, thought, seen, touched, said, and read throughout our lives."[95] The precise origin of the translator's accent remains out of Abu Hamdan's reach. But their exchange shows how the act of listening *for* an accent can give way to a more challenging but ultimately more satisfying listening *with* an accent that broadens the listener's audit rather than narrowing it: a listening receptive to how that which it does not understand can reveal its hitherto-unknown preconceptions and open up new itineraries.

"Interview," etymologically derived from the French *s'entrevoir*, or "to see each other," refers to face-to-face discourse. Abu Hamdan suggests that every filmed interview offers an opportunity to accentuate or to neutralize the complexity of multiple resonant voices (interviewer and interviewee, certainly, but also camera operator, filmmaker, editor, and audience) *listening to one another*. Nothing less than political speech is at stake in any forum, juridical or cinematic, that claims to listen but elides the truth of interlistening. Abu Hamdan suggests as much in the conclusion of *The Freedom of Speech Itself* when he asks, "Shouldn't the freedom of speech be expanded to include the ways in which we are heard?" I think what Abu Hamdan is calling for here, and demonstrating the need for in the sequence above, is similar to what Eidsheim, in a different context, has called "just recognition."[96] This is all to say that each accented accent needs to be heard and acknowledged (as opposed to marked, named, and classified) in its multiplicity, complexity, and humanity.[97] Like neutral listening, accented interlistening is formed through practice and practiced through form. I therefore hear another provocation within Abu Hamdan's question: Shouldn't documentary efforts to give voice to those who "speak with an accent" be expanded to train audiences to listen with an accent?

ACCENTED CINEMA IN THE AGE OF ACCENT DISCRIMINATION

In the introduction to his canonical 2001 book, *An Accented Cinema*, Naficy describes the experience of watching Mohsen Makhmalbaf's *A Time to Love* (Nowbat-e Asheqi, 1991) at a Paris production studio in the mid-1990s. The film, banned in the director's home country of Iran, had been shot in Turkey. The fast pace of the Turkish dialogue, subtitled in French, required Naficy to rely on a friend who, reading the French subtitles quickly, would whisper the Persian translation into Naficy's ear as he took notes in English and Persian. This distinctive spectatorial experience, involving simultaneous acts of watching, listening, reading, translating, and writing, leads Naficy to coin the term "accented cinema": a cinema whose textual features bear the marks of its migratory authorship, whether exilic, displaced, or diasporic. As he writes elsewhere, "If the dominant cinema is considered universal and without accent, the films that diasporic and exilic subjects make are accented. This accent emanates not so much from the accented speech of the diegetic characters—although this is part of it—as from the displacement of the filmmakers and their artisanal or collective production modes."[98]

Naficy uses "accent" to delineate a particular set of films produced by diasporic, exilic or émigré filmmakers working mainly within a fictional or narrative mode. I have extended this term to describe the unmarked and routinized accentuating activities of documentarians and their audiences. The vocabulary I have elaborated in this chapter—*neutral listening, audit, accented interlistening*—does not repudiate Naficy's argument so much as expand its ambit to address the documentary genre's distinctive and often standardized modes of speaking. Documentary speech, I have argued, has a standardized accent. So does documentary listening—and its far-reaching and often debilitating impacts are hard to discern. This is precisely why the documentary audit deserves our critical attention. The speaking and listening conventions now universally recognized as distinguishing features of the documentary genre were developed in an interwar context that Naficy would plausibly consider "interstitial." Like Makhmalbaf, Grierson and other GPO filmmakers produced their instructional films across social, geographic, and cinematic contexts. What is more, their films were thoroughly accented even as they modeled a neutral and accentless listening comportment. GPO filmmakers developed this listening vantage—this audit—in response to complexly racialized, gendered, and classed linguistic ideologies, and their neutral listening habits, in turn, trained audiences to audit an audiovisual and narrative taxonomy of documentary accents.

The alliance that early GPO films forged between documentary form and societal operations of auditing accented speech has endured in ways their makers could not have possibly anticipated. The accent hierarchies and listening habits cultivated by their vocal innovations resound in corporate and juridical practices that are powerfully shaping twenty-first-century migration and diaspora. It is in this context, of accelerating technological developments around accent monitoring and monetization, that I have sought to emphasize the contributions of documentary artists such as Sonali Gulati and Lawrence Abu Hamdan. Gulati and Abu Hamdan do not merely document practices like accent neutralization and forensic accent analysis. They actively illustrate how documentary forms are complicit in constructing hierarchies of accent. In bringing her own embodied listening to the fore, Gulati demonstrates how conventional documentary representations of accented speech function, even in the hands of accented filmmakers, as techniques of accent neutralization that appeal to an abstract, disembodied listener. Abu Hamdan reaches from within the compromised aesthetic of documentary prosopopoeia, or the forensic art of "giving voice," for an idiom that acknowledges how listening, like speech, bears witness to movement, displacement, diaspora, exile, and migration. Gulati and Abu Hamdan reveal, in the process, that a different type of speaking is possible in documentary, as well as a different type of listening: one that collects traces of the accented interlistener's journey through language, social class, geography, and other tracts of stigmatized social identity.

To listen with an accent is to acknowledge that listening is migratory by definition. To listen with an accent requires mindfulness of the "place" from which one has been taught to listen (especially when that place is a nonplace), as well as a willingness, in Sundar's words, to "go to, and listen from, a new or different place."[99] *Nalini by Day, Nancy by Night* and *The Freedom of Speech Itself* are exercises in accent retraining for neutral listeners. If call center agents can attempt to rehome their tongues, they show that neutral listeners can very well attempt to leave the comforts of their listening habitus. The results are disorienting: In tuning our own accented ears, we come tumbling down to earth from the auditory nonplace that is the locus of documentary's audit. The fall is both an exposure of the acts of deception in which we engage when we deploy neutral listening and an awakening to the open horizons of accented interlistening.

2

LISTENING IN CRIP TIME

THE ABLEISM OF THE DOCUMENTARY AUDIT

Amanda wasn't looking for a form of rescue from the state of her body. She wanted this lectern to do its work not only as a solution but as a question, a designed question in material form: Who fits in and moves through space? Who gets into the room, moves through the door or down the street, yes, but also—who gets the education, acquires and keeps the job? Who steps up to reach the microphone, the one saying Listen to me?[1]

This is Sara Hendren, who until recently taught design for disability at an engineering school. Hendren is reflecting on how a design brief for a portable lectern shared by art historian and curator Amanda Cachia, who is a Little Person, led her students to understand disability as a provocation rather than a problem to solve. The obvious misfit of Cachia's body with the classroom's contents—the heights of the light switches and media outlets, the sizes of the tables and chairs, and of course, the proportions of the lectern—cast into stark relief for Hendren's students (most of whom identified as nondisabled) the "standard" bodies and social interactions for which the classroom was designed, making many of them see their own bodies anew in their particularity. Disability accented—stressed or highlighted—the access norms of the classroom.² Hendren explains the significance of this defamiliarizing encounter by evoking cinema's capacity to reveal the limitations of human perception. She asks us to imagine that the moment of encounter between flesh and stuff, of bodies coming up against stairs, sinks, or subway platforms, was being documented on camera, revealing imperceptible aspects of habituated gestures and activities: "If you could slow down the tape right at the instant of connection," she writes, "you'd see it packed with information."³ Cachia's design brief was an exercise not only in defamiliarization but imagination. It posed questions: What if the world was built otherwise? What can bodies and minds do in a world that accounts for disability?

This chapter transposes these questions to the plane of documentary listening. In what follows, I consider how disability aesthetics crip the access norms of documentary speech and listening, and the embodied experiences that these norms implicitly accommodate and validate. Walter Benjamin, writing in 1936, argued that cinema, then only in its fourth decade of existence, could register "the optical unconscious," or what the human eye could not consciously perceive about its own limited perception.⁴ Benjamin may not have put it in these terms, but he was describing cinema's capacity to awaken the senses to experiences of dilation, overload, and distraction that have historically been the province of disability. Writing in the wake of an established disability culture, Hendren is alive to disability's aesthetic capacity to enlarge conservative perspectives of human variation, difference, and beauty.⁵ I too am invested in this capacious social vision. But the stakes for me do not concern what Hendren, following Benjamin, might call the ableist (discrimination in favor of the able-bodied) unconscious of mainstream design. Rather, I'm after *the ableism of documentary's auditory unconscious*, that which exceeds and conditions documentary hearing and organizes the field of documentary audibility. I want, in other words, to understand how ableist values orient the documentary audit.

Documentary's least conspicuous oral and aural grammars have historically presumed a sighted and hearing audience without physical, intellectual, or sensory disabilities. In place of Hendren's classroom fixtures, I have in mind common conventions of documentary sound and the assumed relationships, values, and practices that they house and voice. Some of these conventions, such as the cropped framing known as the "talking head," or commentary that is spoken over images and other sounds, have become fixtures in their own right. Others might be described as common-senses that have solidified through formal and informal pedagogy. The injunction against commentary voiced in a nonstandard or "accented" accent is one to which I am especially alert, having spent decades in U.S. classrooms where I sound out of place. Another is the dictum that text and spoken commentary should be kept to a minimum so as not to "spoil" the image or render it redundant.

This chapter traces a crip counterhistory of the documentary audit through the contributions of three documentarians: the Japanese filmmaking partners Hara Kazuo and producer Kobayashi Sachiko and the American filmmaker and artist Jordan Lord, who have reckoned with the out-of-sync and misfitting temporal experiences that disability scholars call "crip time."[6] As I consider their contributions to the disability documentary canon, which precede and follow more canonized representations of crip culture that emerged during the intervening, key decades of disability self-advocacy and legal activism, this chapter asserts the historical significance of their efforts to recenter disability expertise in documentary conversations about access. My reading of Hara's *Sayōnara CP* ("Goodbye CP," 1972) reveals how the access activism of people with mobility and speech disabilities in Japan inspired the post-vérité aesthetic of coerced access that Hara is widely regarded to have pioneered. Turning to Lord's *Shared Resources* (2021), I show how the film confronts the enduring afterlives of the vérité dictum "show don't tell" (at its core, a defense of ableism and inaccessibility) even amid efforts by streaming platforms and art venues to make film and video offerings more accessible by adding sensory access features such as captions and audio description.[7]

When I speak of "crip time," I am referring to the social capacities that can be cultivated, in Alison Kafer's words, by "bending the clock to meet disabled bodies and minds" away from the ableist (which is also to say capitalist) values of productivity, self-sufficiency, independence, and achievement.[8] "Disability and illness," Ellen Samuels elaborates, "have the power to extract us from linear, progressive time with its normative life stages, and cast us into a wormhole of backward and forward acceleration, jerky stops and starts, tedious intervals and abrupt endings."[9] I became disabled in the course of writing this chapter. A delayed diagnosis of a life-threatening breathing disorder that I have lived with since childhood brought with it the vertiginous realization that I had aged prematurely but that treatment might reverse this course, adding years to my life. The wormhole of "crip time" is familiar, certainly, to people whose bodies and minds have been medicalized as untimely (chronic, terminal, advanced, delayed, premature) and to their caregivers. Crip time is also disproportionately experienced, as the crip-of-color scholars Jina B. Kim and Sami Schalk have reminded us, by those whose debilitation by incarceration, poverty, state violence, colonial occupation, pollution, and other forms of organized abandonment renders them vulnerable to premature death.[10] "All of us now are living in crip time," write Samuels and Elizabeth Freeman, referring to the reorganization of work and life schedules the world over as the impacts of the COVID-19 pandemic spiral and evolve.[11]

"Crip" is a word designed to shock. "Cripple" was once used as an insult for people with visible physical disabilities and remains prevalent as a mainstream metaphor for ruin (as in "she was crippled with student loan debt"). Over the past four decades, people with not only physical but also sensory and mental impairments have reappropriated this index of the dominant culture's deficit view of disability as a defiant expression of disabled pride that embraces the valuable forms of creativity, interdependence, pleasure, and noncompliance that disability experience can yield.[12] The harshness of "crip" relative to "handicapped" or "disabled" explains its appeal in U.S. disability culture.[13] As a noun, verb, and adjective, the word bristles with "an urge to shake things up, to jolt people out of their everyday understandings of bodies and minds, of normalcy and of deviance."[14] Robert McRuer and Carrie Sandahl have emphasized the simultaneously confrontational and invitational quality of crip provocation, understood as a political and conceptual intervention in productive reciprocity with queer activism and queer theory. Sandahl describes "cripping" as an everyday practice of confronting oppressive norms, building community, and maintaining the practitioners' self-worth, while McRuer stakes out a contestatory and disidentificatory positionality for "crip theory" relative to social and scholarly norms (including those that govern disability studies and queer studies)—one that identifies with disability as a transformational experience and ethos while remaining vigilant to how the ableist logics of neoliberal capitalism defang and coopt disability identity.[15] Founded on the tenets of nonidentitarian solidarities and unlikely dis/identifications across identities, cripping and crip theory have sustained critiques and coalitions that push beyond McRuer's and Sandahl's articulations and have inspired feminist and crip-of color reading methodologies that I employ here.[16] These are methods that, to paraphrase Kim, use disability as a lens to 1) unearth able-bodied assumptions or ableist ideologies and 2) further a critical disability ethos or vision. Crip methods are available even to those who may not claim crip identity and are applicable even to texts that are not ostensibly about disability or crip-identified.[17]

What can documentarians accomplish, then, by listening in crip time? My pursuit in posing this question is something other than a perceptual "fix" for ableism. I don't focus on films that use special camera lenses, microphones, or digital postproduction effects to evoke the perceptual experiences of, for instance, D/deaf or blind protagonists. Recent high-profile documentaries such as *Touch the Sound: A Sound Journey with Evelyn Glennie* (2004), *Hear and Now* (2007), *Planet of Snail* (2011), *Notes on Blindness* (2016), and *Vision Portraits* (2019), which represent blindness, deafness, and deafblindness, have done much to raise awareness around disability experience and to trouble narrative arcs ballasted by discovery, loss, or shock. They have elevated the audiovisual disability simulation—an exercise that can unhelpfully frame disability as individual and sensational (as a "knowable fact of the body," to borrow Kafer's phrase) rather than socially located, complexly embodied, and multiply mediated—to the status of crip phenomenology.[18] I am interested instead in the value shifts that documentary representations can catalyze when they bend their audit to crip time. All documentarians manipulate sound. They stretch, bend, layer, amplify, and remix verbal and nonverbal sounds. But Hara and Kobayashi and Lord do so not in service of whittling meaning from sound or repurposing recorded speech to fit a message. They stage listening encounters in solidarity with disability as a political experience that crip ableist assumptions about access and consent that underpin conventional documentary listening.

Access remains a foundational but undertheorized concept in documentary. In her field-defining study of media and disability, Elizabeth Ellcessor writes that "access" is colloquially understood in two contradictory ways: as a commodity and as a public good. The second, more collectivized understanding of access as a shared resource and responsibility is a frequent topic of discussion in disability communities, where it has been theorized as a revolutionary practice of anticipating what others need in order to participate in the social world—what the disability justice activist Mia Mingus terms "access intimacy."[19] Beyond these circles, however, access is generally understood in the first, more commoditized sense of an individual benefit—that is, as something that can be obtained rather than a relational process.[20] This is true of U.S. disability law, which defines "access" as the ability to enter, move within, and operate a device, service, environment, or facility, and "accommodation" as a design or protocol modification that enables access.[21] Documentary subscribes to the same propertied imaginary of access. This commoditized understanding of access is generally understood to have entered documentary discourse around the midcentury vérité turn, when the filmmaker's ability to enter, move within, and record people's everyday private environments came into conflict with the right to privacy. Access has since been characterized in industry parlance in transactional and extractive terms: as the leveraging of money, force, reputation, or trust to acquire entrance to private or intimate realms deemed to harbor documentary value. The industry refers to this kind of "intimacy access" to people's private lives as a form of "added value" that makes a film especially appealing to potential funders.[22] In recent years, a growing conversation among socially committed documentary filmmakers, scholars, and nonprofit arts workers has located this extractive imaginary of access as the underlying malady of a documentary field increasingly driven by predatory market demands. These diagnoses have been accompanied by manifestos advocating the reorganization of documentary forms and industry practices: Alexandra Juhasz and Alisa Lebow have called for formal innovations beyond the "story form" favored by commercially viable documentary, and Sonya Childress and Natalie Bullock-Brown have demanded new systems of accountability that combat extractive practices and advance socially responsible filmmaking.[23] Brett Story has envisioned collectivized structures for sharing resources and risk that could make the field as a whole more accessible, imagined along the lines of community land trusts that remove land from real estate speculation and hold it in a trust for community use.[24]

This chapter excavates the role of disability activists in agitating the norms of documentary access and championing a crip counterpractice of access understood as a shared resource, risk, and responsibility. Hara and his disabled partner Kobayashi made *Goodbye CP*, their first film, in collaboration with members of Aoi Shiba no Kai ("Green Grasses" group) in Kanagawa, a self-organized advocacy group of people with cerebral palsy (CP) who played an important role in instigating the disability rights and independent living movements in Japan.[25] Hara and Kobayashi translate the Green Grasses' disability pride and harsh critiques of ableist social norms and welfare policies into a deliberately outrageous and obstreperous crip documentary aesthetic of wrested access and unaccommodated listening. Hara has been both reproached and lionized for exploiting intimacy access as a form of documentary value. He honed an almost principled disregard for his collaborators, his audiences, and even his own private life into an invasive and exhibitionist style in its own right, which he dubbed "action documentary."[26] In *Goodbye CP*, Hara goaded his disabled collaborators into reckless access performances by encouraging them to "throw away your wheelchairs and take to the streets" (see fig. 2.1). But few have considered how the resulting crawling performances by people with CP provoked Hara, in turn, to develop a form that would force normate audiences to reckon with the discomfort of delayed and denied access to social participation. By rejecting the accepted logic of subtitling the voices of people with disability-affected speech, *Goodbye CP* aggressively confronts the entitled expectations of nondisabled documentary listeners as a sanctioned form of unwelcome and excessive auditory access on par with staring. Hara and Kobayashi's exploits forcefully crip the access norms of sync-sound realism, which dominated U.S. and European documentary at the time. The film's mismatched dissonance forces normate listeners to accommodate to the physical unease, risk, and discomfort that comes from listening in the provisional and delayed presence of linguistic access—or what I describe as *disentitled listening* in the mode of *crawling* rather than staring.

In utopian spirit, if not in tactics or tone, Hara and Kobayashi's adversarial redistribution of access anticipates Lord's more generous embrace of access as a potentially transformative attack on documentary

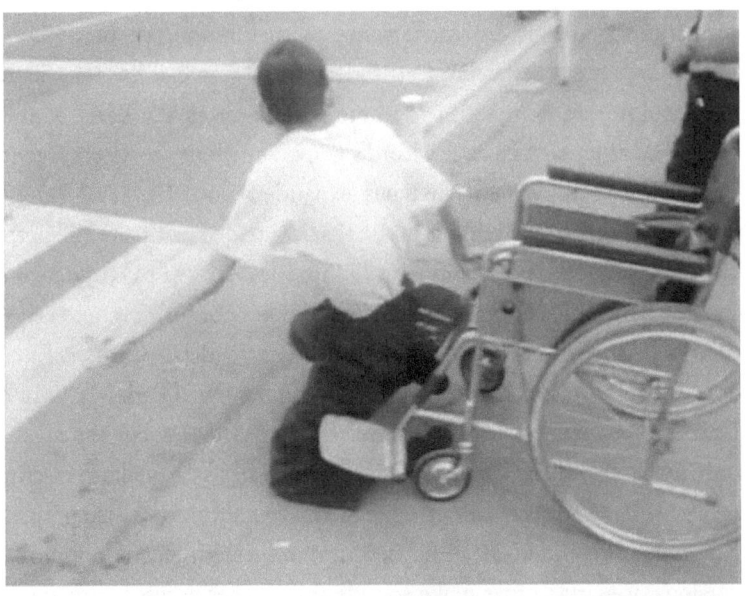

FIGURE 2.1 Two screenshots from *Goodbye CP* depicting Yokota descending from his wheelchair and crawling across a crosswalk.

forms and values in *Shared Resources*. A meditation on their white, Southern father's self-reliant attitude toward war debilitation, debt, and bankruptcy, Lord's film reframes disability as the basis of the social and cinematic contract. Lord's work contributes to an emergent disability arts movement that has expanded since the COVID-19 pandemic—a mass-disabling event that coincided with the thirtieth anniversary of the Americans with Disabilities Act (ADA) (1990)—to include a cohort of crip, queer, trans/gender nonconforming, and crip-of-color American artists working in film and video.[27] Carolyn Lazard, Constantina Zavitsanos, Christine Sun Kim, and Park McArthur have all used sensory access features to decry the low bar for meeting legal accessibility standards in art venues and as a medium of crip creativity. Lord directs this critique at documentary form, using open captions and burned-in audio description—essentially, nonoptional versions of features that make sounds and images accessible to audiences who cannot hear or see—as the building blocks of a new documentary language (see fig. 2.2). By rethinking access as a queer and crip

FIGURE 2.2 Screenshot from *Shared Resources* illustrating Lord's use of audio description and open captions. Courtesy of the artist.

practice of sharing resources or what Mingus calls "access intimacy," the film invites a *sideways* listening: an attention and an appetite for access understood not as a resentful legal obligation but as a collective practice of care that swells documentary meanings and horizons. Listening sideways rehearses a "much more conceptual, much more collaborative" form of access.[28] It is an exercise in enacting a social vision that understands disability as the "ground state of life."[29]

Sounding out the tonal differences of these films against each other allows me to amplify the varied inflections of confrontation and care that critical disability studies scholars have attributed to "crip" as a noun, verb, and practice for contesting ableist norms while also inviting people into disability community. Access intimacy enfolds these contradictions. When transposed to the documentary realm, it removes documentary relationships from the propertied realm of contracts, compliance, audits, liability, and risk management and holds them in trust. It fosters a more capacious understanding of access as the necessarily incomplete and improvised work of building the supports for social inclusion across conflicting needs and asymmetries of power. Access, reframed as relational promise rather than transaction or theft, stands as the cornerstone of a crip social vision grounded in care and interdependence. But this vision cannot be realized without breaking some habitualized documentary bonds and expectations. Access understood in the crip sense of shared enterprise operates not as seamless integration but as a frictioned, leverage-generating device, or what Aimi Hamraie, referring to the initiative of disability activists and their allies in "editing" their built environment, calls a "crip curb cut."[30] Hara, Kobayashi, and Lord crip access in ways that are *propositional*. Their experiments with access offer ways to see and listen anew through the camera, opportunities to pull back the curtain on the collaborative basis of cinema, and mechanisms for building solidarity across conflicting access needs.

The problem of solidarity also runs through this chapter as a question of method. I come to this chapter both as someone coming to terms with disability identity and as an accented immigrant working in the U.S. academy. I wrote in the previous chapter and in my previous book *Immediations* about how documentary filmmakers make nonnormative speech accessible to their imagined audience through textual supplements (burned-in subtitles for nonstandard or nonnative accents) or vocal surrogates (explanatory commentary that speaks for or makes sense of neurodiverse communication). Both of these "solutions" represent access norms: They reinforce compulsory language standards and compulsory able-bodiedness even as they operate under the guise of "giving a voice to the voiceless."[31] Accent studies has taught me that documentary practitioners perpetuate the myth of neutral listening when they mark or accentuate the otherness of disability-affected speech. My accented interlistening (a term I introduce and define in the first chapter) has taught me to hear documentary grammars that model and invite an ableist audit as part of a historical strategy of minoritizing colonized populations as untimely by denying their coevalness.[32] Disability studies offers a related insight: Selective linguistic access accommodates able-bodied listeners and disables those whose speech and listening has been marked as impaired. Disability, understood through the lens of crip-of-color critique—that is, as a social system and relationship to power that intersects with and is mutually constituted by other social identities and vulnerabilities—reframes the documentary soundscape as a type of built environment that offers fits to majority bodies and creates misfits with minority forms of embodiment.[33]

Goodbye CP and *Shared Resources* both refuse the access norms that might allow them to circulate more easily within an ableist mediascape. In my previous book, I referred to these access norms as "immediations," or audiovisual conventions that incorporate minoritarian participation by winnowing experiences and worldviews that do not fit a humanizing story arc. *Goodbye CP* is not accessible to most viewers in its intended form, and *Shared Resources* is not available through a distributor. As such, their ambitious commitments to redistributing access and dilating time stand in inverse relation to their commercial marginality and invisibility. This is why I devote so much space to describing the soundscapes of these films in detail; I respond to their invitation to listen in crip time by documenting their listening modes.

DISENTITLED ACCESS AND CRAWLING LISTENING

Two scenes from *Goodbye CP* scaffold its cinematic deconstruction of the manufactured distinction between what Hara calls "the healthy and the disabled." Both scenes are set in trains and feature Yokota Hiroshi (1933–2013), who, along with Yokotsuka Kōichi (1935–1975), was a leader of the Kanagawa Green Grasses chapter and a protagonist in Hara and Kobayashi's film. Yokota disembarks a train without assistance in the first, hair-raising scene, which is less than two minutes long but a frequent highlight in discussions of the film. In the second, less-discussed scene, which takes place later in the film, just before Yokota's poetry reading in a vehicle-free space designated as a "Pedestrian Paradise," Yokota argues that listeners need no assistance to understand his performance. The two scenes form a diptych that compares the unexamined (and always accommodated) access needs of able-bodied documentary listeners to those of nondisabled city dwellers navigating urban infrastructures designed to exclude the participation of people with disabilities.

Scene I: Yokota has boarded a train without his wheelchair. Bespectacled and dressed smartly in a blazer and pants, Yokota appears at the end of a long low-angle tracking shot: Hara, holding the microphone and camera (an Arri ST, which shoots 100-foot silent 16 mm rolls of 46–47 seconds each), walks across several train cars to arrive at the spot where Yokota sits on the floor of the train, his atrophied legs folded beneath him. The legs of other seated passengers can be seen around Yokota; Hara is presumably crouching to keep the camera at Yokota's level (see fig. 2.3). The moving train sounds like a continuous rumble of thunder, interrupted periodically by creaks, loud hisses, and a ringing bell when it slows to a stop and the doors open to allow passengers to file in and out. Yokota is also moving. His body is animated by involuntary facial contortions and head and arm movements. These are all symptoms of CP, which can impact a range of muscle groups, including the respiratory, facial, and tongue muscles required for forming speech, resulting in the loss of muscle coordination and control and a range of mobility and speech impediments. At one point, Hara pulls back and crosses over to Yokota's other side, and Yokota begins crawling on his knees toward the exit. Hara backs out of the train, his camera framing the door. The conductor announces the stop, and Yokota, lurching forward, suddenly falls out of the frame. Hara runs out of film at this point, but the microphone continues to record. The bell peals over a freeze-frame image of the train door, Yokota no longer in view.

Scene 2: Yokota is helped out of the backseat of a car and onto the back of a young man. The camera follows behind them as Yokota's assistant carries him up a steep flight of stairs, across a busy platform, and onto a train where he deposits Yokota on a seat. When it is time to disembark, the assistant hoists Yokota back onto his back, out of the train, across the platform, and up another flight of stairs, where they wait for and board a second, more crowded, train (see fig. 2.4). This time they remain standing, holding a drop-down ceiling handle for support. A recorded exchange between Hara and Yokota plays over the scene. Hara's speech is even and clear; Yokota's is slurred and punctuated by gurgles, keening sounds, and elongated syllables. I have transcribed the exchange below from the DVD subtitles provided by the film's distributor (Facets), but as I soon elaborate, Hara insists on

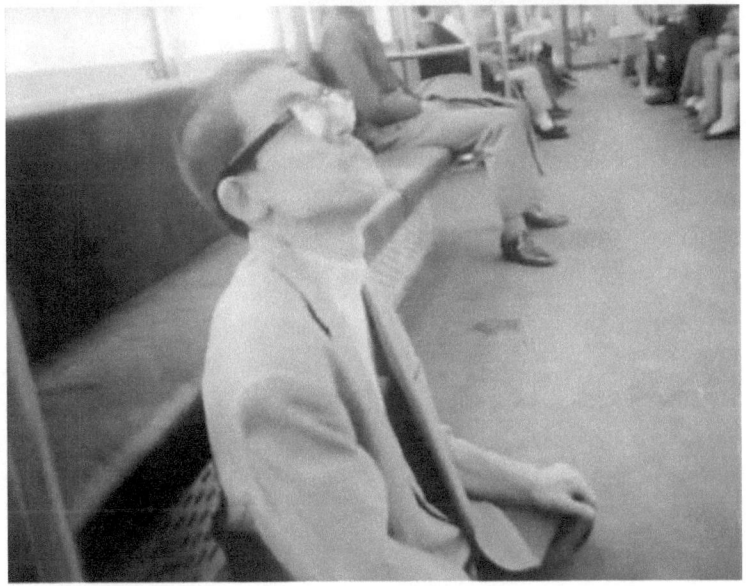

FIGURE 2.3 Two screenshots from *Goodbye CP* depicting Yokota on his knees on a moving train.

FIGURE 2.4 A sequence of three screenshots from *Goodbye CP* depicting Yokota being carried onto a moving train and across a platform by his assistant while a subtitled conversation with Hara plays over the scene.

no subtitles when the film is screened in Japan, preferring to circulate a pamphlet containing a transcript:

> HARA: You say people don't understand what you say. You really think so?
> YOKOTA: How can they?
> HARA: So you'll be doing this just to satisfy yourself?
> YOKOTA: No, that's not it. I think they will understand something . . . even if they don't understand every single word.
> HARA: How's that?
> YOKOTA: They'll wonder what I'm doing.
> HARA: You don't want them to know you're reciting your poems.
> YOKOTA: Well, if they're really listening, they'll understand.
> HARA: You think so? So we don't need to set up? Should we make a sign that says "Poem Reading?
> YOKOTA: Yokota Hiroshi Poem Reading . . . Meeting?
> HARA: Poem reading meeting?
> YOKOTA: I guess not a meeting. Yokota Hiroshi Reads Poems.
> HARA (repeats): Yokota Hiroshi Reads Poems.

I hear these two scenes as a call and response, or an instigation and counterinstigation that shapes what I have come to understand as Hara and Kobayashi's cinematic philosophy of disentitled access. Scene 1 is a staging of what Rosemarie Garland-Thomson calls *misfitting*, or the process whereby people with minority forms of embodiment are disabled by environments designed to harmoniously "fit" and sustain normate bodies.[34] In 1972, train stations in Japan offered no automatic gates, ramps, or electric lifts for passengers in wheelchairs or with other mobility disabilities. These are all examples of what the ADA terms "reasonable accommodations," or modifications and provisions that make existing facilities or workplaces accessible to and usable by people with disabilities.[35] Equivalent antidiscrimination legislation was only introduced in Japan in 2013.[36] The Green Grasses' spectacular protests against inaccessible buses and segregated facilities are widely acknowledged to have paved the way for a new generation of activists who have challenged the segregationist impulse of Japan's traditionally welfarist approach to disability policies with demands for social participation, barrier-free access, and integration grounded in the discourse of disability rights.[37]

Hara's challenge to Yokota to board a train without his wheelchair or a personal assistant was inspired by a book popular among student activists of the time: Terayama Shūji's *Throw Out Your Books and Head for the Streets*. Hara has described this provocation, which he had previously rehearsed with high-school students at the Kōmyō School for Handicapped Children, as an attempt to upend nondisabled people's unexamined perceptions and values regarding disability and to agitate his Green Grasses collaborators (who had already achieved national prominence for speaking out against eugenicist attitudes regarding disability) into more extreme and dangerous physical actions that involved leaving their domestic confines and interacting with city infrastructures.[38] Yokota's crawling performance produces public and private frictions. He demonstrates how the space-time of the train station offers fits to ambulatory bodies and creates a misfit that not only excludes but mortally endangers him. Because Hara runs out of film during the last shot, we don't find out until the next scene, when Yokota's wife Yoshiko violently opposes his involvement in the film, that Yokota has exited the train without harm. The tense asynchrony of the frozen image and ringing bell in the final shot amplifies the misfitting and out-of-time-ness of disabled life.

In Scene 2, Yokota, a poet, responds with his own philosophy of noncompliant friction. As in the previous scene, Hara's provocation places the burden of personal risk on Yokota, but this time Yokota pushes back. The onus of bridging the gap between his CP-inflected speech and the comprehension of his audiences should—like the gap between the train and the platform—not be on him, says Yokota, but on nondisabled people. He reasons that not understanding will make his audience wonder what he is doing. That wondering could, he speculates, lead to a deeper listening that appreciates the bravery of a person with severe communication impediments performing poetry in public even if the content of their speech remains somewhat opaque. Importantly, Yokota locates that deeper listening ("if they're really listening") as untimely: a listening that continues after the event of speech has concluded and which may perhaps require a reflection upon itself.[39] Hara has noted that Yokota was influenced by the teachings of Rev. Osaragi Akira, the Socialist Buddhist monk and philosopher who established Maharaba Village, a rural commune for people with CP where Yokota and Yoshiko had met and married. Yokota's philosophy of listening swims diagonally against the currents of Osaragi's revolutionary separatism and Yoshiko's desires for respectable integration, which inform her disapproval of Hara's antics and eventually lead Yokota to quit the film.[40] It also undeniably influences Hara's decision to craft a nonsync antirealist aesthetic that offers no easy fit or linguistic access to nondisabled audiences. Hara's initial plan for confronting ableist attitudes places the burden on disabled bodies—he writes, "My camera would persistently and relentlessly gaze upon Yokota Hiroshi's body"—but Yokota's intervention pushes him toward strategies that confront the unsanctioned visual *and* auditory access of normate audiences to disabled bodies.[41]

This mutually transformative collaboration among fledgling filmmakers and activists not only shaped the global disability movement and the career of an important documentary filmmaker but also, crucially, a crip documentary aesthetic that may be more familiar to many in its more mainstream iterations. The centrality of sound and listening to this aesthetic has much to do with the fact that the disability movement in Japan was led by people with CP with disability-affected speech. Many of them (including Yokota and Yokotsuka) dropped out of or did not attend school and were not involved in the student movements that spurred their own activism.[42] They shared this outsider status and class identity with Hara, who had dropped out of photography school to support himself, and Kobayashi, a polio survivor whose leg disability and rural schooling excluded her from studio-based film apprenticeships. Kobayashi, a feminist who attributes much of her thinking around gender, bodies, and liberation to Takeda Miyuki (Hara's first wife, a radical feminist and the subject of Hara and Kobayashi's second film), nevertheless persisted in enrolling in a low-tuition night program for screenwriting. She approached Hara to make the film that would become *Goodbye CP* after seeing a solo show of Hara's photographs of disabled students at Kōmyō.[43] The collaboration was fruitful for all parties: *Goodbye CP* had a very limited theatrical release in Kanagawa due to budget constraints, but the film gained a brisk following across Japan thanks to the Green Grasses, who screened it at residential institutions, hospitals, and "roadshows" while Hara and Kobayashi targeted universities and leftwing student groups. These screenings increased the membership of the Green Grasses and led to the formation of regional chapters and spinoff advocacy groups; it also resulted in *Goodbye CP* becoming Hara and Kobayashi's most-rented film.[44] The decision of the Green Grasses and Kobayashi to join forces with Hara recalls another storied coalition: that of polio-surviving disability activists and nondisabled allies who are said to have taken sledgehammers to sidewalks in Berkeley, California, under cover of night in the late 1960s, recementing them to make crude but effective curb cuts.[45]

In a 1995 publication reflecting on his feature collaborations with Kobayashi, Hara describes action documentary as a philosophy of mutual provocation or attack. Hara begins by initiating an action with his camera; this action is then taken up and filtered through the bodies of those who are provoked; they then act, and in turn, their actions become a provocation to Hara, who is able to examine what is made visible as a result.[46] Hara's relational and activist ethos, evocative of Brechtian estrangement, was shaped by national and international currents: both the U.S. civil rights and Black Power movements as well as Japanese filmmakers such as Hani Susumu, Ogawa Shinsuke, and Tsuchimoto Noriaki, who were among the first in Japan to practice intersubjective documentary approaches that emphasized durational, immersive-collectivist, and long-term collaboration.⁴⁷ Though he was enamored of these precursors (Ogawa in particular), Hara sought a more combative and dissonant approach to cinematic collaboration. He found this in the political avant-gardism of Matsumoto Toshio, who rejected factual documentary claims and saw the camera as a means of interrogating unconscious perceptual biases and foregrounding cinematic mediation as a process of fragmentation and disorientation.⁴⁸

Hara's disabled collaborators (Kobayashi, Yokota, Yokotsuka, and other members of the Green Grasses) must be named among his political and aesthetic influences. Their decision to leave the ghettoized confines of residential facilities for people with disabilities and forcefully enter public spaces and conversations indelibly shaped the impulse of public self-exposure (confronting protagonists, intruding in personal lives, exposing vulnerabilities) for which Hara's "private cinema" has been canonized.⁴⁹ Yokota's manifesto for the Green Grasses, which functioned as a founding document for the movement, champions the principles of "aggressive self-assertion" and "endless confrontation" with "able-bodied civilization."⁵⁰ These disabled artists and activists played an integral role in crafting the confrontational, dialectical aesthetic of disagreement, debate, and public performance that would become a hallmark of performative post-vérité film and video in the 1980s and 1990s. This confrontational post-vérité aesthetic tends to be attributed, on one hand, to internationally renowned documentarians outside crip culture who pay homage to Hara (Michael Moore, Errol Morris) and, on the other, to trailblazing U.S. and UK-based crip video artists such as David Mitchell, Sharon Snyder, and Stephen Dwoskin, who may not have been aware of Hara and Kobayashi (though Mitchell and Snyder name Morris among their inspirations).⁵¹ Hara's influence on more popular and globally renowned documentarians has already been recognized by film scholars—he has enjoyed a critical resurgence following the 2007 release by the nonprofit distributor Facets of a number of his documentaries on DVD, including *Goodbye CP*, several of which are now available through the subscription streaming platform The Criterion Channel—and cultural historians have acknowledged his role in further radicalizing the Green Grasses.[52] What I want to emphasize here is the impact of disability knowledge and experience, including what contemporary disability scholars such as Kim and Schalk might call Kobayashi's feminist crip-of-color vision, in collaboratively shaping Hara's philosophy of "action documentary."[53]

Action documentary's emphasis on physical and sensory ways of knowing and being, what Lúcia Nagib calls its "corporeal realism," can be understood from this standpoint as a crip-of-color methodology that embraces disabled bodyminds as aesthetic resources.[54] By documenting the encounter between Yokota's body and the built environment, the film registers what nondisabled onlookers have stopped noticing, or never acknowledged, about its ableist design. Other scenes crip the "fly on the wall" conventions of vérité-style photography. Hara gives Yokotsuka a still camera and challenges him to photograph strangers up front and uncomfortably close, from a distance of no more than one meter (see fig. 2.5).[55] The film is punctuated by sequences in which Yokotsuka, camera raised to his eye by shaking hands, lurches unsteadily toward pedestrians in a crowded mall, on the street, or at a bus stop. Usually read as a reclaiming of the nondisabled gaze upon the disabled body, this exercise is experienced by Yokota as physical unease: a combination of terror and exhilaration that comes, as he says in one scene, from "catching someone's eyeline" and breaching the safety of distance. "If they are far away," he says, "it's easy." At its core, then, action documentary examines how crip discomfort and risk—complexly embodied sensations, knowledges, and feelings produced by wresting access from ableist situations and spaces—take a sledgehammer to realist aesthetics and demand a new system of documentary value.

What might it mean for film audiences, especially nondisabled audiences accustomed to having easy and nonthreatening access to

LISTENING IN CRIP TIME 99

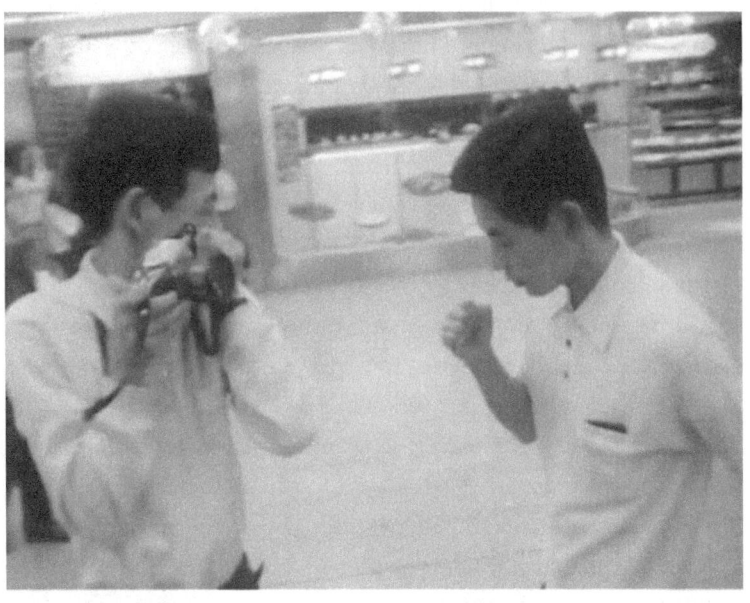

FIGURE 2.5 Screenshot from *Goodbye CP* depicting Yokotsuka engaging in the "one meter exercise."

disabled bodies and voices, to be cripped by such embodied risk and discomfort? Can documentary get normate listeners to accommodate to bodies moving, speaking, and living in crip time? These are the challenges Hara and Kobayashi set for themselves and for the audiences of *Goodbye CP*. If Yokota and Yokotsuka can throw out their wheelchairs and head for the streets, they reason, then the audiences of their film can very well plunge into it without the supports—the audiovisual and textual accommodations—that transform crip experience into accessible images and soundbites. When *Goodbye CP* was shown in Japan, Hara insisted that it be shown without subtitles. Instead, he would circulate a pamphlet about the film that contained a transcript in Japanese. "The effect," the Hara scholar Joel Neville Anderson writes, having seen the film in a variety of contexts, "is that if a viewer is not accustomed to communicating with people with CP, they are likely to struggle to understand their speech, and have to refer to the transcript." He continues, "Thus, the experience of watching a Hara film, and especially this one, is a markedly different experience when viewed with foreign subtitles offering immediate translation in a familiar and comprehensible format."[56] This is borne out in the testimony of the film critic Satō Shigechika, who describes the film's "largely unintelligible dialogue" in a 1972 review.[57]

I have come to understand these choices as access obstacles that acquaint nondisabled audiences with the unpredictable compressions and dilations of time and space involved in negotiating access. These negotiations entail a type of collective power-sharing in which nondisabled audiences give back by accommodating people with disabilities. Hara and Kobayashi's refusal to cater to listeners unaccustomed to verbal and auditory impediments shapes a crip aesthetic of disentitled access that I would describe as *crawling listening*. Subtitles conventionally offer linguistic access to nonnative speakers of the language spoken in a film, but when they are used to translate disability-affected speech, they alleviate the temporary or situational disability of listeners, in this case, those unaccustomed to speaking with people with CP. They accommodate majority bodyminds seeking access to people with minority embodiments even as they accentuate CP-affected speech as untimely and slow.

Accommodations, Jay Dolmage notes, have a "chronicity—a timing and time-logic."[58] They are retrofits; they come after the fact. Anyone who has requested, say, a wheelchair bus or a modified teaching schedule can attest that accommodations are "slow to come and fast to expire."[59] They routinely involve painful inconveniences of space (poorly located accessible entrances; too-small elevators) and harmful delays (bureaucratic systems may move slowly or refuse to acknowledge the problem; using accommodations may be time-consuming). Margaret Price calls the material costs of these workarounds "time harms." As she writes, the arduousness of repeatedly traversing the "accommodations loop" can cost disabled people time, money, and emotion (paying for one's own accommodations; giving up opportunities or inaccessible jobs; exhaustion from reasserting access needs).[60] Hearing and sighted audiences rarely encounter such obstacles in accessing disability-affected speech. Accommodations such as proper synchronization and timely translation are provided to them by default without their ever having to ask. This is a result of what the design scholar Aimi Hamraie has identified as an ableist interpretation of Universal Design since the late 1990s as design that accommodates nondisabled people and disavows disability, despite its roots in the work of disability activists and disability rights efforts preceding the ADA.[61] In contrast, captions and audio description are often unavailable even when they are explicitly requested by people with disabilities. Even when they *do* work, their chronicity is not straightforward.[62]

Thanks to Anderson, who has arranged 16 mm screenings of the film in North America, I have seen *Goodbye CP* projected without subtitles or transcript (to my knowledge no English-language transcript exists) and subsequently as a subtitled DVD from Facets. The subtitled version in which the film circulates internationally fundamentally changes the politics of the film even as it retains, for non-Japanese speakers such as myself who are more familiar with Euroamerican vérité of that period, something of the challenging opacity of the untitled print. *Goodbye CP* is obdurately out of sync. Absent or erratic synchronized sound was not unusual for small-crew and low-budget social documentaries made in 1970s Japan: Hara shot on borrowed Arriflex and Filmo windup cameras, and the edit is cheap and rough.[63] Even so, the mismatch of image, sound, and subtitles in *Goodbye CP*, especially during interviews with Green Grasses members, stands apart because of the laborious engagement it demands: It engages me in an accented listening activity of which I have often been at the receiving end. I can best describe this listening as an auditory equivalent of staring: a highly focused, intense, and excessive listening-scanning-looking-reading in which the listener, encountering speech that is foreign to their ear (a foreignness or estrangement that may also be inflected by the listener's perception of the speaker's visual appearance, along with expectations regarding what such a person may plausibly sound like), leans in, *too close for comfort*, and asks the speaker to repeat what they have said, *differently*, and comprehensibly.

Staring, as famously theorized by Garland-Thomson, refers to an ableist mode of looking to which visibly disabled people are often subjected. It is an intense, sustained looking whose profligate interest is usually socially inappropriate.[64] Garland-Thomson maintains, as does Anderson, that staring can be socially productive because it demands a response: She argues that "starees" are often adept at taking charge of the staring encounter and engaging starers in ways that can be mutually transformative. My sense, however, is that Yokota and Yokotsuka are leery, as am I, of burdening the staree with transforming the relational dynamic under circumstances in which they (the staree) have already been robbed of consent. Staring-listening is entitled listening—it presumes a listener who wants but does not need access. It puts the onus on the stigmatized speaker to accommodate the normate listener and to grant access where the listener cannot enter. I would distinguish staring-listening from the effort that accented and D/deaf listeners have to exert, for instance, when they bend their perception to accommodate and apprehend speech that is coded as "neutral" or "normal."

I keep returning to one sequence of the film, featuring close-up confessionals with men with CP speaking about their delayed, furtive, failed, and nonconsensual first sexual experiences, to grasp what is at stake in staring-listening. It is a disturbing sequence punctuated by jarring tonal shifts. The men speak frankly about being coerced into abstinence and sexual predation because of their disability. Yokota speaks of being denied the status of a sexual being by his uncle and guardian. An unnamed man recounts being bullied by classmates into raping a young woman. Toward the end, Yokotsuka describes feeling disarmed by the tender hospitality of a sexual partner to his disability after nearly three decades of rejection: "I couldn't get it up, I had suppressed it for so long. I tried so many times, I thought I was impotent. *I had no idea where to put it.*" The testimonies paint a picture of consent as a negotiation of access across confounding and asymmetrical inclines of power that can quickly turn violent. Sitting with these profound meditations on the forced misfitting of disability as a political experience, I find myself meditating on the oblique pertinence of Yokotsuka's statement to the documentary listener witnessing Hara and Kobayashi's out-of-sync testimonies. To listen in the provisional and delayed presence of linguistic access is to be put in the position of listening not as a starer but as a crawler. It is to listen without the expectation or certainty of being granted access. In an interview describing his "crawls," performance pieces in which he physically crawled on cement, dirt, and asphalt in solidarity with homeless and disabled people, artist William Pope.L describes crawling as an act that "performs both humility and willfulness."[65] To listen in this mode is to listen in acknowledgement of the reciprocity, interdependence, and unevenness of access, and with the conviction that the physical unease, risk, and discomfort of being put out are worthwhile—especially if we understand the normate acceptance of disentitlement as hospitality to the access needs of people with disabilities.

To listen as a crawler—to wait for a transcript that may or may not be available, for a mouth to form itself around a sound, for a textual translation that comes after a sound that precedes or follows its corresponding image—is to learn to listen in crip time. Crawling listening might mean becoming attentive to how documentary time is measured, edited, aligned, and made valuable, which is often at odds with what Hendren, paraphrasing Samuels, calls "the out-of-sync plotting of life in its mismatched state."[66] It might mean accepting the lag between listening and understanding to which Yokota refers in Scene 2. It might also entail practicing what Lisbeth Lipari calls an "otherwise" listening that is hospitable to the unfamiliar without holding, grasping, or inserting it into "some tidy box of 'understanding'" that satisfies the "insatiable appetite for the familiar."⁶⁷ Listening otherwise can be a listening out of time: It can have the effect, as one ethnographer reports, upon interviewing someone with extremely slow language production, of slipping into an "altered sense of time."⁶⁸ Above all, crawling listening might mean reflecting on the extractive entitlement of listening that takes access for granted and presumes that disabled accents will be retrofitted, discretely and violently, to the norm. The Indigenous studies scholar Dylan Robinson (xwélméxw) invokes a structurally analogous "hungry listening" when describing the insatiable settler colonial appetite for Indigenous sonic resources deemed palatable.⁶⁹ Hungry listening, Robinson writes, is acquisitive and appropriative; it is a listening *for*. It satiates through familiarity (the satisfaction of identification and recognition) and certainty (the "fit" of content within a predetermined framework). It is hungry, to borrow Robinson's words, for "the felt confirmations of square pegs in square holes, for the satisfactory fit as sound knowledge slides into its appropriate place."⁷⁰ Staring-listening is also hungry for familiarity and certainty. It mines the content of documentary speech without care for the relational acts of hospitality, exchange, or theft involved in the negotiation of access.

Crawling listening confronts nondisabled audiences with the fact that their access to disability experience is not guaranteed but contingent. Disentitled access intimates that access is a more-than-two-way street and that negotiating access as a shared responsibility, far from being a drain on resources, may result in collective gains, even if those gains are temporary and laborious. What if such listening were the default rather than the anomaly in documentary? What might it mean to approach access not as a retrofit but as the bedrock of the documentary encounter? What would documentary form look like if access were a framing consideration and the basis of ethical, aesthetic, and narrative decisions? To answer these questions, I turn now from Hara and Kobayashi's reactive approach to listening in crip time to the work of Jordan Lord, whose proactive contributions to an ongoing conversation on transformative access among disabled U.S. artists follow in the path of *Goodbye CP*.

LISTENING SIDEWAYS

Shared Resources begins where vérité films in the reflexive mode sometimes end. Lord's mother and father, both principal participants in the film (Lord has said the film was made "in consultation" with them) sit in their living room and react to an early cut of the film. "I didn't just dislike it, I loathed it. Hated it, despised it," says Albert, Lord's father. Albert is objecting to a pivotal scene in which he appears weak and vulnerable after a hospital visit. Lord's mother Deborah interjects that Albert was, in fact, weak at the time, but her protest has little impact. Later in the film it is revealed that Albert lives with life-threatening chronic illnesses caused by Agent Orange exposure during the Vietnam War, including retinal damage that could culminate in blindness. We learn that Albert, formerly a debt collector, has been debilitated by a series of losses: the loss of the family's home to Hurricane Katrina and the subsequent loss of his job and his Veterans Affairs (VA) disability benefits after filing for Chapter 13 bankruptcy. Notorious for being nearly impossible to complete, Chapter 13 bankruptcy leads to a three- to five-year debt-repayment plan during which debtors must live on a fixed income.

The scene to which Albert objects immediately precedes the reaction scene. It is the first in the film, and what it depicts, indicated below in parentheses, is only later identified and set in context. Crimson light fills the screen (Lord has covered the lens with their finger to occlude the weakened image of himself that Albert so resents, so the light, passing through flesh and skin, registers in shifting hues of red) (see fig. 2.6) while three voices (belonging to Deborah, Lord's sister Ashley, and Lord) coax a fourth (Albert) to drink a glass of

FIGURE 2.6 Screenshot from *Shared Resources* in which Lord has placed their finger over the lens, producing a crimson image that is described in a yellow open caption. Courtesy of the artist.

milk. Albert's disorientation is discernable only from how the others interact with him, repeating their words, demonstrating how to lift the glass, and laughing to break the tension. An even-toned off-screen voice (Lord's) describes the images and text that appear on screen. The descriptions say both less and more than what I perceive as a sighted and hearing person. Some clarify what is happening: "A reddish pink frame fills the screen, pulsing from dark to bright"; "On the screen what's being said appears in a yellow open caption on top of a black bar." Others add complexity, pointing out details that my perceptual habits lead me to miss or dismiss as insignificant: "On the table between my parents, a pair of headphones and a recorder are visible"; "Throughout the film, yellow text designates someone speaking off camera; white text designates someone speaking on camera."

For sighted and hearing audiences unaccustomed to watching a film with access features such as open (or nonoptional) captions and a verbal description of what is shown (commonly called audio description), Lord's anticipatory, accommodating vision can be disorienting. Lord interprets Albert's objection to his portrayal as weak or vulnerable as a statement of his access needs—that is, accommodations and adjustments that Albert requires in order to fully participate in the film and the world in which it will circulate. Lord responds to these needs by occluding Albert's image. In verbally describing that occlusion ("a reddish pink frame fills the screen, pulsing from dark to bright"), Lord anticipates Albert's future access needs were he to lose his vision, as well as those of blind and deaf viewers. The ethical and creative possibilities of open captions and burned-in audio description allow Lord to link Albert's disavowal of his disability experience to the very ableist forces that justify neglecting or segregating the needs of audiences with sensory differences.

In assuming, imagining, and calling forth a crip audience, *Shared Resources* affirms disability as the "ground state of life."[71] As Lord puts it, disability, like dependency, is a form of social wealth and relational possibility, "a bond that grows." The design of the film, apparent in its opening scene, foregrounds access as a practice of mutual care and dependency rather than a burden. The film invites a *sideways listening* less interested in precision or clarity than in how meaning grows thicker, slower, and stranger when it is mediated through the pathways of another person's embodied particularity and access requirements, circuitous and time-consuming as this may be. Listening sideways is not about the point so much as getting to the point, or simply getting around. It cultivates an appetite for access intimacy, or what Mia Mingus calls "that elusive, hard to describe feeling when someone else 'gets' your access needs."[72] This is a powerful act of solidarity. When access needs are treated not as inconvenient afterthoughts but as the building blocks of narrative form, transformative shifts in documentary relationships follow.

I have come to think of Lord's relational and formal commitment to "baked-in" access as a refusal of the austerity thinking that leads documentarians to conceive of participants in their films as liabilities that threaten their access to sources of documentary value. Liability concerns lurk, unstated, when filmmakers admit backstage negotiations and relational dynamics into the diegesis or paratext of their films after the fact. In *Goodbye CP*, for example, Hara keeps his camera running during a fight in which Yokota's wife Yoshiko angrily objects to Yokota's crawling performances. She resents that Hara and Kobayashi have forced their way into her home to capture their private discord. When asked to account for his decision, Hara claims that Yoshiko granted him permission to use this footage in the film despite her disapproval and that Yokota and Yokotsuka have defended the film as a "collaboration."[73] Lord's insistence on access as a primary cinematic principle prompts me to understand such ex post facto efforts at accountability as retrospective accommodations or retrofits. Documentarians often compensate for the harm they have caused by devising makeshift structures to redress complaints and protect their investment. But as Hara's case exemplifies, these gestures routinely come too late and offer too little. Retrofits designed to meet a minimal legal interpretation of access (in this case, permission, or what documentary "appearance release" forms treat as a liability waiver) become defeat devices that perform access even as they preserve the structures that perpetuate exclusion.[74] Repetition can turn retrofits into self-defeating convention. The trope of the reaction scene is one such convention; the justification of directorial decisions by film participants in post-screening Q&As is another. The appearance release form similarly produces the appearance of access equity even as it is legally designed to outsource risk to documentary subjects.

Shared Resources moves away from such adversarial and litigious approaches to access as risk management. These are themes already set up by Lord's previous short film, *After . . . After . . . (Access)* (2018), which questions the medico-legal logic of common documentary practices around access. The film documents the filmmaker's preparation for open-heart surgery and concludes with cell phone footage shot inside the hospital. Lord tells us that this footage was shot surreptitiously by a friend and caregiver after Lord's months-long petition to film their care networks during their surgery and recovery was denied—the hospital refused to sign a release that would permit Lord to film their care and to use the filmed record indefinitely. As Lord has observed elsewhere, the documentary appearance release form is modeled on the form that patients are required to sign indicating their informed consent. This effectively releases the medical provider from responsibility for any potential harm to the patient.[75] As the "stolen" footage plays, Lord reflects that the modern, legalistic meaning of access, understood as the ability to enter, has superseded its medieval meaning as a fever or altered state, understood more broadly as an attack or breach. "The perspective has changed," Lord muses, "but not the dynamic." Lord is referring to how the enclosure of life-supporting resources as private property transforms access from a public good into an individual benefit. Access without permission or consent—even, and indeed especially, for the common good—is deemed a theft and a punishable offense.

Shared Resources explores this neoliberal, transactional understanding of access and its implications for the documentary form through an interview with Albert about his work as the head of the collections department at a bank. Albert responds to Lord's queries about his work and his bankruptcy as a spokesperson for the very system that left him without a social safety net when he was fired. Good lenders and collectors, Albert reasons, have a responsibility toward their people to whom they lend, and good borrowers owe it to their creditors and to themselves to make good on their debt. Even though his own father (whom Albert cites as a victim of predatory lenders) left his mother with a staggering amount of credit card debt, Albert states that he does not regret the massive loans he borrowed for Lord's college tuition, believing this to be his responsibility as Lord's parent, which he has now fulfilled.

Reflecting on Albert's insistence on holding himself to account, Lord muses that in documentary, too, it has become commonplace to hold people to account. Indeed, as previously noted, the function of the appearance release form is to outsource risk to the subject. Interview subjects are "framed," held individually accountable for their words just as insurance and the creditors hold debtors accountable for their health and education. Lord comments, "The process of interviewing, which is also involved in applying for jobs, schools, and loans, most closely resembles the sense of applying that means to join or adhere like one might apply glue. The interview sticks with the person being interviewed. Though it can always be recut and recombined, it creates a record. The record produces a kind of evidence that the person may later be held to. We might call this their story, but it might as likely be called their account." Brett Story offers a different perspective on the logic of accountability undergirding the concept of "story" by calling attention to how the ascendant, commercially viable documentary forms that center individuals' stories suppress or edit out aspects of shared reality. She writes, "The story form as it is most commonly heralded—owned, belonging, contained, resolvable—does useful work for recuperation precisely because it dovetails with the individualism at the heart of neoliberal capitalism and the property form alike. The hero, the resilient individual, the villain, the charity case: these are all variations on an already existing and pernicious ideological preference for the individual over the social, the "character" over the condition, experience over consciousness."[76]

Against the neoliberal logic of their commercial contemporaries, Lord edits with an eye to the larger structures of violence that Albert elides in the telling of his story. The film intercuts Albert's responses with verbal commentary on how editorial decisions (miking bodies to separate voices from their surroundings, changing the order in which things are said, removing extraneous material, combining different images with a voice to conceal cuts) perform an *invisible audit*, enabling documentarians to extract an account from a life in which bits and pieces of information are deemed valuable ("values, knowledge, past experience, expertise, trustworthiness"). Before and during the interview with Albert, Lord cuts back in scenes from his daily life that reveal the debilitating and ableist logic of this audit. Albert is shown driving to the bank from which he was fired to deposit checks and use the coin machine no less than four times. He visits an ophthalmologist, who tells him the only way to control his retinal damage is to get his diabetes under control. At home, as Jordan's mother Deborah makes soup using canned vegetables (a survival strategy learned during her working-class childhood), Jordan's sister Ashley remarks that their father's health issues would benefit from a fresh-food diet. Insofar as Albert's account suggests that individuals are responsible for their recovery, whether corporeal or financial, these reverse cutbacks imply that recovery is less a return to a prior, pristine state than a series of painful detours through the wormhole of crip time. They stick with the listener, demanding a different kind of accountability, another type of social glue.

Lord answers that demand by rethinking documentary access—beyond the capitalist model of false scarcity and gatekeeping—as a queer and crip practice of sharing resources and building social capacities. Their insistence on open captions and burned-in audio description performs the fundamentally speculative, improvisatory, incomplete, and necessary work of caring and support that Mingus calls "access intimacy." Access for the sake of love, community, and connection—redefined simply and ineffably by Leah Lakshmi Piepzna Samarasinha as "revolutionary love without charity" and "love-work of collective care"—enacts a transformative shift in neoliberal documentary values.[77] As Mingus puts it, access intimacy approaches access not as something that is begrudgingly given up but as an anticipation of need that generates a kind of social wealth. She continues, "Access shifts from being an individual responsibility to a collective responsibility . . . from being silencing to freeing; from being isolating to connecting; from hidden and invisible to visible; from burdensome to valuable; from a resentful obligation to an opportunity; from shameful to powerful; from rigid to creative. It's the 'good' kind of access, the moments when we are pleasantly surprised and feel seen. It is a way of doing access that transforms both our 'today' and our 'tomorrow.'"[78]

The way Lord practices access intimacy departs from a long cinematic tradition of austerity thinking that frames linguistic access (subtitles, dubbing) and sensory access features (captions, audio description) as burdensome additions that distract or subtract from aesthetic experience. The widespread acceptance of subtitles and dubbing in various national contexts, data on elective subtitle use for enhanced narrative comprehension, a robust body of scholarly criticism framing subtitling as an interpretive art, and experimentation with the aesthetic possibilities of text on screen has done little to budge the mainstream perception of linguistic access as a degradation of the "original" cinematic text.[79] Dubbing, we have been told, turns actors into "ventriloquist's puppets," destroying any trace of cinematic authenticity, while verbose subtitles "drown" or replace the image, producing "resentment" and "fatigue" in audiences toggling between sensory impressions and textual interpretation.[80]

The availability of linguistic and sensory access has historically been a function of interactions among industry interests, consumer desires, technological innovation, and legislative change.[81] However, the relatively recent global expansion of captions and audio description in audiovisual media has been a direct result of U.S.-based disabled self-advocacy and legal activism, especially by D/eaf people, who have been early adapters and innovators of access technologies.[82] Following the COVID-19 pandemic, automated captions have become a near-ubiquitous option across videoconferencing and social media platforms.[83] Nevertheless, increased familiarity with and demand for captions among the general population has not significantly impacted the availability of media offerings that account for disability access as a first principle. The industrial history of sensory access for audiovisual media has been guided since its inception instead by a mandate of invisibility that reinforces the social invisibility of disabled people and the unmarked norm of a sighted and hearing audience. Following an all-too-brief broadcast experiment with open captions, captions and audio description have largely been segregated to an optional track.[84] Making sensory access optional caters to a larger variety of access needs, but the practice of retrofitting access as an optional feature also placates able-bodied investments in cinema as an experience "spoiled" by translation. The default inclusion of access features to facilitate the participation of people with peripheral embodiments remains largely limited to disability film festivals whose vanguardism around access is possible in part because of their cultural marginalization.[85]

To this day, industry norms for captioning and audio description uphold the values of inconspicuousness, discretion, and seamless integration. Style guides consist largely of design and pacing recommendations for retrofitting captions and verbal description to the film or television program in the available space-time between scene changes and dialogue to minimize asynchrony and maximize narrative comprehension. Best practices advise audio describers and captioners to be neutral, accurate, and objective, and to avoid interpretation, commentary, or graphic or technical vocabulary that calls attention to itself.[86] Users of these services have lamented the mystification, misdirection, and shrinking of cinematic experience under the neutrality imperative. The blind disability scholar Georgina Kleege has noted, for instance, how the withholding of information about nudity can, in addition to infantilizing blind audiences, leave them to imagine narrative information made explicit to the sighted viewer.[87] In a related vein, Deaf artist Christine Sun Kim's video *[Closer Captions]* (2020) explains how the translation of music as a single word or symbol depicting a musical note impoverishes D/deaf spectators, suggesting synesthetic alternatives (a tiled floor is captioned "the sound of shampoo scent floating among the fog").

Lord has stated that their intention was to work with access as the "material and form" of their creative practice.[88] They elaborate, "I wanted to get at all the things that happen, not just at the point of projection, but in the relay between people, in order to get the image and sound into someone's perception."[89] Lord shares this investment with crip, queer, trans/gender nonconforming, and crip-of-color artists such as Kim, Lazard, McArthur, Zavitsanos, and Amalle Dublon, who have taken up sensory translation as a medium of formal experimentation, invention, and critique.[90] In addition to providing necessary access to disabled audiences, all of these artists have produced audio and video works that stage institutional critiques of the art world's performative and self-defeating access accommodations and model disability aesthetics inspired by access intimacy. Lazard's *A Recipe for Disaster* (2018), a remix of Julia Child's *The French Chef*, the first TV show to feature open captions, responds to the discontinuation of this practice with a snowball of complaints ("well, your party sucks"; "if you can't share, no one can have any") that accumulate as an increasingly cacophonous scroll of audio described text layered over a captioned recording of the program (see fig. 2.7). The Deaf artists Joseph Grigely, Kim, and Liza Sylvestre echo this aesthetic of complaint. In *Inventory of Apologies* (2019), Grigely compiles apologies he has received from cultural institutions that failed to caption their online events. Kim is shown signing in *Spoken on My Behalf* (2020) while sarcastic captions ventriloquize interpreters and hearing people who have voluntarily or involuntarily "voiced" the artist, and in *Captioned-Channel Surfing* (2017–2018), Sylvestre captions TV programs captured while channel surfing without captions, conjuring a parallel but overlooked spectatorial experience reliant on visual observations, lip-reading, body language, and prosthetics such as hearing aids and cochlear implants.[91] Other artists employ an aesthetic of displacement and substitution to emphasize the positive benefits of exclusion from ableist cultural spaces, widely referred to in disability communities as JOMO (the joy of missing out). For instance, McArthur's audio piece *PARA-SITES* (2018) describes the gallery and artworks in their MoMA exhibition, in addition to off-site and imaginary spaces. Zavitsanos and Dublon similarly employ open captions

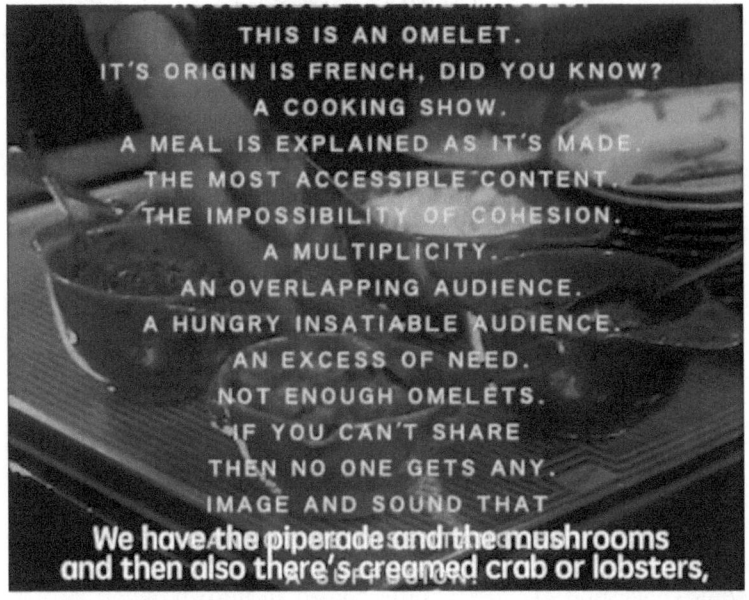

FIGURE 2.7 Screenshot from *A Recipe for Disaster* depicting an open captioned scene from Julia Child's *The French Chef* overlaid with scrolling commentary. Carolyn Lazard, *A Recipe for Disaster*, 2018. HD video (color, sound), 27 minutes. Courtesy of the artist.

as the central medium and material in their minimalist video *April 4, 1980* (2018). The captions are described by Zavitsanos, whose voice is slowed down to fit the speed of caption reading rather than matching the speed of captions to the soundtrack, offering sighted and hearing viewers "the rare experience of a piece not meant to privilege them."[92]

Shared Resources contributes an aesthetic of redundancy to this crip and queer lexicon of access intimacy. What appears on screen is told, and what is spoken or sounded is shown. The look, sound, duration, and feel of the film are rejoinders to the documentary axiom "show don't tell." Popularized by the midcentury vérité turn, this axiom continues to exert pressure on documentary form and carries with it underexamined beliefs dating back to the early sound era. These beliefs affirm cinema's visual essence and the purity of the image as a universally accessible language. Verbal commentary is thought to be tainted by subjectivity, and narration is regarded as a didactic and redundant "double telling."[93] As a theory of narrative economy, "show don't tell" valorizes inaccessibility. The viewer (presumed to be seeing and hearing) is independently responsible for finding their way into the narrative through elegantly disguised and sutured points of entry. If telling reveals these openings, Lord doubles down on its redundancy as the lowest and most obvious denominator of access.

Audio description is often resented and avoided by filmmakers more than captioning: In addition to being expensive and laborious, it requires advance consideration and creative compromise in the form of a well-ventilated soundtrack (too much sound, music, and speech makes it difficult to accommodate verbal description, resulting in sonic congestion). Lord turns this constraint into an opportunity to explore how access features can guide not only the aesthetic of the film, but also its narratological movement. At every moment in the film, beginning with Albert's objection, Lord interprets access needs as formal barriers requiring creative and improvisatory workarounds. The basic principle of audio description is "say what you see." Where best practices and style guides see a covenant of fidelity to an original text premised on able-bodied assumptions, Lord finds a crip philosophy of ekphrasis, a fount of narratorial invention, and a means of activating what is *not* shown.[94] Audio description may appear to emanate as though from an objective, authorless source, but as Kleege has noted, it is often multiply authored.[95] Lord's process honors the unseen labor of access-work as well as its fundamentally collaborative and subjective character. For every scene that appears in the film, Lord asks Deborah, and occasionally Ashley (Albert declined to participate in this process), to watch the footage with and without sound and to record descriptions incorporating three different registers: how they reacted to seeing the footage, how they would describe it to someone who could not see, and what was left out of the frame but important to know. Lord then edits these recordings into one voice-over track, supplementing with their own descriptions and commentary.[96]

Deborah's is the voice we hear most frequently, along with Lord's. Lord's commentary and descriptions, neutrally intoned in the simple present tense, have the effect of zooming out to present analyses of abstract and invisible structures such as the credit economy and internalized ableism. As a combined effect of her willingness (and perhaps need) to open up, her intimate and emotional delivery, and use of the present continuous tense, Deborah's descriptions sound like an internal monologue that takes us inside the film and illustrates how the structures illuminated by Lord are felt and lived. In tandem these two voices demonstrate how audio description functions, per Dolmage and Mara Mills, as ekphrasis. The ancient art of verbally describing visual material, ekphrasis includes such varied and mixed verbal-visual forms as poems about paintings, film analysis, slide lectures, and videographic criticism.[97] Ekphrasis is, as film scholar Erika Balsom reminds, "never tautology." Balsom's reflections on writing about film beautifully capture Lord's approach to audio description: "It attempts to grasp the ungraspable but never fully can, producing an imperfect translation from one medium to another. It excludes some details and amplifies others. . . . It excludes, amplifies, transforms. In trying to stay near, it can go far."[98]

As a sighted and hearing listener, I have experienced this collective description-as-narration as a *sideways growth* of the film, in which the telling of what is shown offers the listener access to a different dimension of the film than the one progressing in the foreground. Creating access, as McArthur and Zavitsanos have written, entails developing relationships with those who work behind the scenes. McArthur writes, "Figuring out together with a person or people who are providing access often means running temporary interference to rules of security, business, and customer service that mediate kitchens, break rooms, and storage areas as work sites. Tina's [Zavitsanos] called this the backstage pass."[99] The backstage is the space of access-work, that invisible and inaudible "relay between people" that literally and metaphorically props up Albert and the story of his recovery. *Shared Resources* unfolds almost entirely in these waiting rooms of life, enfolding the tedium of access-work into its narrative rhythms. In the foreground, the story of Albert's recovery marches along, unsteadily but surely. Meanwhile, Deborah, Lord, and Ashley wait in the bank parking lot as Albert deposits checks, place telephone calls to medical insurance agents, and wait on Albert as he convalesces at home. Responding to their own images, they transport the listener to off-site and backstage spaces of access-work.

Redundancy and repetition facilitate this transit. The occluded opening scene haunts *Shared Resources* like a fever dream. This feels appropriate, considering this scene's role in launching a film that brings us back to an older understanding of access as an altered state, breach, or attack. "When a body gets too close to the camera," Lord reflects during its third iteration, speaking over the image of their finger covering the lens, "it becomes a shutter over the image so that all you can see is that it blocks from view." Lord is describing a practical as well as philosophical dilemma: Albert's blockage to his disability experience produces a formal impasse in that Albert is unable to narrate his account as anything other than a story of overcoming. Here, Lord finds, in Deborah and Ashley's double-telling, an aesthetic and narrative portal to crip time. What Deborah and Ashley say about what they see is not merely sensory translation of what cannot be seen or shown, although we do learn from Deborah that Albert "has no ability to help himself" and that Lord has entered the frame to help Albert to stand up. Their words also swell the scene in a chorus of concern, worry, and love that *tells us what it feels like* to provide care and support—that is, to provide access. "I'm constantly looking at mom.... He's looking like he's going to fall over.... She's incredulous, looking at me for validation," says Ashley. To me, it is incredibly moving to hear Deborah's own perception of her access fatigue grow and evolve through the act of description. This is how she describes a different view of the scene just described, in which Lord closes in on her face as she rocks in a recliner: "My face is, I mean it's telling the whole story. It's telling the story of the stress of how I'm so afraid. There's fear all over my face. The recliner is going back and forth because of the anticipation of what's going on in my home with my husband that I love so, that I depend on so. . . . You capture that, I mean you see it. I felt it, but you see it" (see fig. 2.8).

Kathryn Bond Stockton has described "growing sideways" as a queer orientation with regard to "growing up," which represents a temporal and relational destination normalized by compulsory heterosexuality. Sideways growth, she writes, is "a motion, an emotion, and a growth, even though, from certain conventional angles, it may look like a way of going nowhere."[100] *Shared Resources* grows sideways by cultivating a crip kind of love for access intimacy. Open captioned in yellow to indicate their off-screen status, Lord's audio descriptions materialize an imaginary off-site dimension in tension

FIGURE 2.8 Screenshot from *Shared Resources* showing a close-up of Deborah Lord, the filmmaker's mother, with her description of the image transcribed in yellow open captions. Courtesy of the artist.

with conventional documentary space. At an ontological level, they combine the denaturing effects of what Michel Chion calls *acousmatic* voices without an on-screen source and *athorybal* on-screen text that is unaccompanied by an utterance.[101] At a political level, they do something more. They thicken the listener's sense of access, understood less as perception than as politics, or, as Lazard puts it, "less as legibility than as feeling."[102] If I were to describe my own auditory activity during Lord's film, I might say: I am listening sideways, to the workaround, to what must happen despite and because of all that ableism makes unthinkable and nonsensical. I am falling in love with the thickness and slowdown that comes, in Dublon's words, from "becom[ing] involved with the means of getting around, or communicating, and the poetry or choreography of that means."[103] I am developing an ear for the unaudited and unaccounted love work of collective care that ballasts documentary stories.

WHAT'S THE CATCH?

In their classic study of disability and narrative, David Mitchell and Sharon Snyder argue that literary narratives throughout history have leaned on disability as a crutch. Literature exploits disability as an accent—an aberration that narrative sets out to resolve, correct, or prostheticize—while retrenching its invisibility as a social and political experience. Documentary is no exception to this discursive dependence on disability. To restate this chapter's analytic arc in slightly different terms, documentary encounters are framed by transactions of access, even as the ableist conventions and rules governing their narration train audiences to actively disregard the relational and collectivist meanings of access that have emerged from disability activism and queer/crip-of-color critique. If the unspoken oral and aural grammars of documentary sound are household fixtures, as I proposed at the beginning of this chapter, then disability is the foundation and prop—the "ground state of life"—that documentary listeners kick away at their own peril.

I have attempted to recognize the resonances among both Hara and Kobayashi and Lord's distinct efforts to train documentary listeners to contend with access understood in the crip sense of an attack or breach on the documentary audit. Hara and Kobayashi take aim at the entitled and paternalistic postures of postwar welfarism in Japan. Their insistence on withholding subtitles while exhibiting *Goodbye CP* forces normate listeners unaccustomed to disability-affected speech *and* Anglophone audiences accustomed to timely translation to confront their expectation that disability will be made to conform to ableist norms. Crawling listening demands that these audiences experience the redistributive principle of shared risk (as opposed to the paternalism of welfarism) as a temporal occlusion, impasse, or obstacle to their auditory access.

I see Lord working in the wake of Kobayashi, Yokota, and Yokotsuka, or *after* them, to use the term Lord uses to honor their crip predecessors and comrades in *After . . . After . . . (Access)*. Like Hara and Kobayashi, Lord enlists disability expertise to shape a desegregated documentary aesthetic that bends its audit to crip time. Lord rejects the liberal-inclusionist discourse of rights that frames barrier-free access as a universal benefit that will seamlessly integrate, becoming a benefit to all without hurting the majority or substantially changing the underlying social structure. The DeafBlind poet and writer John Lee Clark conjures a similar sentiment when articulating his rejection of the liberal interpretation of access as "nonreciprocal assimilation." Being delivered a description of a room "on a silver platter" by an ASL interpreter, he writes, is simply not enough: "I want to *attack* this room. I want to own it, just like the sighted people here own it. Or, if the room isn't worth owning, then I want to grab whatever I find worth stealing. C'mon, let's start over. What we'll do is start to touch things and people here, together, while we provide running commentaries and feedback to each other."[104] *Shared Resources* illustrates that to start over, to do access right, is to engage in a practice of creative destruction that rebuilds new forms amid the ashes of the old. The film invites audiences to experience sensory translation not as a simplistic addition but as an occlusion in its own right. Access becomes a frame within the frame that functions, paradoxically, as both a cut and a supplement that grows the film sideways, along the vectors of crip time. Listening sideways is the opposite of listening for the gist. It means listening for the props and supports that have been cut out or kicked away; it means catching what otherwise ends up on the cutting-room floor of film history.

In *Shared Resources* Lord offers their parents a contract that Albert refuses to sign. Lord calls it a "catch" contract because it is designed to accomplish the opposite of the standard documentary appearance release. A "catch" contract, they explain, would serve to shift the burden of risk and responsibility back to the filmmaker and enable Albert and Deborah to renegotiate Lord's access to them in perpetuity. Albert refuses, on principle, to sign a contract with his child and argues that such a contract may get in the way of a future distribution deal for the film. The issue remains unresolved, and Albert's suspicion lingers as a question: What's the catch?

I have tried answering this question for myself, and I offer it here: *There is always a catch*. Somebody has to be willing to take the fall. There can never be a documentary practice, or a practice of listening and accountability, in which nobody has to give anything up. But the risks associated with providing access are unfairly distributed in a capitalist media ecology. The year after its release, Lord's film received an offer from a subscription-based streaming platform whose focus on experimental and arthouse cinema is enabled by a partnership with Amazon Prime Video. The distribution deal ended up falling apart months later due to a policy change by Prime Video that precludes hosting or acquiring films with burned-in subtitles, which interfere with their business model for worldwide release. The decision was explained to Lord's producer Abby Sun as a preference by Amazon (which then accounted for a third of the niche streamer's revenue) for a "cleaner image."[105] To be sure, there are sound technical and practical reasons for this preference: Broadcast and broadband conditions can produce variations in the quality of open captions that impact legibility, and the default placement of nonoptional captions can interfere with the translation of a given program into multiple languages. But thinking purely in terms of pragmatics also limits our capacity to imagine a political and formal language that grasps the interdependence of sensory and linguistic access rather than viewing them as adversaries in a zero-sum game.[106] As of this date, Lord has been unable to secure a distributor that will retain the open captions and burned-in audio description that grounds the film's ethic and aesthetic; *Shared Resources* can only be accessed for now by directly emailing Lord. *Goodbye CP* is accessible today thanks to Criterion and Facets but not in the more challenging form intended by Hara and Kobayashi, which confronts viewers unaccustomed to disability-affected speech with access challenges. It seems to be a design feature of our conservative and austere documentary media ecology that, in Story's words, "the films whose forms most resist commodification disappear into the ether."[107]

This is why it is important to build the political capacity and muscle memory for the type of listening these films practice—a listening whose difficulty is in direct proportion to its collective gains. This, to me, is the paradigm shift at stake in listening in crip time.

3

LISTENING LIKE AN ABOLITIONIST

WHAT DOES A PRISON SOUND LIKE?

Brett Story's *The Prison in Twelve Landscapes* (2016) opens with a familiar soundscape. Muffled telephonic voices waft over twilight scenes shot through the windows of a moving bus (see fig. 3.1) occupied by mostly Black and brown bodies. A woman tells her partner she has figured out their router was messing up their machines; a father tells his son he caught a catfish for dinner; and a chorus of nieces and nephews tell their uncle they love him. They sound like voicemails. But like the overnight bus, there is something unnatural about these quotidian transmissions: They too are transporting messengers from the outside world across vast distances to listeners in faraway prisons. Their accumulated intensity of loss ("I'm missing you so much; "We'll be here waiting on you"; "God loves you, and you know your g'ma do") reveals, as does the address of the final missive ("This is a shoutout to Devon from Roanoke, Virginia"), that these intimacies are being publicly broadcast—to a call-in radio station in Kentucky, it turns out, to which incarcerated people tune in to hear from loved ones free of extortionate phone charges.

A film that interprets the inaccessibility of prisons—their remote locations, their fortress-like impregnability, their "disappearance" of those inside—as a methodological invitation to understand how

FIGURE 3.1 Screenshot from *The Prison in Twelve Landscapes* showing trees seen from the windows of a prison bus. Photo Maya Bankovic.

prisons shape outside spaces and lives, *The Prison in Twelve Landscapes* models a refusal of *juridical listening*, an established documentary listening practice whose carceral imbrications and complicities are not always evident. Story listens for the fugitive listening of prisoners not as a jury or parole board might (that is, in order to determine innocence or remorse) but with the worry and care of concerned communities and chosen family. She inhabits a listening position attentive to the "carceral aesthetics" of these distant communiqués, defined by the art historian Nicole Fleetwood as the artful ways in which incarcerated and nonincarcerated people work under conditions of unfreedom to produce relational possibilities that disrupt the punishing constraints of penal space, time, and matter.[1] In *Listening to Images*, Tina Campt similarly describes her counterintuitive decision to "listen beneath" the institutional frames of photographs produced for the regulatory or classificatory purposes of the state as an act of filial care inspired by the quiet refusal of Black communities, one that attempts to understand "the way their subjects—sometimes even prisoners—used these images to telegraph statements about themselves that the genre itself was trying to suppress."[2]

Like Campt, Story refuses the forms of visibility, capture, and framing reified by the carceral state. She listens beneath them for the defiant modalities of testimony and witnessing born out of the everyday struggles of people whose lives and relationships are diminished, reorganized, and extinguished by prisons. The prison, as Fleetwood has written, serves modern states as a structure of visuality that determines who sees and what can be seen by making incarcerated people both unseeing and unseen.[3] Story refuses this dominant structure of visuality; she refuses to see like a state. Her film redeploys the frame of the cage or cell, ubiquitous in prison documentaries that humanize the suffering or regret of the individuals inside, allowing us to see the state at work by seeing and hearing the prison out of place. From this analytical vantage the prison appears not as an aberrant building "over there" but as the organizing logic of familiar spaces of everyday life taken to be "free," such as radio stations, interstate highways, and the overnight buses that ferry visitors to and from faraway prisons to their loved ones, in uncomfortable conditions that replicate those of a holding cell. Hiding in plain sight, these everyday spaces are where the social and spatial relations of property, wage labor, and racialization that sustain carceral violence and dispossession are reproduced, even as prisons themselves disappear.[4] The film models a politics of listening that refuses the forms of mystification that sustain the carceral order, in search of relational possibilities that the prison keeps out of sight but not out of reach.

Set in this context, the auditory reorientation of the film's opening broaches a provocative and generative set of questions about the documentary audit, understood as a structure of audibility subtended by habitual listening practices. When and how does documentary listening reify the prison in our political landscape? How are we, as audiences, diminished in understanding our relationships with one another and to the prison when documentary agents listen, and invite us to listen, like emissaries and deputies of the carceral state—invite us, that is, to inhabit the audit of a cop, detective, prosecutor, public defender, witness, jury, or judge? What possibilities for relating and world-building can documentary projects open up when they refuse the state's omnipresent audit—or listen despite its constraints—in ways that, in Fleetwood's words, "do not aim to reproduce or preserve prisons, but to visualize the end of human captivity, devaluation, dispossession, and the carceral logics that tether bodies to penal systems?"[5] What must happen in documentary, at the level of form, at the level of social process, and at the level of political stakes, in order for us to relate to one another in ways that do not feed and increase reliance on the carceral state? Can politically committed documentary audiences learn to listen like an abolitionist?

To frame the documentary audit as a site of struggle against the carceral state is to question a long-standing jurisprudential consensus in documentary discourse that has tended to equate justice with criminal justice, and liberatory listening with juridical listening. The formation of this consensus dates back to the publication of Shoshana Felman and Dori Laub's landmark 1992 treatise on the historic trauma of World War II, *Testimony: Crises of Witnessing in Literature, Psychoanalysis, and History*, which established the figure of the witness testifying to the truth of events silenced by sovereign power, even under conditions of unspeakable trauma and great personal risk, as *the* political subject par excellence. In so doing, Felman and Laub described the act of listening to testimonial claims in pursuit of oppressed truths—and by implication, in judgment of criminal wrongdoing, especially but not only by agents of state power—as the highest ethical responsibility of justice-seeking publics. The impact of these ideas on media and political theory is difficult to overstate. In the wake of this book, scholars working at the intersection of these fields have proclaimed that the act of bearing witness has been critical to the emergence of human rights—indeed, the very notion of the human—and the concept of justice as modern political ideals.[6]

Felman, a literary critic, and Laub, a Holocaust survivor, practicing psychoanalyst, and cofounder of Yale's Fortunoff Video Archive for Holocaust Testimonies, respectively, also instigated a trend-setting interest in film as a humanitarian medium, which is to say, a medium that outsources the punitive power and responsibility associated with juridical listening beyond the purview of the sovereign nation state. Felman invokes a metaphorical trial when she writes in the book's concluding chapter that Claude Lanzmann's *Shoah* (1985) "embodies the capacity of art not simply to witness, but to *take the witness stand*."[7] Felman's subsequent writings clarify that she was comparing the impact of *Shoah* to the Nuremberg trials of 1945–1946. In expanding the carceral remit of international law for the purpose of prosecuting Nazi officials for crimes against humanity, the trials also, crucially, inaugurated the emergence of "humanity" as a justification for simultaneously criminalizing and qualifying warfare.[8] Thus, although the title of their book emphasizes the therapeutic dimension of listening, Felman and Laub locate the ultimate stakes of bearing witness to mediated testimony in the democratization of juridical listening beyond the legal trial and the expansion of the right to proclaim a guilty verdict on sovereign power itself.[9]

Over the last thirty years, appeals to documentary audiences as arbiters of public truth have overwhelmingly been couched in terms of the democratization of the authority to adjudicate and sanction human rights violations by malign state, military, and corporate actors on the basis of evidentiary claims—the democratization, that is, of what I would call a distinctive mode of listening *like* a state. The ascendence of investigative research agencies such as Forensic Architecture (founded in 2010), whose work I discuss at some length in this chapter, marks the most recent episode in this tradition of documentary accountability. Many documentary scholars take this tradition to include the work of human rights media organizations and activist collectives such as B'Tselem (a Jerusalem-based Israeli nonprofit founded in 1989 that works to document human rights violations in the occupied Palestinian territories; it is also discussed further in this chapter), Cop Watch (a network of autonomous activists founded in 1990 in Berkeley, California, that monitors and produces video documentation of police misconduct), and WITNESS (a Brooklyn-based nonprofit founded in 1992 whose early emphasis on empowering communities through video has since evolved into media literacy campaigns, policy advocacy, and collaborative initiatives employing emerging technologies). Others locate within this tradition the sharp uptick, beginning with Errol Morris's trendsetting 1988 film *The Thin Blue Line*, of justice-driven true crime that puts the criminal justice system on trial by, in some cases, advocating for the release of innocent people who have been wrongfully convicted, or in others, holding accountable powerful perpetrators who have harmed with impunity.[10]

To be sure, these media practices are quite varied in terms of their aims and political stakes—for instance, the Netflix series *Making a Murderer* (2015–2018) and community-based initiative Cop Watch both seek to reform the criminal justice system, but the former trades on the entertainment value of penal spectatorship, whereas the latter practices a form of embedded resistance that hinges on the situated effects of pointing a camera at police. They operate at vastly different scales, and not all circulate in forms or exhibition contexts that are necessarily "marked" with regard to their documentary status, even as they strategically employ documentary methods and modes of address to accomplish their aims. My interest in using the framework of listening like a state to think through this disparate range of practices is grounded in two analytical strategies. First, the loose form of relationality implied by the simile "like" is productive: It allows me to highlight the growing and uneasy investment among a broad range of media practitioners in stabilizing, in the name of justice, concepts such as "truth," "reality," and "evidence," whose categorical instability and deconstruction provided the very foundation for documentary studies during its emergence as a discipline in the 1990s, even though, today, what "counts" as documentary is far less certain.[11] Second, this framework allows me to displace the emphasis on "visible evidence" that has led the documentary field to focus overwhelmingly on visual strategies and metaphors of exposure as civilian tactics for holding state power to account.[12] These approaches have been tremendously generative for the field, but they have also obfuscated the constitutive role of juridical listening in the formation of justice-seeking documentary publics. My analytical efforts are therefore focused on listening beneath the overt visual structures and strategies of the works that I examine. I seek to understand how the interpretive work involved in the evaluation and assessment of their evidentiary truth-claims schools audiences in habits of juridical listening that not only familiarize them with what the sound studies scholar James Parker calls the "law's sonic imagination" but also implicitly or explicitly rehearse faith in legal systems based on carcerality.[13]

I find it notable, in this regard, that the "golden age" of juridical listening has coincided with the rise, in the late twentieth century, of what the anthropologists Didier Fassin and Mariela Pandolfi have dubbed an era of humanitarian intervention (military intervention justified by the aim of saving innocent lives) as well as the exponential growth, since the 1980s, of the largest system of jails and penitentiaries in the history of the world: namely the United States prison system or the social experiment known as "mass incarceration."[14] This period has brought untold numbers of predominantly Black and brown people into carceral and custodial systems, whether through imprisonment, detention, asylum, or other forms of humanitarian supervision. As a scholar of humanitarian media intervention, I have found this coincidence difficult to reconcile. In my previous book, *Immediations*, I wrote about how humanitarian structures of governance both sustain and receive sustenance from documentary platforms that invite representations of endangered life. In a similar vein, I have wondered if practices of juridical listening have been accomplices—if not necessarily equal accomplices—to the proliferation of what the abolitionist disability scholar Liat Ben-Moshe, referring both to physical spaces of containment and to the logics and discourses that sustain them, calls "carceral enclosures."[15] After all, incarceration does not happen only in prisons. It is, as Ben-Moshe argues, "a logic of state coercion and segregation of difference" that is enacted through a wide variety of enclosed settings, including settler colonies, psychiatric wards, and refugee camps, that structure group-differentiated vulnerability to social death.[16] Much like its close media cousin, penal spectatorship, juridical listening traffics in what the prison studies scholar Michelle Brown calls cultural scripts and meanings about carceral punishment.[17] When documentary media deploy these scripts as models of accountability, they enlist listeners in vicarious and impactful forms of judgment that involve "exploring and trying out justifications for the infliction of pain or its prohibition."[18]

This chapter seeks to understand and remake, from an abolitionist perspective, the carceral logics and structures that scaffold habits of juridical listening, specifically (1) the paranoid concept of truth underpinning the adversarial trial system; (2) the exclusionary politics of state-driven systems of recognition; (3) the securitized perceptual logic involved in assessing forensic evidence; and (4) the punitive orientation of criminal justice. Abolition, as understood by Ben-Moshe and other activist-scholars whom I follow, is not only a pragmatic project about ending prisons (though this project has a distinct and important history); it is an ambitious political, analytical, and methodological framework for ending a world that could *have* prisons—namely one organized by carceral enclosures and relationships. Abolition offers a political horizon and a method for building social capacities that takes its lead from those whose experiences of surviving organized abandonment offer another understanding of how our relationships to one another and to life-supporting resources could be otherwise organized. I take up abolition as the broad coalitional liberation movement that it connotes today, anchored in the radical Black feminist tradition and critiques of U.S. carcerality, and developed in solidarity with global Indigenous and decolonial freedom struggles.

In learning from these movements, I understand abolition as a project grounded in the transformative generativity of refusal. "Refusal," writes Campt, is a "rejection of the status quo as livable and the creation of possibility in the face of negation, i.e. a refusal to recognize a system that renders you fundamentally illegible and unintelligible."[19] The Mohawk scholar Audra Simpson differentiates refusal from resistance as "a symptom, a practice, a possibility for doing things differently, for thinking beyond the recognition paradigm that is the agreed-upon 'antidote' for rendering justice in deeply unequal scenes of articulation."[20] Kareem Estefan and LaCharles Ward have built on these insights in calling, respectively, for approaches to Palestinian and Black testimony that refuse the violent omissions of legally recognized forms of speech and evidence under racist and settler-colonial regimes.[21] Many abolitionist feminist activists and practitioners refuse punitive or retributive justice and pursue alternatives that prioritize healing, repair, and community accountability at different scales. Some have sought to revive the restorative approach of Indigenous justice systems in emphasizing the importance of repair when violations occur within relationships between people, with the land, and with the environment.[22] Proponents of transformative justice advocate approaches for responding to harm that do not rely on the state or create more violence and which actively seek to cultivate skills, values, and behaviors that involve "getting in 'right relation.'"[23]

With these accounts of refusal in mind, I am interested in what it might mean to produce documentary media that refuse modes of listenership that circumscribe the truth, political recognition, testimonial presence, and the horizon of justice from a vantage premised on the necessity and maintenance of carceral enclosures. If refusals "illuminate limits and possibilities, especially but not only of the state and other institutions," how might refusing to listen like a state sever the mutually generative relationships among the carceral state and the documentary form and thereby free documentary to imagine and support fugitive forms of sociality and affiliation?[24]

To realize a documentary practice that refuses the carceral justice of juridical listening is difficult and messy because the abolitionist project of holding agents of carceral power and state violence accountable and chipping away at their impunity is often motivated by very real desires for vengeance that lead back to carceral enclosures. Juridical listening lends itself to abolitionist accountability projects, but it also obfuscates the carceral garb into which audiences are asked to step when they are jurified and engaged in righteous assessments of innocence and guilt. Refusal is as fraught as the contexts within which it is articulated. As noted by the scholar of Palestinian cinema Nadia Yaqub, refusal can take many forms; dispossessed people make recourse to multiple and sometimes contradictory political strategies, and this is their prerogative.[25] I therefore tread a careful line in this chapter, seeking not to cast judgment on these strategies but to pay close attention to their differences and high stakes. To do so, I employ the distinction between *listening like a state* and *listening like an abolitionist*, inspired by the distinction drawn by prison abolitionists between reformist reforms (reforms that provide temporary relief but ultimately widen the net of carceral control) and nonreformist reforms (reforms that shrink the net of carceral control by orienting toward a more difficult horizon). In order to elaborate the stakes of these listening modes, I have structured this chapter around two projects that confront the internal contradictions of the juridical impulse in documentary listening in formally compelling ways. The first is Ra'anan Alexandrowicz's *The Viewing Booth* (2019), a film that interrogates the complicity of the mode of video activism practiced by Jerusalem-based leftist Israeli human rights media organization B'Tselem with Israel's ongoing occupation of Palestine. The second is *The Killing of Harith Augustus* (2018–2019), a collaboration between the London-based investigative research agency Forensic Architecture and the Chicago-based activist media organization Invisible Institute, which both instrumentalizes and challenges the social and epistemic forms of authority associated with forensic truth-claims.

My choice of these two case studies, which respectively concern settler-colonial violence in the occupied West Bank of Palestine and state racism in the segregated South Shore neighborhood of Chicago, reflects the abolition movement's understanding of how carceral forms, systems, and structures have moved between the United States and other sites and the centrality of Palestine as a rehearsal space for an apartheid legal system based on the settler-colonial punishment of an entire population. It also reflects my effort to trace the compromised and yet potentially emancipatory role of documentary listening practices in this traffic.

The Viewing Booth stages a tribunal on an established approach for hailing documentary audiences as jurors deliberating on audiovisual evidence of human rights violations. In a litmus test of his own waning faith in the power of witnessing, Alexandrowicz, a pro-Palestine Israeli activist-filmmaker, invites Maia Levy, a pro-Israel U.S. university student, to record her responses to videos depicting confrontations between Palestinians, the Israeli Defense Forces and security personnel, and Israeli settlers in the occupied West Bank that have been circulated online both by B'Tselem and by IDF spokespeople and Zionist groups.[26] The resulting film is as much a portrait of Alexandrowicz's own listening as it is that of his skeptical interlocutor. Maia's defensive preoccupation with finding audiovisual proof of Palestinian guilt to refute B'Tselem's criminalizing portrayals of Israel allows her to disavow the larger political crime of occupation. Alexandrowicz listens to Maia in acknowledgment of his own fraught positionality, as an émigré to the United States who was once enlisted as a soldier charged with enforcing the very laws that exculpate IDF and settler violence and criminalize Palestinian resistance. His is an unsettling listening, rehearsed in his previous film, *The Law in These Parts* (2011), in which Alexandrowicz interrogates the architects of the legal infrastructure that has sustained Israel's settler-colonial occupation of Palestine. The questions he poses to Maia bring into relief the complicity both of the defensive mode of Maia's juridical listening and of the prosecutorial impulse of human rights witnessing—including his own—with the ongoing occupation.

The scales of violence obfuscated by juridical listening are made differently perceptible in the work of Forensic Architecture (henceforth FA). FA employs architectural and digital techniques to generate "counterforensic" evidence of war crimes, environmental harm, police killings, and other human rights violations. One of its signal interventions has been to center the concept of the "forum" (the Latin root of "forensics," which refers to the art of public persuasion and debate) through wide-ranging collaborations that present evidence of state and corporate crimes in not only legal courts and tribunals but also art venues, investigative news outlets, and community gatherings. I take up *The Killing of Harith Augustus*, a six-video investigation of the fatal 2018 shooting of Harith Augustus, a Black barber by a white Chicago police officer, in order to think through how FA, in collaboration with the Invisible Institute, have reckoned with the epistemic violence of their counterforensic tactics. The first five videos, which reconstruct Officer Dillan Halley's unjustified use of lethal force down to the millisecond, invite an auditory equivalent of the securitized mode of visuality that Lisa Guenther calls "seeing like a cop."[27] The culminating video breaks free from the carceral forum relations replicated by *listening like a cop* to embrace the *outlaw listening* enabled by informal local forums assembled out of necessity. This final video convenes Black South Chicago residents to speak not as witnesses testifying to individual police crimes but as members of a criminalized community of care who are attuned to the expanded timescales of anti-Black violence and experts in the relationships and resources they require for survival.

Despite their sincere investments in juridical listening, *The Viewing Booth* and *The Killing of Harith Augustus* surface profound concerns regarding the scales of justice sought by juridical listening and its difficulty in connecting incidences of harm to the structural conditions and relations that create and perpetuate anti-Palestinian and anti-Black violence. I find these projects valuable because they allow us to grasp the complexity and generativity of refusal as a practice that requires us, as Campt might put it, to remake the political vocabulary of what it means to struggle from the perspective of those whose refusal of carceral justice is "neither utopic nor autonomous, and neither pessimistic nor futuristic."[28] For Alexandrowicz and the Invisible Institute, listening like an abolitionist is not only about getting rid of carceral enclosures and their institutional and social supports but about asserting desired forms of presence. They listen in pursuit of liberatory forms of justice, relationality, and evidence that are not fully worked out but which already exist in our documentary landscape, in the words of Ruth Wilson Gilmore, as "fragments and pieces, experiments and possibilities."[29]

LISTENING TO MAIA'S VIEWING IN *THE VIEWING BOOTH*

"You can use the controls to choose what videos you want to view, you can stop when you please, pause and look at details. And I'd like you to please try to verbalize whatever comes to mind. It can be feelings, questions, emotions, basically any thought you have." These are Ra'anan Alexandrowicz's instructions for Maia Levy, a student at Temple University. The year is 2017 and Maia has just sat down to watch and respond to a curated selection of web videos documenting the conflict zone of Al Khalil (more commonly known by its Hebrew name, Hebron) in the south of the occupied West Bank.[30] The largest Palestinian city outside Gaza, with Israeli settlements clustered in and around its historic center, Hebron is one of the most surveilled and militarized parts of the West Bank, only a small portion of which has been governed since 2006 by the Palestinian Authority. Following Israel's disengagement from Gaza and consolidated occupation of the West Bank in 2005, Gaza has been rendered "bombable," whereas the West Bank has been subject to settler-colonial violence. Movement restrictions imposed by the Israeli state in 1991, following the first Intifada, have authorized the active debilitation of the Palestinian populations of both Gaza and the West Bank by restricting their access to food and medical care and through raids, skirmishes, and attacks.[31] These conditions of confinement, deprivation, and targeted attack have further intensified in the West Bank after Israel began its military offensive on Gaza on October 7, 2023, now widely recognized by the international community as a genocide.[32] Palestinian residents have described daily life in Hebron as "a prison in a prison," while human rights activists continue to warn of the "Hebronization" of the West Bank.[33]

Completed in 2019, shortly before I began drafting this chapter, *The Viewing Booth* reads at the time of revision in 2024 as a grim precursor of the now-prevalent willful repudiations of Israel's genocidal actions by its supporters. The film, as Alexandrowicz later describes it in one of the few contextualizing statements that comprise its spare commentary, is ostensibly about Maia's viewing. It was an effort, he has written, to "use the tools of documentary to explore and depict the way meanings are created in the consciousness of viewers."[34] The reflexivity of the project is mirrored in the arrangement of the eponymous viewing booth set up by Alexandrowicz in a university basement (see fig. 3.2). The monitor through which Maia watches the videos in a private booth doubles as an "interrotron" (a setup invented by the investigative documentarian Errol Morris) that records her face, transmitting both her responses and the videos to which she responds to a control room where Alexandrowicz is seated, and from which he dialogues with Maia through an audio system (see fig. 3.3).[35] The Hebrew title of Alexandrowicz's film translates to "Mirror." The title refers to the reflexivity of the film's process: Alexandrowicz wishes to hold up a mirror to his own assumptions regarding the impact of human rights advocacy media. He suggests the same idea to Maia when he invites her to return to the viewing booth to watch

FIGURE 3.2 Screenshot from *The Viewing Booth* depicting Maia inside the viewing booth, as seen through the glass door separating the booth from the control room. Courtesy of the artist.

FIGURE 3.3 Screenshot from *The Viewing Booth* depicting Ra'anan Alexandrowicz in the control room during Maia's initial viewing. Ra'anan Alexandrowicz, *The Viewing Booth*. Courtesy of the artist.

FIGURE 3.4 Screenshot from *The Viewing Booth* depicting Ra'anan Alexandrowicz in the control room during Maia's second viewing, when she returns to review the recording of her first viewing session. Courtesy of the artist.

and discuss an edit of her first viewing session, telling her "it's like looking in a mirror" (see fig. 3.4).

Despite its emphasis on vision and spectatorship, though, Alexandrowicz's film is as much about how he listens to the internal dialogue that accompanies Maia's process of viewing, which is rendered by her as an extraordinary stream of commentary. Maia is asked to describe what she sees. But her responses function not as audio description (a process of making visual media accessible to blind and partially sighted audiences, often shorthanded as "say what you see," discussed in the previous chapter) but as a means of verbalizing how she reads or interprets the videos in order to arrive at a verdict. Maia's commentary offers access to the mechanics of a defensive mode of juridical listening that has become a de facto norm of the so-called smartphone era of video witnessing. The unsettling frame of what Laliv Melamed has called the film's "control room aesthetic," echoed in the recursive structure of the film, functions less as an indictment of such listening than as a model of listening that refuses to side with either the prosecution or the defense.[36] Alexandrowicz's unsettling listening rejects the very premise of criminal justice under a settler-colonial system of legalized racial segregation that has repeatedly resisted the sanction of international criminal courts by systematically criminalizing Palestinians.

Alexandrowicz's fifth feature (and his third dealing with the occupation) represents a turning point in his decades-long commitment to documenting and resisting Israeli state and settler violence. He has described *The Viewing Booth* as an attempt to work through a professional and epistemological crisis regarding the efficacy of video documentation in nonviolent anti-Occupation struggles. The film confronts shibboleths regarding witnessing that have been popularized by the Israeli human rights media organization B'Tselem (founded in 1989) and its more internationally renowned counterpart WITNESS (founded 1992), whose slogan is "See it. Film it. Change it."[37] B'Tselem's project *Shooting Back* (since renamed the *Camera Project*), modeled on the work of WITNESS and initiated in the wake of the second Palestinian Intifada in 2005 (the year YouTube launched), distributed dozens of Handycams to Palestinian residents in the West Bank to capture incidences of violence by settlers or Israeli security forces. These rough and ready, often single-shot, videos, sometimes "packaged" with commentary, were then leveraged by B'Tselem in legal and political forums, as well as on YouTube, international news outlets, and their website, as part of their efforts to challenge the occupation.[38] B'Tselem has historically traded in both "effective" and "affective" forms of evidence: The images they solicit are used (though with limited success) for seeking justice in courts of law, as well as for shifting public opinion and catalyzing collective actions against state violence.[39]

At the time, Alexandrowicz, who contributed video footage to B'Tselem that he shot while organizing with Ta'ayush (a solidarity network of Arabs and Jews working to end the Israeli occupation of Palestine) shared B'Tselem's faith in the still-new technology of videocameras as a "weapon of the weak" and their excitement regarding the unprecedented reach of YouTube.[40] Nearly two decades later, as the occupation continues amid its ever-accelerating documentation, he is less certain of the capacity of such images to affect or effect social change. The proliferation of smartphones and social media tools in the occupied Palestinian territories has, on the one hand, generated a massive Palestinian visual archive of Israeli state violence, often filmed in the midst of IDF attacks or raids, and shared online in close to real time. Indeed, as Kareem Estefan notes, the humanitarian pressure on Palestinians to endlessly document their own suffering is precisely why human rights, to paraphrase Eyal Weizman, has become a problem of managing information abundance rather than scarcity.[41] At the same time—bearing out Weizman's sometimes coauthor Thomas Keenan's prescient analysis of the opportunities created by mediation and transmission for both advocates *and* opponents of human rights—the Israeli state and settler media organizations have become wise to the survival tactics and media savvy of Palestinians and have begun releasing their own competing videos that repudiate the inculpating images shot by Palestinians.[42] In 2021, two years after the release of Alexandrowicz's film, Israel responded to documentation of Israeli war crimes filed by West Bank–based Palestinian human rights organization Al-Haq with the International Criminal Court (ICC) by declaring Al-Haq and five other Palestinian human rights and civil society organizations to be terrorist organizations. This diabolical permutation of what Jasbir Puar has named a biopolitical strategy of preemptively debilitating Palestinian bodies and life-sustaining infrastructures effectively outlawed Al-Haq and made them vulnerable to violent reprisal.[43]

Alexandrowicz's response to what many have diagnosed as a cynical and ever-intensifying mobilization by right-wing forces of "post-truth" discourse over the last decade is somewhat different from the two prevailing approaches that documentary scholars and practitioners have tended to take: doubling down on the importance, for the left, of making truth-claims that legitimate the reality of those experiencing oppression;[44] or reclaiming fabulation, speculation, and fictionalization as minoritarian methodological insurrections against settled reality.[45] Like Estefan, Alexandrowicz operates from the premise that Israel's impunity stems not from a lack of evidence but the absence of an institutional and social context in which Palestinian testimony can be heard and validated. He also shares what Keenan, describing the ethos of FA, has called a "non-naïve commitment to a notion of the truth" that must be defended in a "conflictual battleground of readings."[46] However, Alexandrowicz has serious misgivings regarding the interpretive process cultivated by the polarized belief systems of spectators who view, discuss, and recirculate "happenstance videos." This is a collective noun that Jeffrey Skoller, writing in the U.S. context, has applied to the cinematic and social form of continuous single-shot amateur videos recorded by bystanders or during direct confrontations with law enforcement, which are intended either for livestream or release to advocacy organizations.[47]

Alexandrowicz decided, therefore, to design a cinematic process to test the hypothesis, implicit in the practice of B'Tselem as well as other Israeli, Palestinian, and international human rights media organizations, that engagements with their happenstance videos would change (rather than reaffirm) the perceptions and behaviors of viewers who don't already share their political perspective. He issued an open call at his university for participation in a filmed viewing of forty viral videos chosen by him from among thousands of such videos posted online, half by B'Tselem, and the rest by either Israeli military personnel or conservative YouTube channels. After auditioning seven respondents across the ideological spectrum who answered his call, Alexandrowicz chose to make Maia's viewing the sole focus of the film. Maia's oppositional and even hostile stance toward B'Tselem made her a preferred viewer from B'Tselem's perspective as well as his own.⁴⁸ Furthermore, her willingness to engage videos "from the other side" in an open and emotionally honest way made her an exceptionally dynamic interlocutor. Maia was, Alexandrowicz has said, "*the* viewer for me—someone beyond the choir, yet a curious viewer who doesn't walk away from images, who negotiates them."⁴⁹

I turn now to scenes that show Maia viewing and responding to her filmed viewing of B'Tselem videos to illustrate what I have called her defensive mode of juridical listening because of the way Maia marshals evidence, whether actual or speculative, to exonerate Israel. When Maia initially sits down at the viewing booth, her political position with regard to the occupation is as yet unannounced. However, she is equally conversant with, and cynical regarding, the representational tropes commonly employed on either side of the spectrum. She dismisses with an eye roll the very first video, which opens with an altercation between Palestinians and soldiers in which the former assert their right to film. When the second video begins with an image of a Palestinian dissident on the floor, Maia instantly profiles the person on the floor as a "terrorist" and surmises that the video "will be against Israelis"; later, when soldiers are shown giving the person water, she concedes, "Maybe it's a pro-Israel right video." Recognizing the B'Tselem logo in the third video, she admits that its presence is distracting to her: "As someone with Israeli parents," she states, "it made me feel it would be fake, skewed."

This revelation provides an opening for Alexandrowicz, who asks Maia if she will watch and respond to another B'Tselem video, "Soldiers Enter Hebron Homes at Night." The portion of the film devoted to Maia's initial filmed viewing features eight of the eleven videos she watched, and a hefty third of this portion of the film revolves around the "Soldiers Enter" video, which was filmed in 2015 by Nayef Da'ana and distributed by B'Tselem.⁵⁰ A rough cut of the sequence featuring this video becomes the basis of her exchange with Alexandrowicz when she returns for a second viewing session. Alexandrowicz says nothing to frame the video during Maia's filmed viewing, but he describes it as follows in an essay about his film:

> Da'ana documents, in a single 8-minute shot, Israeli soldiers raiding his home at 3am. He records as soldiers wake his family, search their home, and snap pictures of the adults, children, and the premises. They do not provide the family members with a warrant, nor a reason for their actions, yet they do permit family members to record. Though we see no physical violence, the video understandably shocks many viewers. Images of sleeping children being woken up to a house full of armed, masked military men who then interrogate them, rifle through their belongings, and photograph them without explanation demonstrates the acute vulnerability and precarious living situations that shape everyday life for many Palestinians under occupation. The invaded Da'ana family does not physically resist (apart from filming) and at the same time, it seems evident that the soldiers are taking no pleasure in the task they are performing. In a way, the video is most shocking for how mundane and routine the event appears to be.[51]

Withholding such details and his reading of them is part of the method of the film. Having chosen the video, Alexandrowicz allows Maia to frame its meaning. Alexandrowicz says nothing to refute or counter Maia's reading during her first viewing session, only nudging her on occasion to elaborate. His editorial strategy follows Maia's. He shows us scenes from the video and cuts to different views of Maia when she pauses to comment (frontal as she looks into the monitor/interrotron, from outside the door of the viewing booth, a behind-the-shoulder shot of his own dual-screen monitors in the control room), returning to the video when she hits play again (see fig. 3.5). The rhythm of this cutting back and forth reveals how Maia breaks down the continuous flow of the video into short fragments, producing a new set of framings that allow her to read the video against itself.

FIGURE 3.5 Three screenshots from the sequence of *The Viewing Booth* in which Maia initially watches and responds to the "Soldiers Enter" video. Courtesy of the artist.

What follows is a remarkable sequence that resembles the portion of a legal trial devoted to the forensic examination of evidence, except there are no opening or closing statements, only a tangle of frozen moments abstracted from the larger narrative frame and examined in isolation. Maia argues both sides, in addition to serving as witness and jury. She admits twice that it is "sad" and "difficult to see" the little children being awoken from sleep by soldiers: first, right at the start of the video, when the soldiers order Nayef and his wife Dalal to wake the sleeping children, and again, midway through, when Nayef rouses his eight year-old son, telling him not to be scared. However, she then cross-examines her own sympathetic response to make the case that B'Tselem is exploiting the situation for political gain. When Dalal resists the order to wake the children, protesting that they are little and that it is cold, Maia declares, "I feel like she's lying. They [Palestinians] lie a lot." When Alexandrowicz asks, "How can you tell?" she elaborates, "She's being dramatic. . . . It's almost like it's staged a little bit." Maia goes on to cast similar aspersions on Nayef, B'Tselem, the children, and even the soldiers. The soldiers, she complains, are conducting the raid in a performative and cursory manner. When the couple's younger son, Qusai, disoriented, tells the soldiers his name is Mohammed, before correcting himself, Maia suspects him, too, of lying.

It is against B'Tselem, though, that Maia builds her most damning case. Initially, believing that B'Tselem agents are filming, she complains, "They don't give any context as to why they [the soldiers] are doing this." She adds, "What if there was a complaint, like there was a bomb in the house." She also expresses frustration with B'Tselem's "selectful [sic] translation" of what is said and incredulity that B'Tselem always seems to be at the right place at the right time where the action is taking place. It isn't until the soldiers leave that Maia surmises that videos like these are filmed by Palestinian families and given to B'Tselem (Alexandrowicz confirms that's right). Even so, Maia interprets Nayef's decision to continue filming as the

LISTENING LIKE AN ABOLITIONIST 147

children break down in tears as "added drama" designed to "draw out the seriousness of waking up the kids." She settles on this interpretation. When Maia returns to the viewing booth to view a rough cut of this sequence, she maintains that there are "too many flaws" and "red flags" in the video. "That leads me," she says, "to not wanting to believe it, and picking up evidence of all the things they are doing wrong."

B'Tselem has been criticized by Palestinian human rights activists and leftist Israelis for its extractive relationship with Palestinians under occupation, as well as for its role in presenting Israel in a benevolent light.[52] Maia's critique of B'Tselem proceeds from a different basis. Her defensive reading of Nayef's video exemplifies what the media anthropologist Rebecca Stein has called a Zionist pedagogy of repudiation that systematic state-sponsored Israeli media campaigns against videos of Palestinian death and injury have normalized as a social script.[53] Faced with a growing volume of bystander videography that delegitimizes the Israeli state, pro-Israel patriots resort to a familiar script to dispute their veracity and to shift the narrative from Palestinian injury to Israeli victimhood. Maia checks all the conventional boxes of the Zionist repudiation script, which has worked its way from a conspiratorial corner of the internet to the political center of Israeli state and public discourse over the roughly twenty-year lifetime of testimonial videography; indeed, this very discourse has been used to justify Israel's genocidal siege on Gaza.[54] Maia accuses B'Tselem of cynically using children for political leverage; she describes the tactical skills developed by people living in conflict zones (what Alexandrowicz calls "an ambush for an ambush") as a conniving lure designed to trap and defame IDF soldiers.[55] She alleges manipulation at the level of the image (a favorite accusation, notes Stein, has to do with "what came before" any particular event of harm or injury) as well as the event (the Palestinians, deemed natural liars, are suspected both of theatricality and of failing to deliver a convincing performance).[56]

Stein has traced the origins of the Zionist repudiation script to the campaign to discredit the viral footage of the infamous September 2000 shooting of twelve-year-old Muhammad al-Durrah, killed in crossfire in Gaza during the early days of the second Intifada, when a team of "self-styled forensic experts" went through the material frame by frame, creating a manual and playbook that would be recycled in subsequent keystone repudiation campaigns.[57] I want to dwell, however, on a transnational juridical prehistory and aftermath. Maia's process of breaking down and interpreting the video is disturbingly reminiscent of the 1992 trial of Theodore Briseño, Stacey Koon, Laurence Powell, and Timothy Wind for the brutal beating of Rodney King, which precipitated the formation of WITNESS and other human rights media organizations devoted to using video to challenge legal decisions and influence public opinion.[58] Documentary scholars have analyzed in various ways the failure of George Holliday's video in proving the guilt of the four Los Angeles Police Department officers who were caught on tape beating Rodney King, but there is widespread agreement that the prosecution's downfall came from its belief that the evidence would speak for itself. Keenan sums up the prosecution's strategy this way: They essentially pointed at the video and said "See?" whereas the defense attorneys understood that evidence and proof are not the same.[59] "By breaking up the continuous flow of time in the low-resolution video recording into short discontinuous fragments," Skoller elaborates, "at times slowing down the motion and showing series of freeze frames at others, the defense constructed an alternative reading of the video, and argued on this basis that one could see how King was resisting and even attacking the police who were doing their job making the arrest."[60]

If B'Tselem's video makes the implicit claim, as the prosecutors of King's assailants did, that seeing is believing, then Maia's close but decontextualized readings employ what Kimberlé Crenshaw and Gary Peller, describing the defense's formalist interpretive strategy, have called a process of "narrative disaggregation."[61] By redirecting the jury's attention from the real time of the video to disaggregated stills of King and the police, each of which they inserted into a different narrative of threat, the defense effectively divorced the effects of white supremacist power from their social context and historical meaning. In essence, the defense hijacked the formal maneuver associated with what Stuart Hall calls "oppositional reading," evacuated of its political content.[62] Hamid Naficy has, in a critique along these lines, fingered the defense's "dissected vision" for violating the spatial and temporal integrity of the images and turning them into abstractions with no referent.[63]

The usual reading of such a "dissected" and "disaggregated" mode of perception and interpretation, of which the LAPD defense is regarded as exemplary, has been to frame it as a symptom and harbinger of a postmodern turn characterized by the devaluation of reality as subjective, as well as a contradictory form of overinvestment in and disenchantment with the epistemological stability of documentary images.[64] Stein views the Zionist repudiation script as a logical culmination of this impulse, noting that it resembles the Trumpist accusation of "fake news" that barricades against counterevidence.[65] Indeed, this is how Alexandrowicz makes sense of Maia's oppositional viewing. When discussing the film, he has evaluated the process whereby Maia reframes images challenging to her worldview in terms of absent but plausible circumstances—"unseen somethings"— that "lie *outside* the visible content of the frame" as the dismaying but predictable result of a media climate crowded with disinformation and dominated by streaming platforms that present documentary and fiction as depoliticized equivalents.[66] He often points to a symptomatic moment from Maia's second viewing to substantiate this analysis. Asked to elaborate on the source of her speculation as to whether a bomb threat might have justified the raid, Maia answers that she had seen a similar situation in the hit Netflix show *Fauda*, which dramatizes the adventures of an IDF soldier. She stands her ground even as she concedes that "using that [a fiction show] as a guide or reference to this [documentary video] can be dangerous."

I want to offer a different, and ultimately more disturbing, framework for understanding Maia's interpretive stance. My proposal troubles the consensus that pernicious legal fictions must be countered with persuasive truths, or what Keenan, describing the "hard, technical, rhetorical work of persuasion, the claiming of public truths and of rights" calls "counterforensics."[67] Juridical listening of the kind that Maia practices—adversarial, fragmented, forensically driven, speculative, disaggregated, and doubt-cultivating—is not the unfortunate result of postmodern derealization: *It is its engine.* The adversarial trial, as Carol Clover has written, is a "machine for the production of paranoid speculation."[68] With roots dating back to the stateless world of German antiquity, the adversarial trial structure common in much of the Anglo-American world, as well as in Israel and the occupied Palestinian territories, is grounded in rules and protocols for maintaining fairness in the absence of sovereign authority: a duel-like structure for separately collecting and presenting evidence; differential burdens of proof for the prosecution and defense; and a jury responsible for arriving at a verdict. These protocols proliferate scenarios or "theories" as to what might have happened, encouraging jurors' habits of close attention, intricate analysis, and paranoid imagination.[69] These perceptual and interpretive habits would give rise, in the late nineteenth century, to the "forensic gaze"—defined by Tory Jeffay as a mode of looking that mines images for information beyond that which is verifiable by the human eye—and with it, the conviction that the scrutiny of the image will yield incontrovertible truth.[70] Maia's process of rehearsing the worst and best possible interpretations of the facts in order to arrive at the most plausible lie reveals the extent to which juridical listening reinforces what Clover calls the archaic and oddly cynical notion of the truth at the heart of the adversarial trial structure: "a truth of exhausted possibilities."[71] Understood in this light, Maia's defensive speculations are not exceptional or even particularly modern. Juridical listening schools audiences in the anxious, defensive practice of making up competing versions or stories of what could have happened. Forensics, as I will argue further in the next section, is merely the prevailing form of expertise for claiming the truth of a particular version or exposing others as fraudulent. In fact, defensive listening can be understood as the reigning ideological paradigm for denying culpability in a media climate where prosecutorial accusations have become a default countermeasure against abuses of state power.[72]

It is powerful, in this context, that Alexandrowicz does not speak for Nayef and B'Tselem by constructing an alternative counternarrative. Instead, by inviting Maia back to review her own filmed viewing, his film constructs an unsettling structure for reflecting on the complicity of juridical listening, whether prosecutorial or defensive, with the settled truth of the occupation. This is a structure rehearsed in his previous film, *The Law in These Parts* (2011), a meditation on the parallels between independent documentary and the Israeli Supreme Court as failed bulwarks against military violence in the occupied Palestinian territories.

The setup of this film is simple. Alexandrowicz sits across a table from Meir Shamgar, a former chief justice of the Israeli Supreme Court, and seven other retired judges, prosecutors, and legal advisers—all high-ranking members of the Israeli military legal corps—and interrogates each of them regarding their role in engineering the two-tiered legal system that has been used to administer, prolong, and defend Israel's military occupation of Palestine for over forty years (now fifty-seven and counting). Referring to a deep archive of legal orders, opinions, and rulings, Alexandrowicz confronts these men, one by one, regarding the outcome of little-known laws that have justified the detention, dispossession, incarceration, and torture of Palestinians by the Israeli military. These include the establishment of separate identity cards and military courts for trying Palestinians outside the civilian courts reserved for settlers; the denial of prisoner of war status to Palestinian liberation fighters; and the revival of Ottoman-era laws to enable land seizures to build Israeli settlements, border walls, and military posts.

Much of the film is devoted to eliciting speech from the judges and lawyers (who, perhaps perceiving Alexandrowicz as an ally, nakedly admit their Zionist loyalties and speak with disarming frankness) to tease out how their rulings in defense of the military's targeted killings and bombings constructed a legal snarl that has further disenfranchised Palestinians. The film builds to a culminating crescendo when Alexandrowicz, channeling the tactic of an "ambush for an ambush," asks the retired Lieutenant Colonel Judge Jonathan Livny to listen to testimony by a Palestinian schoolteacher regarding his brutal torture during interrogation by the General Security Services (an independent commission has alleged that judges were aware of the torture, which GSS has denied). Alexandrowicz keeps the camera tightly framed on Livny's face while he listens to Alexandrowicz read from the testimony about how the man was beaten and sodomized to the point of paralysis. As Alexandrowicz reads, we cut to the faces of other justices, who were also made to listen to excerpts from other testimonies of people who were tortured. Finally, Livny, his lip twitching, spits out that he was aware of the torture but unable to stop it. "You serve a system . . . you represent the IDF, the majority of the Israeli public with set opinions of us versus them, it's hard to shake that off," he says. Another retired colonel and military judge, Oded Passenson, adds, chillingly, "I believe when a detainee says what was done to him but I am suspicious of his motives, so I believe the interrogator because his job is to protect me."

Alexandrowicz makes no secret of his politically motivated decision to portray a partisan and contravening reality; in fact, the documentary fabrication of reality is a persistent theme of the film. But in the film's conclusion, he dwells on the futility of demanding recognition for Palestinians under a legal system created out of lethal force, theft, and dispossession—one in which there is no pretense or possibility of their equality under the law. "In the situation we've reached, my security depends on the violation of others," he reflects.

"The making of this film and its viewing are happening under the protection of people responsible for this security and freedom."

The Viewing Booth is, in many ways, an analysis of the partisanship of juridical listening under these conditions. Alexandrowicz invites Maia to listen to her filmed viewing, and in a refrain of the scene with Livny and the other judges, he prompts Maia to acknowledge the powerful implications of what she chooses not to acknowledge (for instance, the fact that the soldiers are wearing masks to avoid camera detection) and of the new details she notices (such as the green color of the Da'ana family's passports, which identify them, in her own words, as a legally disadvantaged "category" of person). And in a refrain of the judges' defensive listening, Maia momentarily flinches before doubling down on her position. When she states that B'Tselem's videos have the effect of reinforcing her beliefs rather than changing them, Alexandrowicz deems her response "a harsh mirror." But this visual metaphor occludes as much as it reveals about the dynamics of Alexandrowicz's listenership relative to Maia's. Alexandrowicz has said that he did not wish to betray Maia, his politics, or the makers of the B'Tselem videos shown in the film—and indeed, his interview persona in this scene lacks the prosecutorial aggression of *The Law in These Parts*.[73] He refuses not only to take sides but also the very idea of sides under settler law. He engages in what Simpson calls a refusal of the politics of state-driven recognition by refusing, to paraphrase Estefan, to enter a discursive forum in which a fiction of justice is built on the betrayal, erasure, and dispossession of one side.[74] That refusal is inscribed in an unsettling mode of listening that is aware of its own compromised space of articulation. This is a listening that unsettles the very terrain of cinematic judgment by refusing the fundamental exclusion on which the latter's concept of the political is premised. It is a listening that reveals what juridical listening refuses to hear about its own listening. There is nothing cynical about such listening; it calls for an altogether different way of imagining the political beyond sides, beyond the adversarial logics of legal forums of recognition. The next section of the chapter asks what it would mean to convene such a forum, finding an imaginative response to this call in a collaboration between Forensic Architecture and the Invisible Institute.

OUTLAW LISTENING

Over the past two decades, the London-based investigative research agency Forensic Architecture has emerged at the forefront of a so-called "counterforensic turn" in human rights media activism. FA's founder, Eyal Weizman, writing in collaboration with Thomas Keenan, has diagnosed, theorized, and helped to popularize the notion that an epistemological shift in the realms of law, science, and popular culture has demoted the testimonial credibility of witnesses. If the Jerusalem trial of 1961 (also known as the Eichmann trial) inaugurated what Felman and Laub call the "era of the witness," their argument is that the discovery of Joseph Mengele's skeleton in 1985, and the battery of forensic analysis to which these remains were subjected, announced the beginning of a new aesthetic and juridical sensibility, the "era of the thing." The authors propose that the "era of the thing" has not only changed what counts as evidence but also the methods whereby evidence is constructed and accepted as fact.[75] The outcome, they state, is that expert technoscientific claims on behalf of human remains and other material objects (such as buildings, bones, and bullets) have become the gold standard of juridical evidence. The investigation of such objects and their presentation as evidence in legal proceedings is colloquially known as "forensics."

Architectural analysis was the impetus for FA's formation in 2010—Weizman rose to prominence for his field-shaping collaborative research with B'Tselem on the architectural politics of Israeli settlements in the West Bank—but does not encompass the range of its practice.[76] Today, the agency engages in research creation through a

PhD program at Goldsmiths and operates as a shifting configuration of teams of academics, artists, designers, lawyers, programmers, and data scientists. Working in collaboration with human rights activists, international NGOs, and victims of state and environmental violence, these teams employ a range of digital tools (such as architectural models, open-source intelligence, pattern analysis, and synchronization) to produce and present evidence of human rights violations in legal, journalistic, and artistic forums. Some of FA's best-known investigations have focused on the Syrian torture prison Saydnaya, environmental racism in Louisiana, the use of U.S.-manufactured tear gas on civilians along the U.S.-Mexico border, and numerous instances of Israeli war crimes against Palestinians, including, most recently, Israel's organized destruction of life-sustaining infrastructure in Gaza. FA's trendsetting example has inspired a throng of investigative and accountability media agencies (Bellingcat, the Visual Investigations unit of the New York Times, SITU/Research, VFrame, Mnemonic, and DFRLab) contributing to the promulgation of "forensic aesthetics," defined by Weizman as an insistence on the aesthetic dimensions of investigating and presenting truth-claims.[77] FA's commitments to theorizing its own evolving practice, and increasing its reach by exhibiting in artistic contexts, makes the organization an outlier and barometer in this landscape. The agency has been celebrated and criticized in equal measure for the contradictions underlying its practice, which seeks simultaneously to destabilize and instrumentalize forensic truth-claims: it has been featured in major biennials and was nominated for the prestigious Turner Prize, even as scholars have questioned the mismatch between the interpretive openness of aesthetic judgment and the positivist and didactic address of its presentations, which are tactically designed to withstand future legal scrutiny.[78]

In a book introducing FA's mission and its major investigations, Weizman frames counterforensics—a term borrowed from Allan Sekula, a fellow believer in coopting state techniques of surveillance and biometric governance in collective struggles—as a civilian practice of truth-making or "open verification" that repoliticizes the forum, the archaic Latin root of *forensis* ("pertaining to the forum").[79] While forensics in its contemporary understanding has come to be narrowly affiliated with legal and scientific methods of investigation, Weizman reminds us that in ancient Rome, the forum was not restricted to scientific gatherings or courts of law. The archaic forum was "a chaotic and multidimensional domain" of judgment in which "both people and things participated and were presented."[80] Forensics, he writes, is a state tool, and as such, it has been hoarded and monopolized by states and their proxies (police, military, and corporations) to cover up state violence and stabilize truth in the interest of ruling powers. Weizman therefore theorizes counterforensics as a tactical project of seizing the technoscientific means for producing evidence that incriminates malign state and corporate actors, which is done through mediatized speech acts that are scaled for a latent public that has the will to listen—*an audience*—rather than being narrowly addressed to courts of law.[81]

The auditory imaginary underpinning this remediation of the forum has remained surprisingly undertheorized despite the explicit aural metaphorics of forensic discourse. Keenan and Weizman describe the art of making forensic claims as a rhetorical skill or argumentative practice. For them, forensic aesthetics are an example of what the Roman rhetorician Quintilian called *prosopopoeia*, in which the speaker artificially endows inanimate objects with a voice, thereby "giving a voice to things to which nature has not given a voice."[82] It is this formulation that authorizes Keenan and Weizman's activist commitment to intervening on behalf of those whose voices have been stripped of their humanity ("We are using prosthetic tools not to replace the human voice but to complement it" is a frequent refrain of Weizman's).[83]

FA characterizes the objective of political agency as being able to find a voice, which in turn implies finding a listening public, but the listening attitudes, habits, and comportments called into being by their modes of verifying evidence—forums, as FA notes, are often retrofits, assembled around the evidence after the fact—have yet to be parsed. This oversight is in some ways characteristic, as Kate Lacey has noted, of theories of the public sphere.[84] It is also a function, in this case, of the ocularcentric politics of display in which FA and other forensic media agencies partake.[85] Display is a central concern of the galleries, museums, and biennials that represent the predominant type of forum (other than their own website and the occasional community space or university classroom) at which the agency has tended to exhibit testimony and evidence that is inadmissible or denied in courts. As Weizman notes, cultural and art venues can function as a complement, alternative, or catalyst for fractious juridical processes, as well as a space for theorizing and putting pressure on forensic epistemologies and practices. In other instances—as with the temporary truth commission ("Ground Truth") that FA, in collaboration with displaced residents and the Israeli NGO Zochrot, constructed at the site of a demolished Bedouin village in the Negev desert—artistic venues have provided a more durable home for materials at risk of destruction: The temporary structure where Bedouin residents presented proof of their ownership over lands seized under the pretext of the Ottoman Land Code of 1858 was dismantled ahead of its bulldozing by Israeli police, but the materials were later supplemented and reassembled as a transitory museum at a Vienna gallery.[86] Weizman freely admits that the juridical forums (national and international courts, tribunals, and the United Nations) in which FA seeks to present research findings are not always accessible or viable. But the forums that he invokes at his most utopian are neither juridical nor artistic; Weizman emphasizes the tactical importance, rather, of convening or constructing "alternative, informal forums . . . in the field and on the street" when the necessary forums do not exist. He elaborates, "We can thus not limit the presentation of our evidence to any single context, but must seek to migrate it between several different forums. At other times, we must search for alternative, informal forums. Tactical and operative, they can take place in the field and on the street. At yet other times, when the necessary forums do not exist, we must conceive, assemble, or construct new ones."[87]

In the following analysis of a collaboration between FA and the Invisible Institute (henceforth II), I turn away from the prevailing emphasis of scholarly writing on counterforensics on evidence and aesthetics (or on objects and their mediation) to the neglected problem of the forum and its attendant listening relations.[88] The forum is at the fulcrum of Keenan and Weizman's tripartite description of forensics as comprising an object, a mediator, and a forum. Described by Weizman as "a shifting triangulation between three elements—a contested *object or site*, an *interpreter* tasked with translating 'the language of things,' and the assembly of a public gathering"—forum is better understood as a *relation* than a space or domain.[89] The project of remaking the social relations among those who are given a voice and those who listen is therefore a *forum function*. That relationship—and not the humanity of those who have been wronged—is ultimately what is at stake in the act of convening an audience to deliberate on counterforensic evidence of human rights violations. Voice, as I have argued throughout this book and in previous writing, is not a preexisting thing out there that precedes the act of being heard, recognized, or admitted into a domain (say, humanity) that remains unchanged by its admission. Like forum, voice is a relation that emerges in shifting triangulation with mediation and listenership. Listening relations—whether carceral, reformist, or abolitionist—and the forum are, in other words, mutually constitutive.

FA's first U.S.-based investigation, of the killing of Harith Augustus, offers a unique opportunity to confront the carceral entanglements of counterforensic listening, which are usually subordinated in critical discussions of FA's practice to concerns regarding their investigative aesthetics and technofetishist politics of display.[90] These entanglements were made explicit in negotiations among FA and its collaborators at II around what it means to verify Black testimonies of anti-Black violence.⁹¹ My reading of this project will show that these negotiations, though complex, come down to the distinction between two distinct practices of listening and forum relations. Prison abolitionists frequently employ the distinction between *reformist reforms* and *nonreformist reforms* to distinguish police reforms that unravel the net of social control (e.g., reforms that disarm police, increase civilian oversight of police, increase data transparency, or redirect policing and prison funds toward social goods) from those that tighten it through criminalization (e.g., reforms that allocate more money to policing, reforms that are primarily technology focused, or reforms that focus on individual "bad apple" police).⁹² The French-Austrian social theorist Andre Gorz, credited by Ruth Wilson Gilmore with originating these terms, notes that reformist reforms subordinate their objectives and demands (however deep the need) to the rationality and practicality of a given system, while nonreformist reforms imagine a different horizon based on those needs and are not limited by a discussion of what is possible at present.⁹³ I have found this distinction helpful in elaborating what is at stake in the way FA's collaborations have pushed the horizons of the agency's evolving discourse and practice.⁹⁴ Building on Gilmore and Gorz, I offer the following (useful, if slightly crude) heuristic for parsing the two modes of listening and forum relations at work in *The Killing of Harith Augustus*: "listening like a cop" and "listening like an outlaw community of care."

Initially produced for exhibition in the 2019 Chicago Architecture Biennial, the Harith Augustus investigation led to a reckoning among FA and its collaborators at II, including Trina Reynolds-Tyler, a data researcher and native of Chicago's predominantly Black South Side neighborhood, regarding the stakes of turning Augustus's death into an artistic exhibit for a largely white audience. Their decision to migrate the visual materials associated with the investigation out of the Biennial exhibition space onto the FA website and II's South Side community space exemplifies the aesthetic strategy that LaCharles Ward, in a recent essay on Black artists dealing with themes of anti-Black violence, has called "Black redaction." Whereas redaction in the legal sense functions as a form of state or corporate censorship, Ward describes Black redaction as the "presentation of a new version of a text" undertaken by "Black people and those committed to and caring for Black life."[95] By calling on spectators to decode the official record and produce another record that centers on Black life, Black redaction functions, Ward argues, as a form of Black testimony that offers new ways of interpreting evidence and the law's violent omissions from the positionality of Blackness.[96] As a practice of refusal, Black redaction invokes Saidiya Hartman's refusal of modes of witnessing that spectacularize the violated Black body and thereby reinforce its status of "thing" in the very act of speaking for it, as well as Campt's definition of "black visuality" as "a radical modality of witnessing that refuses authoritative forms of visuality which function to refuse blackness itself."[97]

Viewed through the lens of Black redaction, the Harith Augustus investigation becomes a project in pursuit of a listenership adequate to the task of caring for Black testimonies of anti-Black violence, from a vantage that refuses the law's violent redactions. This pursuit emerges as a minor refrain throughout the six videos that comprise this project but becomes amplified in the final, belated video produced by II, which summons an abolitionist forum grounded in a Black listenership of connection and solidarity. This abolitionist forum stands in contrast with the listening relations constructed by the first five videos, which underscore the tensions bound up in the sousveillant oversight of police by civilian witnesses—an abolitionist project that procedural justice is designed to hamstring—in their reformist appeal to audiences as members of a suspicious and securitized "neighborhood watch" on the lookout for "bad policing" requiring punitive sanction. The carceral modality of listening modeled at times by these videos functions as an extension of the forensically oriented perceptual practice that Lisa Guenther calls "seeing like a cop."

LISTENING LIKE AN ABOLITIONIST 161

Let me offer an overview of the investigation before proceeding further. *The Killing of Harith Augustus* revolves around the 2018 murder by police of a Black man, a barber by trade, in the South Shore neighborhood of Chicago. Subtitled "Six Durations of a Split Second," the project comprises six short videos, which are titled "Milliseconds," "Seconds," "Minutes," "Hours," "Days," and "Years"; each seeks to expose a different dimension of police violence across a distinct timescale. The investigation replicates the methodology of a previous award-winning investigation of an IDF raid on the Bedouin village Umm al-Hiran, in which FA investigated misrepresentation narratives at different scales (this investigation was shortlisted for the 2018 Turner Prize, a major award presented annually to a British visual artist). For their first U.S.-based collaboration, FA teamed up with II to interrogate the logic of the "split-second decision" that is often invoked as a legal defense by police accused of lethal force in tense or uncertain situations in which the safety of the officer or of bystander civilians is deemed by police to be compromised. This was how the Chicago Police Department defended the actions of Dillan Halley, the young, white rookie cop, newly qualified and still on probation, who shot Augustus for appearing to touch his holstered gun. Augustus was stopped by a police patrol on suspicion of being armed in a state that permits concealed carry. Quincy Jones, the veteran Black police officer who initially stopped Augustus, is said to have engaged in a civil exchange before Halley and another newly qualified white cop, Megan Fleming, escalated the situation. In an article for *The Intercept* describing the project, Weizman writes that the "cumulative effect" of the videos is to "bring into focus the totality of circumstances that produced the split second in which the police reacted with deadly force."[98] The investigation attempts, in other words, to reassert the historical and social context that is excised from consideration by the invocation of a temporal state of exception.

This may be true of the videos considered in aggregate. However, the mode of the final video, "Years," is difficult to reconcile with the first five videos. All six videos are narrated by Reynolds-Tyler, but "Years" speaks in a distinct voice and invokes and constructs a different mode of listening. The first five videos ("Milliseconds," "Seconds," "Minutes," "Hours," and "Days") use a trademark range of counterforensic rhetorical strategies—didactic exposition paired with a "timeline aesthetic" of cross-verification and synchronization that relies on the performative force of what Orit Halpern calls "beautiful data"—to mount a civil rights case against Halley, who has thus far been protected from litigation by Chicago police, political officials, and powerful lobbying groups such as the Fraternal Order of Police.[99] Using 3D modeling, eyewitness and expert testimony, and audiovisual synchronization, these videos cross-verify, interrogate, and contradict the redacted and suggestively editorialized material that was released by the Chicago PD, revealing a litany of procedural violations on the part of Halley and other members of the patrol.[100] They reconstruct the shooting from absented vantages, often at scales imperceptible to the human eye, producing a counternarrative that implicates Halley and exonerates Augustus. For instance, "Seconds" tracks the five officers' movements from multiple camera perspectives to reveal how they repeatedly profiled Augustus: after the senior officer, Jones, stopped him, Fleming, another newly qualified officer, grabbed at an otherwise cooperative Augustus (see fig. 3.6) without issuing a verbal warning after he had shown that he had a permit to own, but not to carry, his gun; this triggered the series of events that led to Halley shooting Augustus, who never actually drew his gun. In "Hours," Reynolds-Tyler, commenting on excerpts from videos shot by protesters, recounts how police attacked, beat, and arrested protesters who gathered at the site of the shooting (see fig. 3.7). "Days" catalogs how the police narrative—which initially alleged an "armed confrontation" in support of Halley's false incident report—shifted under pressure from activists who demanded that the Civilian Office of Police Accountability investigate the Chicago PD's delayed release of edited bodycam footage, settling on the unconfirmed claim that "Harith Augustus *attempted* to pull a gun."

FIGURE 3.6 Screenshot from the video "Seconds" showing two synchronized perspectives of Megan Fleming accosting Harith Augustus while other members of the police patrol encircle him. Courtesy of Forensic Architecture and Invisible Institute.

FIGURE 3.7 Screenshot from the video "Hours" showing Trina Reynolds-Tyler interpreting a model of the protest that followed the police killing of Harith Augustus. Courtesy of Forensic Architecture and Invisible Institute.

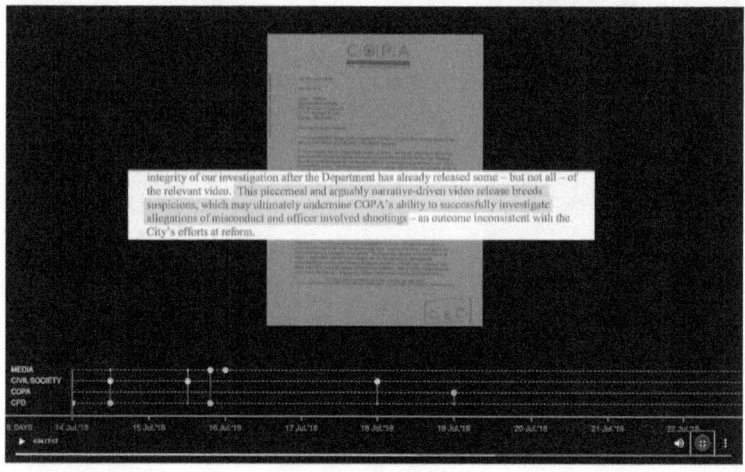

FIGURE 3.8 Screenshot from the video "Days" depicting a memo from the Civilian Office of Police Accountability to the Chicago Police Department Superintendent. Courtesy of Forensic Architecture and Invisible Institute.

I find these videos fascinating because of how their juridical address circumscribes their abolitionist call to "watch the cops." Following the Rodney King trial, the U.S. Department of Justice (DOJ) has become the default recourse for activists who have found local police, political officials, and police oversight boards unresponsive to their demands for censure of police accused of constitutional violations.[101] Even though the Harith Augustus investigation was produced for display in an architecture exhibition, it is addressed explicitly to the Civilian Office of Police Accountability (COPA) (see fig. 3.8), the oversight agency tasked with investigating police shootings in Chicago, and implicitly to the DOJ, the final level of legal recourse. Watching the cops in pursuit of greater openness and transparency in civilian oversight of police is the founding mission of II. The organization's pilot project was a successful lawsuit demanding that the city of Chicago declassify records of over one hundred thousand misconduct complaints lodged against police officers by residents of the predominantly Black and brown

South and West Side neighborhoods. It is noteworthy, in the context of this practice of Black vigilance—keeping vigil through civilian sousveillance—and its attendant critique of policing as a structurally racist institution, to see how the videos operationalize the perceptual logic of "seeing like a cop"—a heightened attention, in this instance, to "aberrant" policing—in support of procedural reforms. Given that the videos are doing double duty in addressing the DOJ in the guise of a broader public, it is not entirely surprising that the reforms for which they argue (improved training, officer compliance in use of dashcams and bodycams, community-based policing, and criminal prosecution of Dillan Halley) are of the procedural variety that the DOJ has tended to institute, all of which leading abolitionist researchers have found to enhance rather than shrink police legitimacy.[102]

Lisa Guenther frames "seeing like a cop" as the perceptual counterpart of James Q. Wilson and George L. Kelling's notorious "broken windows" approach to policing. Wilson and Kelling famously endorsed "irregularity in police practice" (including "informal or extralegal steps" that "probably would not withstand a legal challenge") to ensure "regularity on the street."[103] They advocated for the arrest and removal from public spaces of people whose presence threatens propertied personhood and white, middle-class values based on racist, ableist, and sexist visual cues of impropriety and danger.[104] Guenther describes "seeing like a cop" as a set of perceptual practices (watching for abnormal activity, listening for strange sounds, and tracking the movement of unfamiliar people from a safe distance) that are racialized as white even when they are practiced by people who are not exclusively white. "Seeing like a cop," Guenther writes, "typically leads to calling the cops."[105] To put this another way, seeing like a cop could be called a forensic mode of perception: It is closely linked to the spectatorial actions of scrutiny, squinting, moving closer/zooming in, developing, enhancing, and enlarging that Jeffay associates with the forensic gaze. At the time of its emergence in the late nineteenth century, Jeffay argues that the forensic gaze represented a distinctly racialized mode of vision, arising at a moment when a racialized visual compulsion (exemplified by pseudosciences such as craniometry and physiognomy, which were preoccupied with reading visible bodily details for larger immutable inner truths) intersected with the invention of photography as a new visual technology capable of capturing details imperceptible to the eye.[106] Seeing like a cop is a direct descendent of the late nineteenth-century racist pseudosciences that gave rise to the forensic gaze. A proprietary and securitized mode of looking especially common in gentrifying neighborhoods, it invokes state violence as a necessary condition for feelings of safety and belonging.

FA and II unravel the fatal consequences of this perceptual practice for Augustus, a Black man walking down the street wearing a durag. The two videos that develop a case against Dillan Halley's illegitimate use of lethal force, "Minutes" and "Milliseconds," offer fascinating evidence of how building this case enlists audiences in a suspicious mode of listening that distinguishes between "good" (normal, innocent, unproblematic, or acceptable) policing and "bad" (abnormal, guilty, problematic, or unacceptable) policing requiring censure. Both videos are structured around the absence of sound in the recorded surveillance footage—it was only after Halley had fired shots that he turned his bodycam on to "event mode," a setting that initiates sound recording. "Minutes" and "Milliseconds" counter the police narrative that strategically weaponized this sonic absence against Augustus. "Minutes" opens with a statement from the police superintendent Eddie Johnson, made during the press conference at which he released footage from Halley's bodycam, redacted and editorialized to zoom in on a freeze-frame showing Augustus's holstered gun, a full twenty-four hours after the shooting: "We're not trying to hide anything. . . . The video speaks for itself." Speaking for the people versus the Chicago PD, Reynolds-Tyler retaliates, "No evidence ever speaks for itself, certainly not a silent video."

The manner in which these two videos "speak for" the evidence—telling what is shown—is noteworthy because of how they define the relationship among those who listen and the video of the actually and metaphorically voiceless Augustus. Reynolds-Tyler restates what Keenan has said in another context regarding the forensic dissection and distortion of George Holliday's video of Rodney King's near-fatal beating by the LAPD by the officers' defense attorneys: "If evidence spoke for itself we would have no need for a jury."[107] No video speaks for itself in U.S. legal forums: A witness needs to authenticate it and speak it into the record, whether an eyewitness testifying that the video represents what they saw or an expert witness certifying that the evidence has not been tampered with.[108] Reynolds-Tyler, a data scientist who arrived on the scene an hour after the shooting, speaks in both capacities and also admits other eyewitnesses and experts into the record: She hails listeners as a jury assessing the persuasive claims of witnesses who speak for the evidence. As such, the videos do not migrate evidence from one forum to another so much as they migrate the acoustics of criminal justice out of the legal forum as the basis of a public listenership. To use language borrowed from James Parker, a scholar of acoustic jurisprudence, they call on our collective knowledge of "the law's sonic imagination" to direct our listening in particular ways through verbalization, the hearing of arguments and evidentiary truths, and the pronouncement of judgment.[109]

What interests me about this directed listening is how witnesses speaking for data-driven evidence shape a domain of audibility that encourages listeners to silence the structural anti-Blackness of policing and tune into the forensic minutiae of "bad" policing in a manner that replicates the outlook of the patrol cop scanning for signs of irregularity. In "Minutes," which syncs information gathered from all of the released surveillance footage and police statements to reconstruct the event's missing soundtrack, it is testimony from a Black security guard, Darren Coleman, who was standing next to Quincy Jones, that, along with Reynolds-Tyler's closing pronouncement ("Harith Augustus was pronounced dead nineteen minutes after shots were fired"), turns Halley's false claims that Augustus "pulled a gun on me" into the smoking gun. Coleman voices support for community-based policing by officers familiar with the neighborhood, arguing, "[Quincy] Jones was basically dealing with the situation, and when they grabbed at him, he panicked. You have these new officers and they're nervous, if I'm dead honest, in a black neighborhood. Like I said, that whole situation could have been different if they never would have grabbed at him."

"Milliseconds" collates expert insight from a neuroscientist on the temporality of instinctive reactions with data derived from a gunshot detection system to establish the exact moment Halley fired his gun, showing that Halley was the only one of the five officers who actively and consciously escalated the situation by shooting Augustus despite the absence of a reasonable threat. Reynolds-Tyler clinches it once again: "All four [of the other officers] shared the same perception of the event but none of them engaged as Dillan Halley did." As a mode of making the evidence evident, then, these messages function as auditory cues for listening like a cop. They deploy audiences to assume the vantage of a neighborhood watch listening for evidence of aberrant, irregular, and dangerous policing, and they secure buy-in for reformist reforms such as enhanced training, culturally sensitive policing, and criminal prosecution that have been shown to *increase* policing in the guise of regulation. Listening like a cop for spectacularly violent policing habituates listeners to the mundane violence of criminal justice reform.

I want to turn, in closing, to "Years." The culminating video of the project was released months after the original investigation, and it departs from the forensic scrutiny, expository didacticism, and timeline aesthetic typical of FA's video investigations by zooming out to analyze the structural conditions that normalized differential policing in Chicago. This enables the video to admit and make audible what Ward, describing testimonial evidence grounded in the daily experience of Black people, calls "Black evidence."[110] "Years" not only follows different protocols and criteria of admission when it comes to the scale and order of evidence we hear—evidence that appeals not to the state but to Black communities—it also effects a subtle but transformative shift in how it asks audiences to listen by insisting on and calling attention to Black testimonies of anti-Black violence.

"Years" was created by FA's collaborators at II because, as the scholar Sasha Crawford-Holland has noted, "They were concerned that an investigation merely replicating the clinical epistemology of the state could be experienced as reductive, insensitive, even harmful, by community members."[111] As with the other videos, Reynolds-Tyler functions as a source of narrative cohesion and local credibility, but she speaks in "Years" not as a data analyst or eyewitness making sense of otherwise inscrutable data but as a community member in the predominantly Black South Shore neighborhood. Unlike the other videos, "Years" has the tone less of a tribunal than of a vigil or wake. Experts are not absent: Adam Green, a historian at the University of Chicago, offers structural analysis of the segregationist policies and restrictive covenants that led to the impoverishment of Chicago's Black neighborhoods, which have paved the way to differential policing. But like the prominently featured local activists Will Calloway and the veteran civil rights activist Timuel Black (now deceased)—who offer firsthand accounts, respectively, of the mood of South Shore neighbors awaiting the trial of Laquan McDonald's murderer at the time of Augustus's killing, and of "Black belt" neighborhoods cordoned off by police in the lead-up to the 1919 Chicago race riot, whose residents banded together for self-protection—Green speaks as a Black community member. Others who live and work in the South Shore also speak, but their function is not as witnesses turning evidence into proof but as specialists in understanding the resources and relationships required for Black endurance and thriving.

Two pieces of testimony stand out here for their emphasis on care and connection as the scaffolds of neighborhood resilience and safety. Rev, Augustus's coworker at the Sideline Studio barbershop, talks about Harith's last haircut: a baby boy's first haircut. He says, "Only a special barber with patience can handle such a small baby." For Rev, Augustus's decision to carry a gun came from the same place of communal care. Asked how he felt when he realized that Augustus carried a gun, Rev says, "He's in a barbershop by himself. I felt more protected when I found out than I felt threatened. I'm not afraid of a man who I work with everyday feeling like he's gotta protect himself. He's gonna protect all of us" (see fig. 3.9). As Green puts it, Augustus—knowing

FIGURE 3.9 Screenshots from the video "Years" depicting scenes from interviews with Harith Augustus's coworker Rev and the poet Audrey Petty. Courtesy of Invisible Institute.

his life was in his own hands—was taking outlaw measures, "voluntarily, individually, drastically," to effect the conditions not only of his own safety but also the safety of his community. Another resident and 11 staff member, the poet and critic Audrey Petty, describes the pull she felt to visit the barbershop where Augustus worked, with her ten-year-old daughter Ella, to pay their respects, "not knowing what we'd find there, but knowing we'd find people who knew him, and that was enough." Petty offers a further reframing of transformative safety without the need for security: "I feel safe because of my connections with my neighbors . . . but also being in Black community, and having that sense of history and connection."

What does it mean to listen like an abolitionist? To listen in ways that, to reprise Fleetwood, do not aim to reproduce or preserve prisons but which enable us, instead, to imagine and bring into presence the values and relationships that are the bedrock of a world without police and prisons? For these Black South Shore neighbors, residents, workers, elders, regulars, and well-wishers, it means speaking and listening as members of an outlaw community of care. Neighborliness and community are not a given—as we have learned repeatedly from cases such as George Zimmerman, who killed his neighbor Trayvon Martin, or Francisco Oropeza, the man accused of killing five of his neighbors in Texas after they asked him to stop shooting his rifle so that a baby could sleep—their conditions have to be created through struggle. Mariame Kaba, who spent twenty years organizing against the prison industrial complex in Chicago, reminds us that these conditions have to be fought for, nurtured, and defended by building relationships founded not on carceral security but on the hard-earned safety of mutual trust:

> You can have security without relationships, but you cannot have safety—actual safety—without healthy relationships. Without really getting to know your neighbor, figuring out when you should be intervening when you hear and see things, feeling safe enough within your community that you feel like, yeah, my neighbor's punching their

partner, I'm going to knock on the door, right? I'm not going to think that that person's going to pull a gun on me and shoot me in the head. I don't believe that because I know that person. I know them. I built that relationship with them, and even though they're upset and mad, I'm taking the chance of going over there.[112]

In this rearticulation of what it means to listen like an abolitionist, Kaba also reframes verification as a practice not of securing the truth but of confirming the solidity of relationships. It is significant that the place where Black community members with a range of relationships to the South Shore neighborhood—propertied as well as unpropertied and belonging as well as unbelonging—congregated in order to reconfirm their relationships was a barbershop. Barbershops have long served Black men across social classes, including those excluded from the formal economy, as customary spaces of refuge outside the punishing constraints of white surveillance, daily discrimination, and penal time. They are spaces of informal learning where relationships of trust are fostered by the duration of awaiting one's turn, which is filled with ranging talk and debate about mundane troubles and pleasures, political issues, and movement work. As the South Chicago-based scholar Quincy T. Mills writes, quoting George Schuyler, a Black journalist and critic who visited Southern barbershops across the 1950s, "the barber shop is a forum," and the barber is a crucial conduit within that forum.[113]

Perhaps part of the work of building relationships of trust and care, then, involves the nurturing of informal, necessary forums in which recognition, belonging, and accountability are organized not around punitive assessment and judgment but acts of speech, address, and listening that strengthen social capacities and solidarities. Forums are often thought of as retrofits—something that comes after the harm, after the fact. Too often, the act of listening is also understood this way, as something belated and reactive. What we witness in "Years" is an apprehension that listening can be constructive and generative of social relations. In gathering together testimony that seeks not to uphold the whiteness of the law and of juridical listening, "Years" hails listeners committed to looking out for Black life not as agents of law enforcement or judgment but as outlaw agents of a more audacious abolitionist vision.

ABOLITIONIST LISTENING AS GATHERING TOGETHER

I have charted, in this chapter, minor refrains within two prevailing modes of documentary accountability that call on audiences to listen not in order to censure, shame, or punish but in order to bring into presence abolitionist values and relational modes that juridical listening routinely disbars. By way of a conclusion, I would like to reflect on the different registers at which *The Viewing Booth* and *The Killing of Harith Augustus* refuse the concept of witnessing that tends to orient documentary efforts at challenging state violence, settler impunity, and other harms. This is a concept of witnessing that, by jurifying audiences and engaging them in exploring and trying out justifications for punishment, reinscribes a punitive understanding of sovereign power as the structuring basis of social relationships.

In thinking about the alternative understanding of witnessing at stake in this refusal, I find myself returning to the work of the xwélméxw scholar Dylan Robinson, introduced in the previous chapter. In his discussion of the watershed *Delgamuukw* land claim trial in which Gitxan and Wet'suwet'en people sought jurisdiction over their territories in northern British Columbia, Robinson—recounting an instance in which a judge objected to the performance of a Gitksan song and asked for it to be submitted as a written transcript because he had "a tin ear"—describes the refusal of Canadian settler courts to acknowledge Indigenous songs (whether as living historical documents or as functional law) as a failure of witnessing.[114] Robinson goes on to explain that he understands "witnessing" not in the visually grounded Western sense of the "eyewitness," which emphasizes the gathering, display, and instrumentalization of content, but in the Indigenous, aural sense, as in the Halq'eméylem words *xwlálám* (meaning "to witness and to listen") and *xwélalà:m* ("listening"), described as a practice of respectful and non-goal-oriented listening that Robinson likens to the practice of "gathering together" around various communal tables, whether in the longhouse, or over dinner, to share conversation and connection.[115] Robinson locates the emphasis of *xwélalà:m* on embodied connection and the bringing together of dispersed knowledges, histories, and life narratives as a counterpoint to the distinct but similarly alienated forum relations schooled both by the Canadian settler courtroom and the museum as venues of Indigenous expropriation.[116] "To effect a decolonial crisis in the act of listening," Robinson writes, "cannot simply entail a willful approach to kick colonial listening habits. Instead, it means shifting the places, models, and structures of how we listen."[117]

The Viewing Booth and *The Killing of Harith Augustus* offer a glimpse of documentary practitioners grappling in distinct but related contexts with the carceral forum relations and enclosures that are replicated by the attitudes, habits, and comportments of juridical listening. As *The Viewing Booth* unfolds, Alexandrowicz's unsettling listening begins to function as a mirror not only for Maia's defensive mode of witnessing Palestinian suffering but also for his own listening positionality, understood less as a stable state than as a process and evolving practice whose settler complicity is not in any way easily resolved by his activism. By designing a process that is as dialectical as the form of the film, Alexandrowicz asks an abolitionist question rather than fighting repudiation scripts on their own terrain: What can a listening that refuses the false pretense of "two sides" *do* in its own right? As a political activity, what can it teach us about the limits of prevailing models of documentary accountability?

The Killing of Harith Augustus offers a different articulation of this question. And like *The Viewing Booth*, it is propositional in how it offers an answer by designing and modeling an abolitionist structure of listening. I want to return here to "Years." One of the noteworthy features of this final video is that it does not—as the other five videos do—relentlessly rake over the final moments of Augustus's life and the image of him in death in order to work against the various legal tactics and temporalities of redaction (on the scene, after the fact) leveraged by the Chicago PD. "Years" both withholds and holds a candle to this absent presence, practicing what Ward calls Black redaction. This is a practice not of censorship but of creating a new form for presenting the harm that was done to Augustus: a form that insists we gather together to attend to what is absent, what is present, and what *must be made* present (see fig. 3.10).[118] There is no other way to listen for this simultaneously absent presence and present absence— the sound of life ongoing despite the prison—than as an abolitionist.

FIGURE 3.10 Screenshot from the video "Years" depicting a memorial to Harith "Snoop" Augustus in front of Sideline Studio. Courtesy of Invisible Institute.

CODA

Listening Without Impact

As filmmakers, we are often asked to write applications for funding that include frustrating speculations about how our films will have "impact"—a form of boilerplate writing where we are encouraged to imagine the ways that our future films will influence politicians, change minds, or change policy. I always wish I could remind funders that creating new kinds of listening and conversation space is, in itself, a critical kind of impact—maybe the most critical impact.
—Irene Lusztig, Facebook post

If we listen rather than extract, the story reveals itself.
—Cecilia Aldarondo, "All That Glitters"

Over the last two decades, conversations about accountability in documentary, especially but not only in the United States, have reoriented around the concept of *impact*. A growing number of grantors now earmark "impact funds" for films deemed capable of shifting attitudes or policies around pressing social issues through community engagement. Filmmakers, in turn, hire consultants with backgrounds in areas such as education, law, activism, or public broadcasting as "impact producers" charged with optimizing the potential of documentary content for social change.

Impact campaigns—also called "outreach" or "engagement" campaigns because they strategically engage communities, professionals, or organizations connected to a film's issues (for instance, an impact campaign for a documentary on the criminalization of sexual assault victims might seek funds for engaging closely with journalists, first responder nurses, victims' advocacy nonprofits, and police officers)—can span years; some begin even as a film is being conceived. Funding for documentary films is increasingly contingent upon illustrating intended impact.[1] Impact can determine whether a film has value and even whether it gets made at all.

The rise of the impact industrial complex is a cultural barometer of an increasingly risk-averse and corporatized documentary landscape. In a time of shrinking public support for the arts, demonstrable impact, illustrated through concrete benchmarks, metrics, and deliverables (including quantitative measures of projected "eyeballs" or numbers of screenings and qualitative surveys of audiences) assures philanthropic foundations or private investors that a film will do social good even if does not generate revenue. To be sure, many of impact's proponents disavow its function as marketing or public relations, framing it as a social justice-centered practice organized around the values of care, collaboration, and community accountability.[2] Put somewhat differently, impact justifies the social value of documentary by turning it into a commodity on the speculative market.

Impact is not without its critics. As the first epigraph indicates, many filmmakers find impact exercises frustrating or hollow but go through with them reluctantly even as they seek other, more ineffable forms of encounter. One filmmaker with whom I spoke noted that regulations around impact can paradoxically create barriers where there should be access points both for makers and their potential audiences.[3] Conversely, a vocal minority of impact producers see themselves working in the grassroots tradition of distribution, education, and community engagement that defined social documentary prior to its corporatization. Just as films can have impact without an impact campaign, impact work can also enact the slow transformation of documentary values, relationships, and systems called for by Sonya Childress and Natalie Bullock-Brown.[4] The best examples, like the toolkit for disability-inclusive filmmaking released by FWD-Doc in coordination with Netflix's *Crip Camp* (dir. Nicole Newnham and Jim LeBrecht, 2020) can be powerful arguments for the anticipatory politics of access intimacy explored in chapter 2.[5] Others, like the trans-poetics informed discussion guide produced by POV for *North By Current* (dir. Angelo Madsen Minax, 2021) provide much-needed resources for communities grappling with grief and addiction. There is much to say about the implications of these shifts, both remedial and potentially radical, for documentary. What I want to emphasize, in coming to the close of this book, is the importance of *auditing* to impact and its processes of verifying documentary accountability.

Impact is a cornerstone of audit culture. The colloquial understanding of accountability—"being responsible"—extends outward from the technical meaning of audit introduced early in the book: the duty to present verifiable accounts and to account for what one does. Under the gaze of a growing administrative class of impact managers, the documentary field has been redefined in terms of a logic of accountability in which all aspects of a film's "value proposition" must be optimized in demonstrably measurable ways. The pattern is familiar. A similar transformation has been underway for decades in the realm of higher education, where the exclusionary structures exposed by the inclusion of minoritized students, faculty, and staff have been resolved by adding to the ranks of senior administrators charged with managing demands for meaningful change. There, too, the rhetoric of reform has been introduced by marrying managerial concepts (accountability, transparency, and inclusion) with the socialist values of collaboration and care.[6] Barring notable exceptions, the result has been a wholesale abduction and perversion of these values, as the principles of shared governance, academic freedom, and humanistic inquiry have been dismantled and replaced by a top-down system of managerial control that presents itself as more responsible, scientific, and democratic.[7] What is more, because accountability is a horizon that cannot be reached—one can never have too much of it—this self-sustaining system never reaches its goal.[8]

The impact of audit culture on documentary, as noted by Irene Lusztig, is that verifying impact often comes at the cost of a deeper listening—a listening that eludes capture and is therefore harder to measure. To put it in the terms that I have used throughout this book, the documentary audit hijacks the political potential of documentary listening by turning it into a utilitarian practice with measurable outcomes.

What better figure for a benevolent overseer class that represents the documentary field to itself than a "neutral-accented" commentator? In chapter 1, I introduced this figure as a formal manifestation of the documentary audit, understood as that which exceeds and conditions documentary listening. Nearly a century on, the imperial habits of listening and formal hierarchies discussed in that chapter have found new life in the neoliberal structures of impact. Audit culture seeks to measure the social good of documentary. I have sought instead to trace the deleterious impacts of the documentary audit in a range of institutional domains—from linguistic profiling to retrofitted accommodations and juridical listening—where documentary listening habits are operationalized in biopolitical projects that determine social thriving and legal status. I have, in turn, outlined a range of articulations of the documentary audit: a habitual structure that distributes attentional and material resources (introduction); a normative listening vantage from which recorded sounds can be neutrally regarded as measurable social facts (chapter 1); an acquisitive listening posture constructed by transactional relationships and contractual arrangements (chapter 2); and a structure of cinematic judgment premised on a fundamental political exclusion (chapter 3).

This book has sought to amplify the solidarity efforts of documentarians working alongside communities who have been profiled, neglected, and criminalized to refuse the habitual structures and the discriminatory listening positionalities and conventions endorsed by the documentary audit. Each of the modes of otherwise listening that I have named and elaborated—listening with an accent, listening in crip time, listening like an abolitionist—represents a position and a practice formed through struggle. They are each grounded in the stubborn endurance of communities who have been discursively constituted as deviant, untimely, or absent. They represent noncompliant friction and fugitive ingenuity under conditions of persecution, erasure, and organized abandonment. If conventional documentary listening functions as a means of verifying its own editorialized version of reality, then listening otherwise insists that another world is possible. To listen otherwise is to affirm (rather than confirm) a reality that is hospitable to linguistic errantry, access intimacy, and safety without the safeguard of security. To interlisten to accented itineraries as Sonali Gulati does in *Nalini by Day, Nancy by Night*, to listen sideways for the workaround as Jordan Lord does in *Shared Resources*, and to bear witness to outlaw care as Harith Augustus's coworker Rev does in "Years" is to bend the documentary audit toward relational and formal horizons that may seem, from impact's regulatory vantage, to be capricious, redundant, futile. In a word, *unimpactful*.

To be without impact is often understood in a capitalist society as a "failure to scale." The most frequent line of questioning I have encountered while presenting ideas from this book concerns the scalability of listening otherwise. One of my reviewers, a trusted interlocutor, framed this question as a concern regarding the political impact of nonnormative modes of listening, especially given the pernicious ends toward which the book's main subjects of critique—authoritarian uses of documentary (such as those of border police) and reformist uses of documentary (exemplified by Copwatch and related accountability media)—harness documentary listening habits. The ethical implications of accented interlistening, sideways listening, or listening like an outlaw community of care for audiences and for the subjects of particular films was clear to them. "What is not clear," the reviewer explained, "is how such experiences lead to political action, transformation, or change."

I hear the subtext of this question as follows: If conventional approaches to documentary listening have been used to discriminate, exclude, and incarcerate at such a vast and alarming scale, then how can listening otherwise hope to compete without scaling up—without an impact strategy?

A recent conversation with members of the Forensic Architecture Investigation (FAI) Unit of the Palestinian human rights organization Al-Haq has helped me reflect on the stakes of this book's attention to listening without impact and to work that refuses unprincipled compromise with power as the cost of scaling up. The conversation concerned the status of unverifiable testimony. Al-Haq began a partnership with the London-based research agency Forensic Architecture shortly before it was discredited by Israel by 2021 as a terrorist organization. The partnership, while necessary—especially after October 7, 2023, when Al-Haq was cut off from their field agents in Gaza and had to rely on open-source intelligence—has also produced methodological quandaries. In normative usages of forensic analysis, as the FAI unit explained it, verifiable evidence is paramount; testimony that cannot be corroborated by the technology is faulty testimony. For Al-Haq, though, the testimony of Palestinian people is paramount, and any failure to verify or geolocate is a failure of the listener and not the testimony.

Embedded in this searing insight is a commentary on listening as an ongoing site of struggle. It is precisely the material conditions of that struggle, and the unmeasurable scale at which it must be waged, that is papered over by placing the onus of change on individual filmmakers or listeners. What Al-Haq's FAI Unit articulates above is not a silver bullet but a model and a staging ground for change of the kind to which I have tried to attend throughout this book. Change needs to come not only to documentary forms and institutions but also to the institutional domains—legal, bureaucratic, corporate, and civic—in which its modes of verification resound. Otherwise, listening is doomed to remain a depoliticized and empty ethic.

NOTES

INTRODUCTION

1. Bill Nichols, *Speaking Truths with Film: Evidence, Ethics, Politics in Documentary* (Oakland: University of California Press, 2016), 74.
2. Bill Nichols, "The Voice of Documentary," *Film Quarterly* 36, no. 6 (1983): 18.
3. In *Representing Reality*, Nichols famously classifies documentary among the social sciences, which he dubs "discourses of sobriety" that aim to "effect action and entail consequences," elaborating that unlike fiction film, which operates in the realm of "unconscious desires and latent meanings," documentary attends to "social issues of which we are consciously aware . . . where the reality-attentive ego and superego live." See Bill Nichols, *Representing Reality* (Bloomington: Indiana University Press, 1991), 3–4; Bill Nichols, *Introduction to Documentary*, 3rd ed. (Bloomington: Indiana University Press, 2017), 26, 52. The fourth edition of *Introduction to Documentary* (2024), coauthored by Nichols with Jaimie Baron, was not yet available for purchase at the time that this chapter was drafted and revised.
4. Over the last three decades, scholars writing about wide-ranging documentary conventions and approaches have adopted the "voice" metaphor, and practitioners have engaged it to theorize their own authorial address. See for instance Charles Wolfe, "Historicising the 'Voice of God': The Place of Vocal Narration in Classical Documentary," *Film History* 9, no 2 (1997): 149–67; Trish FitzSimons, "Braided Channels: A Genealogy of the Voice of Documentary," *Studies in Documentary Film* 3, no. 2 (2009): 131–46; Sarah Kessler, "The Voice of Mockumentary," in *Vocal Projections: Voices in Documentary*, ed. Annabelle Honess Roe and Maria Pramaggiore (New York: Bloomsbury

Academic, 2018), 137–52. For a detailed discussion of documentary attempts to theorize "voice," see Pooja Rangan, "Documentary Listening Habits: From Voice to Audibility," in *The Oxford Handbook of Film Theory*, ed. Kyle Stevens (Oxford: Oxford University Press, 2022), 403–20.

5. Lisa French, *The Female Gaze in Documentary Film: An International Perspective* (New York: Palgrave Macmillan, 2021), acknowledges and contends with this absence and proposes, in a series of interviews with women filmmakers, that their perspectives enact what bell hooks might call an "oppositional gaze."

6. For an overview, see the introduction to Pooja Rangan, *Immediations: The Humanitarian Impulse in Documentary* (Durham, NC: Duke University Press, 2017).

7. Nick Couldry, *Why Voice Matters: Culture and Politics After Neoliberalism* (London: Sage, 2010), 2.

8. Brian Winston, *Claiming the Real II—Documentary: Grierson and Beyond*, 2nd ed. (London: Palgrave Macmillan, 2008), 46. Winston argues that the Griersonian tradition of framing working-class people as "social victims" has had a profound influence on realist documentary into the present.

9. Trinh T. Minh-ha, *When the Moon Waxes Red* (New York: Routledge, 1991), 60.

10. As John Corner notes, Grierson, credited with originating the term "documentary," first used the term in a review of Robert Flaherty's *Moana* (1926), a docufictional representation of village life in Samoa that Fatimah Tobing Rony has called "romantic ethnography." See John Corner, *The Art of Record: A Critical Introduction to Documentary* (Manchester: Manchester University Press, 1996), 2; Fatimah Tobing Rony, *The Third Eye: Race, Cinema and Ethnographic Spectacle* (Durham, NC: Duke University Press, 1996), 102.

11. I am invoking James C. Scott's analysis of the emergence of the mode of visuality that he terms "seeing like a state": a simplified, abstract, homogenizing grid for looking at and making sense of complex, illegible, or local social practices in order to make them more amenable to social control. See James C. Scott, *Seeing Like a State: How Certain Schemes to Improve the Human Condition Have Failed* (New Haven, CT: Yale University Press, 1999), esp. chap. 2.

12. John Mowitt, *Sounds: The Ambient Humanities* (Oakland: University of California Press, 2015), 5–6.

13. Jennifer Lynn Stoever, *The Sonic Color Line: Race and the Cultural Politics of Listening* (New York: New York University Press), 11–13.

14. The Métis/Michif scholar and scientist Max Liboiron notes that the theft of land, or what Marx calls "primitive accumulation," is foundational to the

possibility of capitalism. See Max Liboiron, *Pollution Is Colonialism* (Durham, NC: Duke University Press, 2021), 13.

15. James C. Scott writes that taxation, alongside control and conscription, was a driving force of modern statecraft, whose signal achievement was to make previously opaque systems of social organization abstractly legible, manipulable, and, most importantly, profitable. "The shorthand formulas through which tax officials apprehend reality," Scott notes, "are not mere tools of observation. By a kind of fiscal Heisenberg principle, they frequently have the power to transform the facts they take note of." See Scott, *Seeing Like a State*, 47.

16. See Marilyn Strathern, "Introduction: New Accountabilities," in *Audit Cultures: Anthropological Studies in Accountability, Ethics, and the Academy*, ed. Marilyn Strathern (New York: Routledge, 2000), 3–4.

17. See Lauren Berlant, "In a Nutshell: On Her Book *Cruel Optimism*," *Rorotoko*, June 5, 2012, https://www.rorotoko.com/11/20120605-berlant-lauren-on-cruel-optimism.

18. See Paige Sarlin, "Documentary Value," in "Dossier on 'Documentary' (Adj.)," *Millennium Film Journal* 74 (2021): 86–87.

19. See Alexandra Juhasz and Alisa Lebow, "Beyond Story: An Online, Community-Based Manifesto," in "Ways of Organizing," special issue, ed. Jason Fox and Laliv Melamed, *World Records* 2 (2018): 1–5; Alexandra Juhasz and Alisa Lebow, "Introduction: Beyond Story," in "Beyond Story," special issue, ed. Alexandra Juhasz and Alisa Lebow, *World Records* 5 (2021): 9–13; and other contributions to volume 5 of *World Records*. The authors elaborate: "Storied narratives require heroic characters and their neatly linked conflicts and resolutions. This individualistic ideology naturalizes bourgeois values and the economic system that supports them. Similarly, the nearly exclusive corralling of documentary resources in the direction of storytelling, regardless of (or perhaps due to) its lofty humanistic aims, aligns just as neatly with our epoch's neoliberal logics of labor, self, and capital and thus with corporate models for media culture, engagement, and citizenship. Expressed through funding mechanisms, distribution and exhibition circuits, ever-expanding industries, and certain well-lauded, influential films, one little word, 'story,' suddenly carries the day." Juhasz and Lebow, "Beyond Story," 2.

20. Michel Chion famously argues that sound in cinema, unlike the image, has no frame or "auditory container" to stop it from penetrating and enveloping the listening subject. See Michel Chion, *Audio-Vision: Sound on Screen*, trans. Claudia Gorbman (New York: Columbia University Press, 1994), 68.

21. See Shoshana Felman and Dori Laub, *Testimony: Crises of Witnessing in Literature, Psychoanalysis, and History* (New York: Routledge, 1992), 206; the impact of this book is discussed further in chapter 3.
22. See Michael Renov, "Bearing Witness: The Documentary Art of Testimony," paper presented at Expanded Documentary: Extensions, Movements, and Reconfigurations, Paris, May 28–29, 2019; Leshu Torchin, *Creating the Witness: Documenting Genocide on Film, Video, and the Internet* (Minneapolis: University of Minnesota Press), 3, 16.
23. See Elaine Scarry, *Thinking in an Emergency* (New York: Norton, 2011); Craig Calhoun, "The Idea of Emergency: Humanitarian Action and Global (Dis)Order," in *Contemporary States of Emergency: The Politics of Military and Humanitarian Intervention*, ed. Didier Fassin and Mariella Pandolfi (New York: Zone, 2010), 29–58; also see the introduction and chapter 2 in Rangan, *Immediations*.
24. Kate Lacey, *Listening Publics* (Cambridge: Polity, 2013), 7–8.
25. Irina Leimbacher, "Hearing Voice(s): Experiments with Documentary Listening," in "Documentary Audibilities," special issue, ed. Pooja Rangan and Genevieve Yue, *Discourse* 39, no. 3 (2017): 292–318.
26. Gilles Deleuze, *Foucault* (Minneapolis: University of Minnesota Press, 1988), 52.
27. See Mladen Dolar, *A Voice and Nothing More* (Cambridge, MA: MIT Press, 2006); Kaja Silverman, *The Acoustic Mirror: The Female Voice in Psychoanalysis and Cinema* (Bloomington: Indiana University Press, 1988). Dolar writes that voice, in the Western metaphysical tradition, is often regarded as "the material support of bringing about meaning, yet it does not contribute to it itself. . . . It [this material support] makes the utterance possible, but it disappears in it, it goes up in smoke in the meaning being produced." Dolar, *A Voice and Nothing More*, 15. In her 1988 feminist study of classical narrative cinema's sonic structures, Silverman argues that the masterful interiority associated with the disembodied, acousmatic voice-over is usually coded as masculine while the utterances of women are embodied, synchronized, and "pinned to" the body, which is relegated to the role of spectacle. Silverman, *The Acoustic Mirror*, 42–71.
28. Jonathan Sterne, *The Audible Past: Cultural Origins of Sound Reproduction* (Durham, NC: Duke University Press, 2003).
29. See Dylan Robinson, *Hungry Listening: Resonant Theory for Indigenous Sound Studies* (Minneapolis: University of Minnesota Press, 2020), 10. In chapter 2, I take up Robinson's account of the appropriative settler listening that he terms "hungry listening" as a close relative of the ableist entitlement that characterizes conventional documentary listening.

30. Lisbeth Lipari, *Listening, Thinking, Being: Toward an Ethics of Attunement* (University Park: Pennsylvania State University Press, 2014), 52.
31. Nina Sun Eidsheim, *The Race of Sound: Listening, Timbre, and Vocality in African American Music* (Durham, NC: Duke University Press, 2019), 39–40.
32. Lipari, *Listening, Thinking, Being*, 187.
33. See Stoever, *The Sonic Color Line*, 11–15. As examples, Stoever points to how popular Black musical genres like hip-hop become essentialized and racialized bearers of connotations such as crime or noise pollution or how the operatic singing styles of white American women in the nineteenth century were believed to embody an idealized "feminine range," while those of their Black American counterparts were associated with masculinity and hypersexuality. The musicologist Nina Sun Eidsheim has likewise argued, in her study of nineteenth-century American opera, that the persistent attribution by reviewers of a "distinctly Black" timbre to the voices of Black women that otherwise meet professional classical standards partakes of an enculturated idea of sound that listens for difference, noting that this tendency may have led to the typecasting of these singers in roles such as maid, slave girl, or gypsy. See Eidsheim, *The Race of Sound*, 51, 61–90. Signifying operations such as these are discussed at length in chapter 1.
34. See John Corner, "Performing the Real: Documentary Diversions," *Television and New Media* 3, no. 3 (2002): 258. Philip Rosen has recently compiled Brazilian and Soviet examples of documentary's use as an adjective from the 1920s (*documentário*, translated by Nilo Couret as "describing aspects of individual films or the potential of cinema as such"; *documentalnost* and *dokumental'nyi'*, which Joshua Malitsky, via Richard Taylor, translates as, respectively, "documentary quality" and the adjectival form of documentary), predating the Griersonian noun form that predominates Anglophone scholarship. See Philip Rosen, "Now and Then: On the Documentary Regime, Vertov, and History," in *A Companion to Documentary Film History*, ed. Joshua Malitsky (Hoboken, NJ: Wiley-Blackwell, 2021), 190.
35. In developing this line of thinking, I am building on the introduction to a dossier that I coauthored with a group of filmmakers and researchers. See Toby Lee, Laliv Melamed, Pooja Rangan, Paige Sarlin, and Benjamín Schultz-Figueroa, "Documentary (adj.): Keywords and Provocations," in "Dossier on 'Documentary' (Adj.)," *Millennium Film Journal* 74 (2021): 82.
36. Josh Guilford and Toby Lee, "Introduction: Documentary World-Making," in "Documentary World-Making," dossier, ed. Josh Guilford and Toby Lee, *World Records* 4 (2020): 163.

37. Takahashi argues that the ongoing proliferation of documentary forms into the expanded field of media and culture is characterized by two mutually reinforcing forms of documentary realism: "'marked' documentary encounters that announce themselves as special events set apart from daily life" (such as those facilitated by feature documentaries or moving image installations) and "'unmarked' documentary encounters that operate within the flow of daily life" (apps, GIFs, data visualizations, unedited drone footage, etc.). See Tess Takahashi, "Digital Magnitude," unpublished manuscript, July 8, 2021, typescript.
38. Rey Chow, *A Face Drawn in Sand: Humanistic Inquiry and Foucault in the Present* (New York: Columbia University Press, 2021), 29.
39. See Rangan, "Documentary Listening Habits," 410; Rey Chow, "After the Passage of the Beast: 'False Documentary' Aspirations, Acousmatic Complications," in *Rancière and Film*, ed. Paul Bowman (Edinburgh: Edinburgh University Press, 2013), 37.
40. See Leimbacher, "Hearing Voice(s)," 293, 314.
41. See Pooja Rangan, Akshya Saxena, Ragini Tharoor Srinivasan, and Pavitra Sundar, "Introduction: Thinking with an Accent," in *Thinking with an Accent*, ed. Pooja Rangan, Akshya Saxena, Ragini Tharoor Srinivasan, and Pavitra Sundar (Berkeley: University of California Press, 2023), 3. We borrow this phrase from the poet Li-Young Lee. See Li-Young Lee, *The Winged Seed: A Remembrance* (New York: Simon & Schuster, 1995), 76.
42. See Sonya Childress and Natalie Bullock-Brown, "The Documentary Future: A Call for Accountability," *Documentary*, July 2, 2020, https://www.documentary.org/feature/documentary-future-call-accountability.
43. In a 2009 study conducted by a member of the recently formed Documentary Accountability Working Group, surveyed filmmakers largely discuss their access to subjects as an investment of time or money in a relationship deemed to have future commodity value. See Pat Aufderheide, Peter Jaszi, and Mridu Chandra, "Honest Truths: Documentary Filmmakers on Ethical Challenges in their Work," *Center for Media and Social Impact* (2009): 1, 7, 9, 13, 14, 20. Aufderheide is a member of the Documentary Accountability Working Group, as are Bullock-Brown and Childress.
44. Ellen Samuels, "Six Ways of Looking at Crip Time," *Disability Studies Quarterly* 37, no. 3 (2017), https://dsq-sds.org/article/view/5824/4684; Alison Kafer, *Feminist, Queer, Crip* (Bloomington: Indiana University Press, 2013).
45. Liat Ben-Moshe, *Decarcerating Disability: Deinstitutionalization and Prison Abolition* (Minneapolis: University of Minnesota Press, 2020), 111.

46. Tina Campt, "Black Visuality and the Practice of Refusal," in "Performing Refusal/Refusing to Perform," special issue, ed. Lilian G. Mengesha and Lakshmi Padmanabhan, *Women and Performance* 29, no. 1 (2019), https://www.womenandperformance.org/ampersand/29-1/campt.
47. Mia Mingus, "Access Intimacy, Interdependence, and Disability Justice," *Leaving Evidence* (blog), April 12, 2017, https://leavingevidence.wordpress.com/2017/04/12/access-intimacy-interdependence-and-disability-justice/.
48. LaCharles Ward, "Black Redaction, Black Evidence: Another Testimony of Black Life," in *A Site of Struggle: American Art Against Anti-Black Violence*, ed. Janet Dees (Princeton, NJ: Princeton University Press, 2022), 90.
49. Lawrence Abu Hamdan, "Aural Contract: Forensic Listening and the Reorganization of the Speaking Subject," in *Forensics: The Architecture of Public Truth*, ed. Forensic Architecture (Berlin: Sternberg Press and Forensic Architecture, 2014), 73.
50. Brett Story, "How Does It End? Story and the Property Form," in "Beyond Story," special issue, ed. Alexandra Juhasz and Alisa Lebow, *World Records* 5 (2021): 88. Also see Sonya Childress, "Beyond Empathy," *Firelight Media*, March 20, 2017, https://firelightmedia.medium.com/beyond-empathy-ad6b5ad8a1d8.

1. LISTENING WITH AN ACCENT

1. See, for instance, Lauren Michele Jackson, "The Layered Deceptions of Jessica Krug, the Black Studies Professor Who Hid That She Is White," *New Yorker*, September 12, 2020, https://www.newyorker.com/culture/cultural-comment/the-layered-deceptions-of-jessica-krug-the-black-studies-professor-who-hid-that-she-is-white; Katrina Gulliver, "Catfishing in the Ivory Tower," *Arc Digital*, September 21, 2020, https://arcdigital.media/identity-fraud-26e05a72fd82.
2. See comments on "Jess La Bombalera (Jessica Krug)—NYC City Council Testimony 6/9/20," posted September 4, 2020, by Cell.Vision, YouTube, 3 min., 49 sec., https://www.youtube.com/watch?v=n4owEIFtImU. The four-minute video lasts the duration of Krug's testimony during a city council meeting held on the videotelephony platform Zoom, whose logo we see in the lower right corner of the frame. Introducing herself as "Jess La Bombalera . . . here in El Barrio, East Harlem," Krug paces in a circle with the camera framing her face as she speaks. She wears a nose ring, hoop earrings, and purple sunglasses that reflect the surrounding buildings. At the top left corner we see an ASL translator.

3. This fantasy or myth could be understood as an auditory analog of Steven Connor's concept of the "vocalic body." Connor explains, "The vocalic body is the idea—which can take the form of dream, fantasy, ideal, theological doctrine, or hallucination—of a surrogate or secondary body, a projection of a new way of having or being a body, formed and sustained out of the autonomous operations of the voice." See Steven Connor, *Dumbstruck: A Cultural History of Ventriloquism* (Oxford: Oxford University Press, 2001), 35.

4. I am building here on a formulation developed by Pavitra Sundar, my colleague, coeditor, and coauthor in the anthology *Thinking with an Accent*. See Pavitra Sundar, "Listening with an Accent, or How to Loeribari," in *Thinking with an Accent: Toward a New Object, Method, and Practice*, ed. Pooja Rangan, Akshya Saxena, Ragini Tharoor Srinivasan, and Pavitra Sundar (Berkeley: University of California Press, 2023), 294.

5. Nina Sun Eidsheim calls this "the myth of vocal essentialism and innateness." See Nina Sun Eidsheim, *The Race of Sound: Listening, Timbre, and Vocality in African American Music* (Durham, NC: Duke University Press, 2019), 23.

6. See Bill Nichols, *Introduction to Documentary*, 3rd ed. (Bloomington: Indiana University Press, 2017), 23.

7. This is because the alternating documentary impulses toward what Thomas Waugh calls *presentational performance* (the interview convention of presenting oneself explicitly for the camera, borrowed from photography) and *representational performance* (the vérité convention of performing nonawareness of being filmed, borrowed from the dominant fiction cinema), which have shaped a variety of documentary modes (expository, observational, reflexive, and so on), have also shaped contradictory and sometimes fluctuating audience expectations. See Thomas Waugh, "Acting to Play Oneself: Notes on Performance in Documentary (1990)," in *The Documentary Film Reader*, ed. Jonathan Kahana (Oxford: Oxford University Press, 2016), 818, 827.

8. On critiques of documentary objectivity, see Erika Balsom, "The Reality-Based Community," *e-flux* 83 (2017), https://www.e-flux.com/journal/83/142332/the-reality-based-community/.

9. See Rosina Lippi-Green, *English with an Accent: Language, Ideology, and Discrimination in the United States*, 2nd ed. (New York: Routledge, 2012), 45–46. Accents, according to Lippi-Green, are "loose bundles" of phonological features, whether prosodic (intonation, pitch contours, stress patterns, tempo, upswings and downswings, etc.) or segmental (how vowels and consonants are pronounced), and distributed across geographic or social space. She further distinguishes between two types of accent: L1 accent (the native variety of a given

1. LISTENING WITH AN ACCENT   191

language, say U.S. English, which is typically "marked" by the speaker's region, superimposed with clusters of features shaped by other elements of social identity such as "gender, race, ethnicity, income, religion"); and L2 accent (the breakthrough of native language phonology into the target language when a native speaker of language A—say, Hindi or Welsh—acquires language B—say, U.S. English). See Lippi-Green, *English with an Accent*, 42, 45–46.

10. Nina Sun Eidsheim, "Re-writing Algorithms for Just Recognition: From Digital Aural Redlining to Accent Activism," in Rangan et al., *Thinking with an Accent*, 136.

11. Although I am focusing on verbalized and sounded accents in this chapter, colleagues in Deaf studies have written about a similar dynamic in which ASL interpreters sign "SHUSA" or "Sorry Hard Understand Strong Accent"—a sign that, they argue, evidences the interpreter's accented listening even as it frames the accent in question as a characteristic of the speaker. I deal with listening in the context of disability-affected speech in the next chapter. See Lynn Hou and Rezenet Moges, "'SORRY HARD UNDERSTAND STRONG ACCENT!': Racial Dynamics of Deaf Scholars of Color Working with White Female Interpreters," in Rangan et al., *Thinking with an Accent*, 151–73.

12. Lisbeth Lipari, *Listening, Thinking, Being: Toward an Ethics of Attunement* (University Park: Pennsylvania State University Press, 2014), 5.

13. Lipari, *Listening, Thinking, Being*, 52.

14. Lipari, *Listening, Thinking, Being*, 5.

15. Bill Nichols, "The Voice of Documentary," *Film Quarterly* 36, no. 6 (1983): 18.

16. See Michel Chion, *The Voice in Cinema*, trans. Claudia Gorbman (New York: Columbia University Press, 1999), 5; Charles Wolfe, "Historicising the 'Voice of God': The Place of Vocal Narration in Classical Documentary," *Film History* 9, no. 2 (1997): 149–67; and James Nicholson, "Vocal Hierarchy in Documentary," in *Vocal Projections: Voices in Documentary*, ed. Annabelle Honess Roe and Maria Pramaggiore (New York: Bloomsbury Academic, 2019), 222–23.

17. See Hamid Naficy, *An Accented Cinema: Exilic and Diasporic Filmmaking* (Princeton, NJ: Princeton University Press, 2001).

18. See Nancy N. Chen, "'Speaking Nearby': A Conversation with Trinh T. Minh-ha," *Visual Anthropology Review* 8, no. 1 (1992): 87; Pooja Rangan, Akshya Saxena, Ragini Tharoor Srinivasan, and Pavitra Sundar, "Introduction: Thinking with an Accent," in Rangan et al., *Thinking with an Accent*, 13; also see 5–6.

19. The anthropologist Shahram Khosravi articulates a kindred approach in an article advocating for accented thinking as a decolonial epistemology grounded in migrant intellectual life. He writes, "Similar to how Naficy uses accented style as an aesthetic response to the experience of exile and diaspora, accented thinking here is a way of knowing that is rooted in the lived experiences of the racial marginalization of academics." See Shahram Khosravi, "Doing Migration Studies with an Accent," *Journal of Ethnic and Migration Studies* 50, no. 9 (2024): 2347.
20. See Rangan, Saxena, Srinivasan, and Sundar, "Introduction," 13.
21. James G. Mansell, "Rhythm, Modernity, and the Politics of Sound," in *The Projection of Britain: A History of the GPO Film Unit*, ed. Scott Anthony and James G. Mansell (London: British Film Institute, 2011), 161–62.
22. For an overview of other recent efforts to challenge traditional accounts of the "beginnings" of documentary, see Jonathan Kahana, "Introduction to Section 1," in *The Documentary Film Reader*, ed. Jonathan Kahana (Oxford: Oxford University Press, 2016), 14.
23. See Marilyn Strathern, "Introduction: New Accountabilities," in *Audit Cultures: Anthropological Studies in Accountability, Ethics, and the Academy*, ed. Marilyn Strathern (New York: Routledge, 2000), 3, 4.
24. John Mowitt, *Sounds: The Ambient Humanities* (Oakland: University of California Press, 2015), 5–6.
25. Mowitt, *Sounds*, 5; also see Jacques Rancière, *The Politics of Aesthetics*, trans. Gabriel Rockhill (London: Bloomsbury Academic, 2013), 7.
26. See Scott Anthony, "An Introduction to the GPO Film Unit," in *We Live in Two Worlds: The GPO Film Unit Collection Volume Two* (London: British Film Institute, 2009), 6. By 1932, the GPO's predecessor film unit, the Empire Marketing Board, was already Britain's largest supplier of educational films. Aided by investments in mobile distribution vans and an education officer for audience cultivation, the GPO vastly grew the EMB's already substantial nontheatrical documentary viewership from 1.5 million in 1934 to an alleged 5 million annually by 1936. However, as Ian Aitken and, more recently, Brian Winston have both noted, these numbers are difficult to substantiate. See Ian Aitken, *Film and Reform: John Grierson and the Documentary Film Movement* (London: Routledge, 1990), 126; Alan Lovell and Jim Hillier, *Studies in Documentary* (London: Secker and Warburg for the British Film Institute, 1972), 16; and Brian Winston, "The Marginal Spectator," in *A Companion to Documentary Film History*, ed. Joshua Malitsky (Hoboken, NJ: Wiley-Blackwell, 2020), 425–27.

1. LISTENING WITH AN ACCENT   193

27. As James Scott has noted, modern administrative functions such as delivering mail, collecting taxes, and planning public transcripts were facilitated by a synoptic, bureaucratic gaze that rendered a complex social reality legible and thus manipulable. See James C. Scott, *Seeing Like a State: How Certain Schemes to Improve the Human Condition Have Failed* (New Haven, CT: Yale University Press, 1999), 3, 11, 56.
28. Priya Jaikumar has similarly highlighted the geopolitical and disciplinary function of seemingly minor British instructional films. Jaikumar reframes a series of short geographical films about Indian towns produced in the late 1930s for British schoolchildren by Gaumont-British Instructional (originally founded in 1919 as British Instructional Films) as colonial documentaries that reveal the formation of a "geopolitical optic"—one that she argues was central to the constitution of a modern British nation that was simultaneously liberal and imperial. See Priya Jaikumar, *Where Histories Reside: India as Filmed Space* (Durham, NC: Duke University Press, 2019), 40.
29. I am drawing both from the BFI website and from the booklets containing essays, film notes, and biographies that were produced as DVD extras to accompany a three-volume set of restored GPO films released by the BFI between 2008 and 2014; see especially *Addressing the Nation* and *We Live in Two Worlds*.
30. See Jeffrey Richards, "John Grierson and the Lost World of the GPO Film Unit," in *The Projection of Britain: A History of the GPO Film Unit*, ed. Scott Anthony and James G. Mansell (London: British Film Institute, 2011), 5.
31. See Lynda Mugglestone, "Accent as a Social Symbol," in *The Handbook of English Pronunciation*, ed. Marnie Reed and John M. Levis (London: Wiley, 2015), 20. Mugglestone notes that the original definition of accent in 1884 already contains class and regional bias, associating mispronunciation of vowels and consonants, and misplacement of stress or misinflection of a sentence, with the speaker's social location.
32. Enregisterment refers to "a cultural awareness of a set of social meanings associated with specific varieties of speech." See Mugglestone, "Accent as a Social Symbol," 27. I would like to distinguish, furthermore, between the suppression of class-marked accents and the suppression of native languages, such as Welsh. There are complex questions to be posed here about how accent suppression has been resisted in the context of class-based social movements and national independence movements (as a case in point, one might consider the work of the independent Scottish experimental filmmaker Margaret Tait, from the Orkney Islands, who notably refused to work with John Grierson). These are, however, beyond the scope of this chapter.

33. Tom McEnany, "This American Voice: The Odd Timbre of a New Standard in Public Radio," in *The Oxford Handbook of Voice Studies*, ed. Nina Sun Eidsheim and Katherine Meizel (Oxford: Oxford University Press, 2019), 98, 101.
34. Rosa and Flores describe "raciolinguistic ideologies" as ideologies that "produce racialized speaking subjects who are constructed as linguistically deviant when engaging in linguistic practices positioned as normative or innovative when produced by privileged white subjects." See Jonathan Rosa and Nelson Flores, "Do You Hear What I Hear? Raciolinguistic Ideologies and Culturally Sustaining Pedagogies," in *Culturally Sustaining Pedagogies: Teaching and Learning for Justice in a Changing World*, ed. Django Paris and H. Samy Alim (New York: Teachers College, 2017), 177.
35. Nelson Flores and Jonathan Rosa, "Undoing Appropriateness: Raciolinguistic Ideologies and Language Diversity in Education," *Harvard Educational Review* 85, no. 2 (2015): 151; also see Vijay A. Ramjattan, "Accent Reduction as Raciolinguistic Pedagogy," in Rangan et al., *Thinking with an Accent*, 41.
36. As Gordon Johnston and Emma Robertson note, the audience for the BBC's Empire Service, initiated in 1932 with English-language service to Australasia, Africa, India, Burma and the Federated Malay States, Canada, Trinidad, British Guiana, and the West Indies, were difficult to categorize or even quantify. "Listeners," they write, "were diverse in gender, race, class and age, as well as being dispersed geographically across the vast and complicated British Empire (and beyond)." And yet, they continue, "The listener of the BBC imagination in the 1930s, at least to direct short-wave broadcasts, was predominantly a white, male English-speaking exile from Britain, isolated somewhere in the colonies." See Gordon Johnston and Emma Robertson, *BBC World Service: Overseas Broadcasting, 1932–2018* (London: Palgrave Macmillan, 2019), 2, 34.
37. Arthur Lloyd James, responsible for training announcers in the early years of the BBC, as quoted in Mugglestone, "Accent as a Social Symbol," 30.
38. Frances Dyson, "The Genealogy of the Radio Voice," in *Radio Rethink: Art, Sound, and Transmission*, ed. Daina Augaitis and Dan Lander (Banff, AB: Banff Center, 1994), 177–78.
39. Grierson, "The GPO Gets Sound" (1934) quoted in Martin Stollery, "Voiceover/Commentary," in *The Projection of Britain: A History of the GPO Film Unit*, ed. Scott Anthony and James G. Mansell (London: British Film Institute, 2011), 172.
40. Stollery, "Voiceover/Commentary," 172.

I. LISTENING WITH AN ACCENT   195

41. Stoever uses this term to refer to the aggregate of structures that funnel the complexity of embodied listening practices into a corridor of "narrow, conditioned, and 'correct' responses that are politically, culturally, economically, legally, and socially advantageous to whites." See Jennifer Lynn Stoever, *The Sonic Color Line: Race and the Cultural Politics of Listening* (New York: New York University Press), 15.

42. See British Film Institute, "GPO Film Unit (1933–1940)," *ScreenOnline*, http://www.screenonline.org.uk/film/id/464254/index.html, accessed November 11, 2020. As Stollery notes, Grierson favored incorporating the idioms and accents of workers in the form of, in the latter's words, "conversational scraps from a street, a factory, from any scene or situation" (Grierson, "Introduction to a New Art" (1934), quoted in Stollery, "Voiceover/Commentary," 173). Stollery elaborates, "Wildtrack, non-synchronized snippets of dialogue or brief passages of synchronized speech were recorded, ideally on location, and subsequently woven into the soundtrack of GPO films alongside the commentary" (173).

43. Jaikumar, *Where Histories Reside*, 45.

44. The repair of undersea cables was a frequent theme in educational films produced in the 1920s and 1930s in both the British and Anglo-American context. In this period, new wireless technologies such as the telegraph and radio were challenging the cable industry's domination of global telecommunications. As Nicole Starosielski has argued, representations of cable repair from this era depart from nineteenth-century representations (in which the cable functioned as a mediator of the ocean's depth) by bringing cables and thus ocean depths closer—in this instance, to the surface of the ship from which cables were laid—thereby framing them as being as accessible as wireless. See Nicole Starosielski, "Depth Mediators: Undersea Cables, Network Infrastructure, and the Deep Ocean," in *Deep Mediations: Thinking Space in Cinema and Digital Cultures*, ed. Karen Redrobe and Jeff Scheible (Minneapolis: University of Minnesota Press, 2020), 274–80.

45. See Annabelle Honess Roe, "Playing God: Film Stars as Documentary Narrators," in *Vocal Projections: Voices in Documentary*, ed. Annabelle Honess Roe and Maria Pramaggiore (New York: Bloomsbury Academic, 2018), 17; John Corner, *The Art of Record: A Critical Introduction to Documentary* (Manchester: Manchester University Press, 1996), 68.

46. The category of the surname, which has been mobilized in state projects of standardization and legibility, is a case in point. See Scott, *Seeing Like a State*, 71.

47. Mara Mills, "Lessons in Queer Voice," *Amodern 9: Techniques and Technologies* (2020), https://amodern.net/article/queer-voice/. Mills draws on the work of the communications scholar Robert Hopper, whose research suggests that the telephone shifted the attention of linguists from writing to the phenomenon of speech.
48. For a review of research currently underway on the underacknowledged and often uncredited role of women film workers in British documentary from 1930 to the mid-1950s, including the work of John Grierson's sister Marion Grierson, see Rona Murray, "British Women Documentary Filmmakers 1930–1955, 5 April 2019: one day symposium at the London School of Economics," *Media Practice and Education* 20, no. 3 (2019): 297–301.
49. See Stollery, "Voiceover/Commentary," 171, 175.
50. Wolfe, "Historicising the 'Voice of God,'" 149; Mills, "Lessons in Queer Voice." Mills describes a "plummy" voice, associated with the educated English upper classes as "drawling, indistinct, as though hampered by plums in the mouth." For Mills, the queerness of the plummy voice is a function of its over-the-top performance of aristocracy.
51. Harun Farocki, "Phantom Images," *Public* 29, no. 1 (2004): 17.
52. I am building here on Jussi Parikka's observations regarding the aesthetics of operational images; in his words, "the discourse of the photographic, but also the discourses of 'education' and work thus become restaged in ways that do not merely resemble the factory or the earlier use of the industrial scene, but as globally distributed across logistics platforms." See Jussi Parikka, "Operational Images: Between Data and Light," *eflux* 133 (2023), https://www.e-flux.com/journal/133/515812/operational-images-between-light-and-data/.
53. Laliv Melamed, "Operative Imaginaries," *NECSUS* (2021), https://necsus-ejms.org/operative-imaginaries/#_ednref2.
54. See Naficy, *An Accented Cinema*, 10–39.
55. Ani Maitra, "The Persistence of the Other: Revisiting the (Post-)Colonial Scene of Fragmentation," 1–8, paper presented at American Comparative Literature Association Conference, Utrecht University, June 7, 2017; also see Raka Shome, "Thinking Through Diaspora: Call Centers, India, and a New Politics of Hybridity," *International Journal of Cultural Studies* 9, no. 105 (2006): 110.
56. See Jan M. Padios, *A Nation on the Line: Call Centers as Postcolonial Predicaments in the Philippines* (Durham, NC: Duke University Press, 2018), 2, 113. Padios argues that the perceived "relatability" of the Filipino accent to American customers, itself a result of the aftermath of U.S. imperialism, has been leveraged

as a form of neoliberal affective capital within the call center industry—one that has propelled the country's rise in the knowledge-work sector despite its infrastructural disadvantages relative to India (5).

57. Aimee Carillo Rowe, Sheena Malhotra, and Kimberlee Pérez, *Answer the Call: Virtual Migration in Indian Call Centers* (Minneapolis: University of Minnesota Press, 2013), 9.

58. Carillo Rowe, Malhotra, and Pérez, *Answer the Call*, 10–11; A. Aneesh, *Neutral Accent: How Language, Labor, and Life Became Global* (Durham, NC: Duke University Press, 2015), 35–52, 64–76.

59. See Edward B. Kang, "On the Praxes and Politics of AI Speech Emotion Recognition," *FAccT* (June 12–15, 2023): 463. Kang notes that call centers represent "the most widely observed commercial use case of SER [speech emotion recognition] led by technology companies" (464). Using an analysis of one such software company, Cogito, whose AI-based "customer experience improvement" tools are employed in U.S. call centers that service the telecom, cable, health insurance, and pharmaceutical industries, Kang argues that Cogito's SER (itself a technology founded on pseudoscientific assumptions) functions as a disciplinary technology that requires workers to "self-regulate their emotional behaviors to be positively read by Cogito's SER system" in what effectively functions as a "reverse Turing-test" (464). He further explains that it is a common machine-learning practice to import data, frameworks, and theories from external scientific domains such as SER research, which are then established as "ground truths" that become the basis of future benchmarks and performance metrics (457).

60. Sanas, https://www.sanas.ai/, accessed August 27, 2024.

61. See Ramjattan, "Accent Reduction as Raciolinguistic Pedagogy," especially 39–41.

62. Aneesh, *Neutral Accent*, 6–8, 62.

63. Aneesh, *Neutral Accent*, 59. As Padios elaborates, the thinking here is that if customers are not able to geolocate their agents' accents, they cannot know where their calls are going. See Padios, *A Nation on the Line*, 113.

64. Lippi-Green, *English with an Accent*, 157.

65. Rey Chow, *Not Like a Native Speaker: On Languaging as a Postcolonial Experience* (New York: Columbia University Press, 2014), 8.

66. Chow, *Not Like a Native Speaker*, 9.

67. Accent neutralization training also remains common in Philippines-based call centers and is centered on American English, even though not all customers are native or fluent speakers of American English. Padios notes,

"The term *American*, despite being the object of pedagogical attention during training, is in actuality an unmarked, undifferentiated category to which racialized Filipino voices register as *other*." See Padios, *A Nation on the Line*, 112; also see 111.

68. I am building on Stoever's concept of the "embodied ear," which she defines as the way each individual's listening practices are shaped by "the totality of their experiences, historical context, and physicality, as well as intersecting subject positions and particular interactions with power (the listening ear)." See Stoever, *The Sonic Color Line*, 15.
69. Email exchange with Sonali Gulati, April 8, 2024. The next chapter engages further with questions of linguistic and sensory access and the assumption that textual congestion distracts from the cinematic image.
70. Open captions, also called embedded or deposited captions, cannot be turned off; they are burned in to the exhibition format, whereas closed captions can be turned on and off, since they are provided as a separate file.
71. See Mara Mills and Neta Alexander, "Scores: Carolyn Lazard's Crip Minimalism," *Film Quarterly* 76, no. 2 (2022): 39.
72. Krug's deception seems to have been premised on the assumption that Afro-Borinqueñas are underrepresented or absent in academic circles; it therefore falls apart under scrutiny by someone familiar with Black Boriqua accents.
73. Although this was not the intent in this case, Gulati says she makes a conscious decision in some of her other films *not* to subtitle certain parts where Hindi is spoken "because I want certain parts of my film to only be accessible to 'my people,' as in only Hindi-speaking people" (email exchange with Sonali Gulati, April 8, 2024). I take up this idea of restricted linguistic access further in the next chapter.
74. See Aneesh, *Neutral Accent*, 64.
75. John Baugh, "Linguistic Profiling," in *Black Linguistics: Language, Society, and Politics in Africa and the Americas*, ed. Sinfree Makoni, Geneva Smitherman, Arnetha F. Ball, and Arthur K. Spears (New York: Routledge, 2003), 155–68.
76. Passports, as noted by the media and migration studies scholar Michelle Pfeifer, are "not only identification documents. They are also media of mobility, globally unequally distributed, that allow or inhibit movement across borders." See Michelle Pfeifer, "Your Voice is (Not) Your Passport." *Sounding Out* (June 12, 2023), https://soundstudiesblog.com/author/mitchpfeifer/.
77. Pfeifer notes that LADO, as it is currently practiced in the UK, Switzerland, the Netherlands, Germany, Australia, Belgium, and Canada, evolved from the pioneering use of linguistic analyses in asylum procedures by Scandinavian

I. LISTENING WITH AN ACCENT   199

immigration authorities in the early 1990s. See Michelle Pfeifer, "'The Native Ear': Accented Testimonial Desire and Asylum," in Rangan et al., *Thinking with an Accent*, 195.

78. See Pfeifer, "'The Native Ear,'" 202; also see Michelle Pfeifer, "Data and Borders: Tracking Media Technologies of Migration Control in Europe," PhD dissertation (New York University, 2022), 96, and Pfeifer, "Your Voice is (Not) Your Passport." LADO's pathologization of people seeking asylum as "untrustworthy" is also reflected in the vocabulary of migration studies, which reinscribes the authority of the state by framing migrants as lacking (for instance, *un*documented, asylum *seeker*, state *less*); see Khosravi, "Doing Migration Studies with an Accent," 2350.

79. Naomi Waltham-Smith calls LADO a biopolitical perversion of a fundamental dilemma of speech, whereby "what is meant to be the support of political representation, self-expression, and agency is turned against the speaking subject." See Naomi Waltham-Smith, *Shattering Biopolitics: Militant Listening and the Sound of Life* (New York: Fordham University Press, 2021), 91. Pfeifer adds that LADO's founding assumptions reproduce the "convergence between migration and criminality and the criminality of migration." See Pfeifer, "Data and Borders," 106.

80. Lawrence Abu Hamdan, "Aural Contract: Forensic Listening and the Reorganization of the Speaking Subject," in *Forensis: The Architecture of Public Truth*, ed. Forensic Architecture (Berlin: Sternberg Press and Forensic Architecture, 2014), 70, 72; Pfeifer, "'The Native Ear,'" 196.

81. Thomas Keenan and Eyal Weizman, *Mengele's Skull: The Advent of a Forensic Aesthetics* (Berlin: Sternberg, 2012), 13.

82. Keenan and Weizman, *Mengele's Skull*, 16, 28. The carceral implications of forensic listening are further discussed in chapter 3.

83. Elaborating on his research, Abu Hamdan notes that "asylum speakers were expected to simply speak for fifteen minutes non-stop. They were free to say anything they wanted, because nothing they said had any relevance. Only their accents mattered." See Lawrence Abu Hamdan, *[inaudible]: A Politics of Listening in 4 Acts* (Berlin: Sternberg, 2016), 21. Also see Pfeifer, "Data and Borders," 98.

84. Pfeifer's research reveals that the software developed by the Federal Office for Migration and Refugees (abbreviated in German as BAMF) is slated for expansion to other European countries despite its 20 percent error rate. They elaborate, "People are asked to describe pictures while their speech is recorded, [and] the software then indicates a percentage of the probability

of the spoken dialect and produces a scoresheet." See Pfeifer, "Your Voice is (Not) Your Passport." Also see Abu Hamdan, *[inaudible]*, 21, and Abu Hamdan, "Aural Contract," 72.

85. See Lorraine Daston and Peter Galison, *Objectivity* (New York: Zone, 2007), 17.
86. For the purposes of this chapter I am focusing only on the audio documentary, which was presented as a sound installation at *The Showroom* in London (February 1 to March 17, 2012) alongside sculptural representations of voiceprints (or voice fingerprints) contoured from foam, illustrating the frequency and amplitude of two different voices saying the word "you." Emily Apter writes, "The cartographic rendering maps the origins of phonemes while the acoustically absorbent foam slabs become a listening agent; both give material form to the fusion of voice and territory." See Emily Apter, "Shibboleth: Policing by Ear and Forensic Listening in Projects by Lawrence Abu Hamdan." *October* 156 (2016): 105. Apter's essay has been reprinted as the foreword to Abu Hamdan's book *[inaudible]*.
87. Jeanne Hall, "Realism as a Style in *Cinema Vérité*: A Critical Analysis of *Primary*," *Cinema Journal* 30, no. 4 (1991): 24; the film theorist Thomas Waugh is quoted in Hall, "Realism as a Style in *Cinema Vérité*, 25.
88. Irina Leimbacher, "Hearing Voice(s): Experiments with Documentary Listening," *Discourse* 39, no. 3 (2017): 293. These concerns were first articulated, as Leimbacher notes, by Bill Nichols and Trinh T. Minh-ha, whose writings from the 1990s criticize filmmakers who ventriloquize their point of view through recorded voices, whether in string-of-interview films, where recruited witnesses or experts speak for the filmmaker, or in ethnographic films claiming to give voice to their subjects (295).
89. Jessica Silbey, "Evidence Verité and the Law of Film," 31 *Cardozo Law Review* 1257 (2010), quoted in Stella Bruzzi, "Making a Genre: The Case of the Contemporary True Crime Documentary," *Law and Humanities* 10, no. 2 (2016): 251.
90. Bruzzi, "Making a Genre," 251.
91. Apter, "Shibboleth," 111.
92. I have not been able to confirm the identity of this speaker with Abu Hamdan; my interpretation is based on the context provided within the audio documentary and the available writing about it.
93. Abu Hamdan, "Aural Contract," 73. Pfeifer adds that language analysis assumes an "ideal background" characterized by "monolingualism and a biography without mobility or a straight migratory movement from point A to point B," which seldom corresponds to refugee biographies. See Pfeifer, "Data and Borders," 105.

94. Sundar, "Listening with an Accent," 291.
95. Lipari, *Listening, Thinking, Being*, 9; also see 157–89.
96. Eidsheim, "Re-Writing Algorithms for Just Recognition," 144.
97. Eidsheim elaborates that "to be justly recognized is to be recognized in relationship to oneself and the multiplicity of histories and communities, that we constantly adopt, reject, and form within multiple relationship. To be recognized justly is to retain protections and human rights. Listeners who recognize justly afford each voice its multiplicity, including its humanity" (Eidsheim, "Re-Writing Algorithms for Just Recognition," 144). Eidsheim offers this intervention in the context of vocal synthesis and voice recognition software that have been algorithmically encoded to render certain accents hyperaudible and others inaudible.
98. Hamid Naficy, "Epistolarity and Textuality in Accented Films," in *Subtitles: On the Foreignness of Film*, ed. Atom Egoyan and Ian Balfour (Cambridge, MA: MIT Press, 2004), 133–34.
99. Sundar, "Listening with an Accent," 284.

2. LISTENING IN CRIP TIME

1. Sara Hendren, *What Can a Body Do?* (New York: Riverhead, 2020), 17.
2. Accent has other meanings beyond the linguistic. An accent can also refer, as Shilpa Davé has noted in her study of Indian accents, to a "contrasting detail"; for instance, an "accent piece" functions as "an accessory or minor piece that highlights the dominant look or feature." See Shilpa Davé, *Indian Accents: Brown Voice and Racial Performance in American Film and Television* (Urbana-Champaign: University of Illinois Press, 2013), 2.
3. Hendren, *What Can A Body Do?*, 3.
4. "With the close-up," Benjamin writes, "space expands; with slow motion, movement is extended. And just as enlargement not merely clarifies what we see indistinctly 'in any case,' but brings to light entirely new structures of matter, slow motion not only reveals familiar aspects of movements, but discloses quite unknown aspects within them. . . . It is through the camera that we first discover the optical unconscious." See Walter Benjamin, "The Work of Art in the Age of Its Technological Reproducibility: Third Version," in *Selected Writings of Walter Benjamin, Vol. 4*, ed. Howard Eiland and Michael W. Jennings (Cambridge, MA: Harvard University Press, 2002), 265–66.
5. See Tobin Siebers, *Disability Aesthetics* (Ann Arbor: University of Michigan Press, 2010), 3; 35. Siebers attributes the success of modern art to its embrace

of disability (deformed bodies, discolored human faces, bent and twisted figures, and themes of alienation, anxiety, fear, sensory overload and distraction) as a "distinct version of the beautiful" (35), and attributes the Nazi preference for representational art to Dada or expressionism to a eugenic rejection of disability.

6. I am following the Japanese convention of citing family name before given name and will use Lord's preferred pronouns (they/them).

7. Captions provide a textual transcript of dialogue, sound effects, and musical choices in audiovisual media and are typically designed for use by D/deaf and hard of hearing audiences. An umbrella term for techniques meant to make visual media accessible to blind and partially sighted audiences, audio description refers in the cinematic context to the verbalization of images and text that appear on screen, usually on an optional prerecorded audio track.

8. Alison Kafer, *Feminist, Queer, Crip* (Bloomington: Indiana University Press, 2013), 27.

9. Ellen Samuels, "Six Ways of Looking at Crip Time." *Disability Studies Quarterly* 37, no. 3 (2017), https://dsq-sds.org/article/view/5824/4684.

10. Jina B. Kim and Sami Schalk, "Reclaiming the Radical Politics of Self-Care: A Crip-of-Color Critique," *South Atlantic Quarterly* 120, no. 2 (2021): 327.

11. Ellen Samuels and Elizabeth Freeman. "Introduction: Crip Temporalities," in "Crip Temporalities," special issue, ed. Ellen Samuels and Elizabeth Freeman, *South Atlantic Quarterly* 120, no. 2 (2021): 246. Under conditions of racial capitalism, however, chrononormativity, or the ableist conception of life stages as linear and timely, continues to be marshaled in the realms of media and medicine in ways that take their deepest toll on disabled, poor, immigrant, queer, gender nonconforming, and Black and Brown people.

12. See Simi Linton, *Claiming Disability: Knowledge and Identity* (New York: New York University Press, 1998), 14–15.

13. See Kafer, *Feminist, Queer, Crip*, 15. Kafer is referring to a statement by the essayist Nancy Mairs: "People—crippled or not—wince at the word 'crippled' as they do not at 'handicapped' or 'disabled.' Perhaps I want them to wince."

14. Kafer, *Feminist, Queer, Crip*, 15.

15. Carrie Sandahl, "Queering the Crip or Cripping the Queer? Intersections of Queer and Crip Identities in Solo Autobiographical Performance," *GLQ* 9, no. 1–2 (2003): 37–38; Robert McRuer, *Crip Theory: Cultural Signs of Queerness and Disability* (New York: New York University Press, 2006), 32, 71–72.

16. For instance, Kafer argues in *Feminist, Queer, Crip* that a coalitional politics grounded in troubling explicit and intersecting identifications requires

2. LISTENING IN CRIP TIME   203

acknowledging the work done by disability and able-bodiedness and -mindedness in different political visions as well as the exclusions enacted in the desire for a unified disability community (17). Kim and Schalk write that the methods crip theory offers for examining disability beyond identity and even embodiment allow them to develop feminist-of-color disability studies (building on crip theory, feminist-, and queer-of-color critique) that enable more acute racial analyses in those studies even though not all crip theory engages effectively with race. See Jina B. Kim and Sami Schalk, "Integrating Race, Transforming Feminist Disability Studies," *Signs* 46, no. 1 (2020): 39.

17. Jina B. Kim, "Cripping the Welfare Queen: The Radical Potential of Disability Politics?" lecture presented at the University of Minnesota's Critical Disability Studies Research Colloquium, October 9, 2020.

18. See for instance Slava Greenberg, "(Dis)abling the Spectator: Embodying Disability Experience in Animated Documentary," in *Documentary and Disability*, ed. Catalin Brylla and Helen Hughes (London: Palgrave Macmillan, 2017), 129–44; chapter 3 ("In Search of New Vocalities") in Jonathan Sterne, *Diminished Faculties: A Political Phenomenology of Impairment* (Durham, NC: Duke University Press, 2021); Anne-Marie Callus, "The Poetics of Touch: Mediating the Reality of Deafblindness in *Planet of Snail*," in *Documentary and Disability*, ed. Catalin Brylla and Helen Hughes (London: Palgrave Macmillan, 2017), 145–58; chapter 2 in Lisbeth Lipari, *Listening, Thinking, Being: Toward an Ethics of Attunement* (University Park: Pennsylvania State University Press, 2014).

19. Mia Mingus, "Access Intimacy, Interdependence, and Disability Justice," *Leaving Evidence* (blog), April 12, 2017, https://leavingevidence.wordpress.com/2017/04/12/access-intimacy-interdependence-and-disability-justice/.

20. Elizabeth Ellcessor, *Restricted Access: Media, Disability, and the Politics of Participation* (New York: New York University Press, 2016), 7.

21. Americans with Disabilities Act of 1990, as amended. https://www.ada.gov/pubs/adastatute08.htm#12101b.

22. I am thankful to Jordan Lord for sharing this insight at the launch event for a special dossier of the journal *Film Quarterly* on February 10, 2023, which featured us both speaking about *Shared Resources*.

23. See Alexandra Juhasz and Alisa Lebow, "Introduction: Beyond Story," in "Beyond Story," special issue, ed. Alexandra Juhasz and Alisa Lebow, *World Records* 5 (2021): 9–13; Sonya Childress and Natalie Bullock-Brown, "The Documentary Future: A Call for Accountability," *Documentary*, July 2, 2020, https://www.documentary.org/feature/documentary-future-call-accountability.

24. Brett Story, "Artist-Run Documentary Studios: A New Form of Trust," *Documentary*, January 29, 2021, https://www.documentary.org/feature/artist-run-documentary-studios-new-form-trust.
25. Postwar political struggle and organizing around disability rights in both the United States and Japan, which was driven in large part by WWII veterans and war debilitation, multiplied in intensity with the emergence of disabled self-advocacy groups: the Rolling Quads formed in Berkeley, California, in the late 1960s, and Aoi Shiba no Kai ("Green Grasses" group) consolidated as an activist movement in Japan in the early 1970s. The activism of these groups separately fueled the independent living movement in both countries at roughly the same time. See Jasbir Puar, *The Right to Maim: Debility, Capacity, Disability* (Durham, NC: Duke University Press, 2017), 75; Reiko Hayashi and Masako Okuhira, "The Disability Rights Movement in Japan: Past, Present, and Future," *Disability and Society* 16, no. 6 (2001): 860; Shin'ya Tateiwa, "Disability Movement/Studies in Japan 1–9," trans. Hiragi Midori (2010): 1 (Beginning), http://www.arsvi.com/ts/20100091-e.htm; Nagase Osamu, "Development of Disability Studies in Japan: A Brief Outline," *Disability Studies Quarterly* 28, no. 3 (2008), https://dsq-sds.org/index.php/dsq/article/view/116/116.
26. As Okada Jun has noted in her essay on Hara's second film, *Extreme Private Eros: Love Song 1974*, Hara became known for his capacity to bring ethical issues into relief "through the representation of an intimate, private space in which the intrusion of the camera into personal relationships sets the tone for exploiting the intimacy of everyday life—particularly of domestic and sexual strife." See Jun Okada, "Hara Kazuo and *Extreme Private Eros: Love Song 1974*," in *Exploiting East Asian Cinemas: Genre, Circulation, Reception*, ed. Ken Provencher and Mike Dillon (New York: Bloomsbury Academic, 2018), 173. Okada elaborates, "Hara's acknowledged and evident aesthetic, then, is inherently exploitative in wanting to expose those things that are not supposed to be seen, whether it is disabled human beings, sexual intercourse, the birth of a child, or his own demasculinized humiliation, on camera (174)."
27. Faye Ginsburg and Rayna Rapp have chronicled the history of the disability arts in New York City since the 1990s, focusing on disabled artists, cultural workers, and activists working across the visual arts, theater, music, film, choreography, and graphic design in a range of institutional contexts, including major museums, arts funding, community organizations, mutual aid collectives, and universities. See Faye Ginsburg and Rayna Rapp, *Disability Worlds* (Durham, NC: Duke University Press, 2024), 154–86.

2. LISTENING IN CRIP TIME   205

28. Amanda Cachia, "The Politics of Creative Access: Guidelines for a Critical Dis/Ability Curatorial Practice," in *Interdisciplinary Approaches to Disability: Looking Toward the Future Volume 2*, ed. Katie Ellis, Rosemarie Garland-Thomson, Mike Kend, and Rachel Robertson (London: Routledge, 2019), 100.
29. Mara Mills and Rebecca Sanchez with Constantina Zavitsanos, "Giving It Away: Constantina Zavitsanos on Disability, Debt, Dependency," in "Disability and the Politics of Visibility," special issue, ed. Emily Watlington, *Art Papers* 42, no. 4 (2018/2019): 63.
30. Aimi Hamraie, *Building Access: Universal Design and the Politics of Disability* (Minneapolis: University of Minnesota Press, 2017), 102.
31. See chapter 3 of Rangan, *Immediations*; also Trinh T. Minh-ha, *When the Moon Waxes Red* (New York: Routledge, 1991), 60.
32. See Johannes Fabian, *Time and the Other: How Anthropology Makes Its Object* (New York: Columbia University Press, 1983), 31. Fabian is referring to the tendency in Western anthropology to deny the contemporaneity of non-Western cultures by placing them in a temporal frame outside the discursive present of the ethnographer and their audience.
33. Rosemarie Garland-Thomson, "The Story of My Work: How I Became Disabled," *Disability Studies Quarterly* 34, no. 2 (2014), https://dsq-sds.org/article/view/4254/3594.
34. Garland-Thomson, "The Story of My Work."
35. Americans with Disabilities Act of 1990, as amended. See Puar, *The Right to Maim*, 191–92, for a compilation of resources detailing the history of activism leading up to the passage of this landmark legislation, which has become a blueprint for other countries enacting disability rights laws, as well for the United Nations Convention on the Rights of Persons with Disabilities (UNCRPD), which was adopted by the UN in 2006.
36. Celeste L. Arrington chronicles the history of activism leading up to the 2013 passing of the Law for Eliminating Discrimination against Persons with Disabilities in Japan. The law was finally put into effect in 2016, after a three-year delay to allow various institutions to design accommodations as required by the law. See Celeste L. Arrington, "Disabled People's Fight for Rights in South Korea and Japan," *Current History* 120, no. 827 (2021): 233–39.
37. In 1977, the Green Grasses staged an infamous takeover of Kawasaki City Station in which more than fifty wheelchair users attempted simultaneously to board buses, resulting in the halting of thirty-eight bus routes. See Mark Ross Bookman, "Politics and Prosthetics: 150 Years of Disability in Japan,"

PhD dissertation (University of Pennsylvania, 2021), 156. The Law for Buildings Accessible to and Usable by the Elderly and Physically Disabled Persons was passed in 1994 following years of protests against the lack of accessibility in Japan's public transportation system by disability activists affiliated with the Japanese branch of Disabled Peoples International (founded in 1986); this organizing was in turn made possible by the Green Grasses' efforts to establish Zenshoren, a coalition of disability rights organizations, in 1976. See Katharina Heyer, *Rights Enabled: The Disability Revolution from the US, to Germany and Japan, to the United Nations* (Ann Arbor: University of Michigan Press, 2015), 125–26; Hayashi and Okuhira, "The Disability Rights Movement in Japan," 860.

38. See Kazuo Hara, *Camera Obtrusa: The Action Documentaries of Hara Kazuo*, trans. Pat Noonan and Takuo Yasuda (New York: Kaya, 2009), 52, 69–70; Scott MacDonald, *A Critical Cinema: Interviews with Independent Filmmakers, Vol. 3* (Berkeley: University of California Press, 1988), 142.

39. Andrew Campana offers a similar reading of this performance in an article that was published around the time that this chapter was first circulated in draft form, writing that this performance invites the audience to "listen otherwise" in order to "come to a different kind of understanding." See Andrew Campana, "You Forbid Me to Walk: Yokota Hiroshi's Disability Poetics," *positions: asia critique* 30, no. 4 (2022): 759.

40. Upon Yoshiko's instigation, Yokota and his family left Maharaba to live independently in Kanagawa prefecture, where they established a Green Grasses chapter. A feminist disability perspective might offer a more politicized and intersectional understanding of the integrationist desires of women in the Green Grasses movement.

41. Hara, *Camera Obtrusa*, 76.

42. Disability activism in the United States propelling the independent living movement originated in the University of California at Berkeley starting in the late 1960s and was dominated, in contrast, by mostly white, college-going, polio-surviving men with upper body mobility and no speech impediments. See Tateiwa, "Disability Movement/Studies in Japan 1–9," 2 (The People) and 1 (Beginning). The Green Grasses' origins were also elite. Initially established in 1957 by graduates of an elite school for children with CP as a social and recreational group, the group's leadership took on a militant and working-class character in subsequent decades following mergers with Maharaba Village and Kurume, another residential institution. See Hayashi and Okuhira, "The Disability Rights Movement in Japan," 862.

43. See MacDonald, *A Critical Cinema*, 143; Nicolás Carrasco, "Interview: Kazuo Hara and Sachiko Kobayashi," *Desistfilm*, August 28, 2019, https://desistfilm.com/interview-kazuo-hara-sachiko-kobayashi/.
44. See Sean O'Reilly, "'Disarmed': Disability, Trauma, and Emasculation in Contemporary Japanese Cinema," *Arts* 7 no. 1 (2018): 9; Kuniko Sadato, *Kansai shōgaisha undō no gendaishi—Osaka aoi shiba no kai o chūshin ni* ("Modern History of Disability Movement in Kansai Area: Focusing on Osaka Aoi Shiba no Kai") (2011), http://www.arsvi.com/o/aoi-e.htm, accessed April 19, 2024; Sachiko Yamashita, "Being Involved in Care for People with Disabilities as a Healthy Person: Focusing on the Ideology of the Able-Bodied People Movement in the 1970s Liberation Movement for People with Disabilities," presentation, 51st National Conference of the Japanese Society of Social Welfare for Persons with Disabilities, October 13, 2003. http://www.arsvi.com/2000/031013ys.htm, accessed April 19, 2024; Hara, *Camera Obtrusa*, 92–94.
45. See Hamraie, *Building Access*, 95.
46. Hara, *Camera Obtrusa*, 237. By 1995 Hara and Kobayashi had produced three more feature documentaries, each in collaboration with a nonconformist provocateur: *Extreme Private Eros: Love Song 1974* (1974) with Hara's ex-wife Takeda Miyuki, a feminist living and loving outside traditional family structures in occupied Okinawa; *The Emperor's Naked Army Marches On* (1987) with Okuzaki Kenzo, a volatile WWII veteran hell-bent on forcing former comrades to confess to war crimes; and *A Dedicated Life* (1994) with Matsuhito Inoue, a novelist dying of cancer who had fabricated his past.
47. Hara and Kobayashi were not familiar with works of direct cinema or cinema verité that emerged in North America and Europe roughly at the same time as they did in Japan, in response to different social forces. Predating these Euroamerican trends by half a decade, Hani came to prominence in the mid-1950s with two films featuring schoolchildren in which he eschewed the prior realist documentary mode combining scripted scenes with undirected footage of nonactors in favor of a fly-on-the-wall observational approach where he filmed his subjects once they stopped reacting to his camera. See Abé Markus Nornes, "Private Reality: Hara Kazuo's Films," in *Rites of Realism*, ed. Ivone Margulies (Durham, NC: Duke University Press, 2003), 149–51; Justin Jesty, "Image Pragmatics and Film as a Lived Practice in the Documentary Work of Hani Susumu and Tsuchimoto Noriaki," in "Developments in the Japanese Documentary Mode," special issue, ed. Marcos Centeno and Michael Raine, *Arts* 8, no. 41 (2019): 2–3, https://www.mdpi.com/2076-0752/8/2/41.

Like Hani, Ogawa and Tsuchimoto got their start with Iwanami Productions (which doubled as a club for film experimentation) making educational and industry-commissioned PR films, but they broke away in the mid-1960s to make social documentaries aligned explicitly with social struggles. Ogawa's *Sanrizuka* series, on farmers fighting eviction, and Tsuchimoto's *Minamata* series, on seaside communities suffering from mercury poisoning, emphasized collectivity in production and exhibition: Ogawa advocated living, working, and fighting alongside farmers; the films were funded largely by donations, rentals, and loans; and filmmakers would travel to village and cities screening their films in nontheatrical community spaces. See Abé Markus Nornes, "The Postwar Documentary Trace: Groping in the Dark," *Positions* 10, no. 1 (2002): 50–52.

48. Yuriko Furuhata, *Cinema of Actuality: Japanese Avant-Garde Filmmaking in the Season of Image Politics* (Durham, NC: Duke University Press, 2013), 29–34. Also a film theorist, Matsumoto offered an idiosyncratic theory of defamiliarization and image opacity that Hara may not have read but seems to have absorbed from seeing films such as *Security Treaty* (1960), in which Matsumoto blurs the boundaries of documentary and the avant-garde by manipulating a variety of materials (found footage, photographs, drawings) to surreal and shocking effect. See Nornes, "The Post-War Documentary Trace," 46.

49. See Okada, "Hara Kazuo and *Extreme Private Eros*"; MacDonald, *A Critical Cinema*, 125–26. MacDonald situates Hara as part of an avant-garde documentary tradition of perceptual liberation, exposé, and candid self-revelation in which he includes such films as Stan Brakhage's *The Act of Seeing One's Own Eyes* (1971), Frederick Wiseman's *Titicut Follies* (1967), and Ross McElwee's *Sherman's March* (1986).

50. Mark Ross Bookman notes that Yokota Hiroshi's manifesto was originally featured in the eleventh issue of the organization's internal bulletin, *Ayumi*. The manifesto was expanded in 1975 into a book-length study by Yokotsuka Kōichi titled *Mother! Don't Kill Me!* (Haha yo! Korosu na!) and has since been translated into English by Nagase Osamu. Bookman translates Yokota's manifesto as follows:

> 1. We Identify Ourselves as People with Cerebral Palsy (CP). We recognize our position as 'an existence which should not exist' in the modern society. We believe that this recognition should be the starting point of our whole movement, and we act on this belief.

2. We Assert Ourselves Aggressively. When we identify ourselves as people with CP, we have a will to protect ourselves. We believe that a strong self-assertion is the only way to achieve self-protection, and we act on this belief.
3. We Deny Love and Justice. We condemn egoism held by love and justice. We believe that mutual understanding, accompanying the human observation that arises from the denial of love and justice, means true well-being, and we act on this belief.
4. We Do Not Choose the Way of Problem Solving. We have learned from our personal experiences that easy solutions to problems lead to dangerous compromises. We believe that an endless confrontation is the only course of action possible for us, and we act on this belief.
5. We Deny Able-Bodied Civilization. We recognize that modern civilization has managed to sustain itself only by excluding us, people with CP. We believe that creation of our own culture through our movement and daily life leads to the condemnation of modern civilization, and we act on this belief.

(See Bookman, "Politics and Prosthetics," 144–45)

51. Morris calls Hara "one of the undiscovered geniuses of documentary" and Moore his "soul brother in Japan." Both are blurb writers for Hara's book *Camera Obtrusa*. Nornes also discusses a film event in Ann Arbor featuring a complimentary exchange among Hara and Moore in his foreword to *Camera Obtrusa* (xiii–xvi). *Vital Signs* (Mitchell and Snyder, 1994) and *Face of Our Fear* (Dwoskin, 1992) protest the stigmatization of disability in the United States and the UK, respectively. They share a collage-like editing style that juxtaposes confrontational sketches by disabled performers with footage from demonstrations, televised charitable campaigns, and denigrating cinematic and literary representations of disability. See David T. Mitchell and Sharon L. Snyder, "Talking About Talking Back: Afterthoughts on the Making of the Disability Documentary *Vital Signs: Crip Culture Talks Back*," *Michigan Quarterly Review* 37, no. 2 (1998): 316–36; Jennifer Chamarette, "Backdating the Crip Technoscience Manifesto: Stephen Dwoskin's Digital Activism." *Film Quarterly* 76, no. 2 (2022): 18.
52. See Okada, "Hara Kazuo and *Extreme Private Eros*," 174.
53. Japanese disability scholars have commented on the marginalization of women within the Japanese disability rights movement and other social movements of the 1960s and early 1970s. As a case in point, Aoi Shiba no

Kai/Green Grasses rose to prominence when they protested the eugenic ableism propelling a petition to pardon a mother who killed her disabled child, but as Hayashi Reiko and Okuhira Masako note, the leaders of this movement did not consider how this woman's situation was mutually constituted by disability. See Hayashi and Okuhira, "The Disability Rights Movement in Japan," 862; also see Tateiwa, "Disability Movement/Studies in Japan 1–9," 9 (Women). The first women's branch of Aoi Shiba no Kai was only created in 1974, two years after the release of *Goodbye CP*; see Anne-Lise Mithout, "Sayōnara CP: The First Filmic Representation of the Japanese Dis/ability Rights Movement," in *Dis/ability in Media, Law and History: Intersectional, Embodied and Socially Constructed?* ed. Micky Lee, Frank Rudy Cooper, and Patricia Reeve (New York: Routledge, 2022), 147.

54. See Lúcia Nagib, "Filmmaking as the Production of Reality: A Study of Hara and Kobayashi's Documentaries," in *Realism and the Audiovisual Media*, ed. Lúcia Nagib and Cecilia Mello (New York: Palgrave Macmillan, 2009), 196–97.

55. Hara often describes the "one-meter assignment" as the most challenging and worthwhile from his brief stint in photography school and an outsize influence on his approach; see Hara, *Camera Obtrusa*, 38.

56. Joel Neville Anderson, "Cinema's Prosthesis: (Dis)ability and the Politics of Hara Kazuo and Kobayashi Sachiko's Personal Documentary Practice," 18 (unpublished manuscript, June 17, 2019), typescript.

57. See Satō, "Hara Kazuo's *Goodbye CP*," 52, quoted in Campana, "You Forbid Me to Walk," 758.

58. Jay Dolmage, *Academic Ableism: Disability and Higher Education* (Ann Arbor: University of Michigan Press, 2017), 70.

59. Dolmage, *Academic Ableism*, 75.

60. Margaret Price, "Time Harms: Disabled Faculty Navigating the Accommodations Loop," in "Crip Temporalities," special issue, ed. Ellen Samuels and Elizabeth Freeman, *South Atlantic Quarterly* 120, no. 2: (2021): 272.

61. Hamraie, *Building Access*, esp. 5–14.

62. A case in point: At a recent Zoom event that I attended with real-time ASL translation and captioning, the Deaf artist Joseph Grigely shared with the audience the strain he undergoes even when the access features he requires have been provided: "My eyebrows will be furrowed a lot during the event—my eyes are moving between seven different contact points in an effort to understand what is being said." See Joseph Grigely and Emily Watlington, conversation at New York University Center for Disability Studies, April 9, 2021.

63. Jesty, "Image Pragmatics," 2; also see Nagib, "Filmmaking as the Production of Reality," 197.
64. See Rosemarie Garland-Thomson, "Ways of Staring," *Journal of Visual Culture* 5, no. 2 (2006): 174–75; Anderson, "Cinema's Prosthesis," 15. Anderson reads Hara's unflinching framing of disabled bodies and faces as a way of instigating, even validating, diegetic and nondiegetic spectators to stare.
65. Alicia Chase, "Learning to Be Human: An Interview with William Pope.L," *Afterimage* 33 no. 4 (2006): 22.
66. Hendren, *What Can A Body Do?* 167.
67. Lipari, *Listening, Thinking, Being*, 102–3, 136. Also see Neta Alexander's discussion of buffered listening in "The Right to Speed Watch (or, When Netflix Discovered Its Blind Users)," in *Interface Frictions: How Digital Debility Reshapes Our Bodies* (Durham, NC: Duke University Press, 2025), which addresses the perceptual uncertainty of waiting for resolution and the awkwardness that comes with uncertainty of an unknown length, both of which she argues are affectively registered in the body.
68. Hartblay, "Disability Expertise: Claiming Disability Anthropology" (2020), quoted in Devva Kasnitz, "The Politics of Disability Performativity: An Autoethnography." *Current Anthropology* 61, supp. 21 (2020): S16.
69. Dylan Robinson, *Hungry Listening: Resonant Theory for Indigenous Sound Studies* (Minneapolis: University of Minnesota Press, 2020), 47–49.
70. Robinson, *Hungry Listening*, 50; also see 48–49.
71. Mills and Sanchez, with Zavitsanos, "Giving It Away," 63.
72. Mingus, "Access Intimacy, Interdependence, and Disability Justice."
73. Hara, *Camera Obtrusa*, 91–92. As Hara has noted, appearance release forms are not standard in Japan. Hara's retrospective introduction of Yoshiko's permission into the record indicates how the logic of the release has been incorporated into documentary negotiations even in non-U.S. contexts where tort law does not apply. See MacDonald, *Critical Cinema*, 136.
74. A technical term from the auto industry, "defeat device" refers to a technology designed to trick emissions systems so that a car that does not meet safety standards is still able to pass emissions inspections. Dolmage uses the term to describe access retrofits designed to meet a legal standard but whose actual purpose is to mask discrimination and prevent positive and ongoing change. See Dolmage, *Academic Ableism*, 73–74.
75. Jordan Lord, "Shared Resources (Contractual Obligations)," MFA thesis (City University of New York School of Arts and Sciences, 2019), 18.

76. Brett Story, "How Does It End? Story and the Property Form," in "Beyond Story," special issue, ed. Alexandra Juhasz and Alisa Lebow, *World Records* 5 (2021): 87, 88.
77. Leah Lakshmi Piepzna-Samarasinha, *Care Work: Dreaming Disability Justice* (Vancouver: Arsenal Pulp, 2019), 33.
78. Mingus, "Access Intimacy, Interdependence, and Disability Justice."
79. On subtitles, see Abé Markus Nornes, "For an Abusive Subtitling." *Film Quarterly* 52, no. 3 (1999): 17–34, and Atom Egoyan and Ian Balfour, eds., *Subtitles: On the Foreignness of Film* (Cambridge, MA: MIT Press, 2004); on dubbing, see Tom Whittaker and Sarah Wright, eds., *Locating the Voice in Film: Critical Approaches and Global Practices* (Oxford: Oxford University Press, 2017).
80. Antje Ascheid, "Speaking Tongues: Voice Dubbing in the Cinema as Cultural Ventriloquism." *Velvet Light Trap* 40 (1997): 33; Peter Thompson quoted in Amresh Sinha, "The Use and Abuse of Subtitles," in Egoyan and Balfour, *Subtitles*, 174. Sinha, writing in 2004, notes that subtitles are regarded, by and large, as an "evil necessity" whose inferior status as "an after-thought rather than a natural component of the film" is indicated by their habitual placement in the "lowest spectrum of the screen" (174). Twenty years later, this placement remains the industry norm, even though it has become increasingly common among arthouse filmmakers to reposition subtitles elsewhere on the screen.
81. Subtitles were introduced in films as early as 1907, but it wasn't until the age of the talkies and their international distribution that subtitles and dubbing came into their own. See Atom Egoyan and Ian Balfour, "Introduction," in *Subtitles*, 4. As Katie Ellis has noted, D/deaf and blind audiences were positioned as competing but also potentially compensating markets with the coming of film sound when sporadic attempts were made to provide audio description for blind audiences to replace the loss of D/deaf and hard of hearing audiences; Ellis further notes that accessibility in the entertainment realm has been largely fueled by Deaf activism, whereas blind activists have tended to prioritize workplace accessibility. See Katie Ellis, *Disability and Digital Television Cultures: Representation, Access, and Reception* (New York: Routledge, 2019), 128–30, 147.
82. Landmark legislative wins include the Americans with Disabilities Act of 1990, which made closed captions mandatory in the United States for educational and governmental announcements; the Television Decoder Circuitry Act of 1990 (effective 1993), which required television screens 13" and larger to include built-in closed-caption decoders; the Telecommunications Act of

1996, which mandated captions for all newly exhibited video programming; and the Twenty-First Century Communications and Video Accessibility Act of 2010, which introduced closed caption and audio description compliance for digital interfaces and streaming protocols across a variety of devices such as smart TVs, laptops, and smartphones. Following a 2012 settlement in favor of the National Association of the Deaf that compelled Netflix to provide closed captioning for all its on-demand programming, and pressure from blind activists ("The Accessible Netflix Project"), the U.S. Federal Communications Commission (FCC) has instituted regulations for streamers, broadcasters, and movies theaters mandating the wider availability of audio described programs and devices. See Emily Watlington, "The Radical Accessibility of Video Art (for Hearing People)," *Future Anterior* 16, no. 1 (2019): 113; Georgina Kleege, "Audio Description Described: Current Standards, Future Innovations, Larger Implications," *Representations* 135 (2016): 89; Mara Mills and Neta Alexander, "Scores: Carolyn Lazard's Crip Minimalism," *Film Quarterly* 76, no. 2 (2022): 39; Ellis, *Disability and Digital Television Cultures*, chapters 7 and 8. Alexander further discuss the impacts of access activism by Deaf and blind people on televisual and digital accessibility in a forthcoming book chapter. See Alexander, "The Right to Speed Watch."

83. Mills and Alexander review the commercial and social interests driving the automation of access in "Scores." Ellis further details the pioneering impacts of YouTube's automated captions and Facebook's video autoplay features on caption uptake in the general population (*Disability and Digital Television Cultures*, 152, 158–59).

84. Following the development of captioning technology in the late 1950s, educators working with D/deaf students were among the first to caption television programs. In 1972, WGBH, the primary public broadcasting service for Boston, broadcast eight episodes of Julia Child's cooking show *The French Chef* with open captions that could not be turned on and off. As Ellis notes, this practice was short-lived since broadcasters expressed concerns—unsupported by audience research—that open captions would alienate the "hearing majority." Today, closed captions (which exist on a separate file and are usually identified by a [CC] symbol in the corner of the screen that allows the viewer to switch them on or off) are the most common type of captions used by major broadcasters and video streaming services. See Ellis, *Disability and Digital Television Cultures*, 147–48; also see Watlington, "The Radical Accessibility of Video Art (for Hearing People)," 117. Audio description as we understand it today originated in the 1960s according to Ellis; pioneering research

followed in the early 1970s (*Disability and Digital Television Cultures*, 129). Audio description services were first offered in live theater performances in the 1980s in the form of headsets worn by blind audience members through which a describer positioned backstage or in the sound booth would transmit brief descriptions of on-stage visual events during natural pauses between the actor's speeches and sometimes before the performance or during intermission. It was also around this time that museums began offering docent-led tours, taped tours, and additional audio tracks for blind people; AD services also began to be offered for theatrically exhibited films via headsets provided by the theater with a prerecorded audio track, as a television setting, or as an option on home videotapes (and later on DVD). See Kleege, "Audio Description Described," 89–90.

85. See David T. Mitchell and Sharon L. Snyder, *The Biopolitics of Disability: Neoliberalism, Ablenationalism, and Peripheral Embodiment* (Ann Arbor: University of Michigan Press, 2015), esp. chapters 4 and 5. Mitchell and Snyder discuss the politics of atypicality of disability film festivals at the level of organizational and administrative structure (chapter 4) and experimental content and form (chapter 5). FWD-Doc, a group of documentarians with disabilities and their allies, has released a toolkit for accessibility in documentary using Netflix's *Crip Camp* (dir. Nicole Newnham and Jim LeBrecht, 2020) as a model of disability-inclusive filmmaking processes. See FWD-Doc, in association with Doc Society, supported by Netflix, "A Toolkit for Inclusion & Accessibility: Changing the Narrative of Disability in Documentary Film," https://www.fwd-doc.org/toolkit, accessed August 8, 2024.

86. Sean Zdenek, "Which Sounds Are Significant? Toward a Rhetoric of Closed Captioning," *Disability Studies Quarterly* 31, no. 3 (2011), https://dsq-sds.org/article/view/1667/1604; Kleege, "Audio Description Described," 92–95.

87. Kleege, "Audio Description Described," 96–97.

88. Interview with the artist, February 11, 2021. Lord is quoting Amalle Dublon in Amalle Dublon and Constantina Zavitsanos, "Dependency and Improvisation: A Conversation with Park McArthur," in "Disability and the Politics of Visibility," special issue, ed. Emily Watlington, *Art Papers* 42, no. 4 (2018/2019): 52.

89. Abby Sun and Jordan Lord, Q&A at The DocYard, Cambridge, Massachusetts, May 14, 2021. I have paraphrased Lord's words based on my notes from the event.

90. Critical engagements with moving image sensory access features as a creative medium are fairly recent. Earlier scholarly interventions by Zdenek and

2. LISTENING IN CRIP TIME 215

Kleege calling for rhetorical and interpretive license and disability-centered design assume that captions and audio description will be retrofitted to existing film or television programs and tend to focus on narrative fiction works produced and distributed by major streamers and studios. See Zdenek, "Which Sounds are Significant?"; Kleege, "Audio Description Described." Watlington has more recently developed a substantial body of art criticism on formal innovations in access-based video art, including works by the artists mentioned here. See Emily Watlington, "Critical Creative Corrective Cacophonous Comical: Closed Captions," *Mousse Magazine* 68 (2019), https://www.moussemagazine.it/shop/mousse-68/, accessed May 17, 2021; Watlington, "The Radical Accessibility of Video Art (for Hearing People)"; Emily Watlington with Victor Cole, "Audio Description, Described," *Voices in Contemporary Art (VOCA)* 10 (2021), https://journal.voca.network/audio-description-described/, accessed May 23, 2021.

91. See Watlington, "Critical Creative Corrective Cacophonous Comical."
92. Watlington, "Critical Creative Corrective Cacophonous Comical."
93. See Sarah Kozloff, *Invisible Storytellers: Voice-Over Narration in American Fiction Film* (Berkeley: University of California Press, 1988), 8–22.
94. Roland Barthes, gesturing to the unconscious or beyond of the frame calls this "the blind field." See Roland Barthes, *Camera Lucida: Reflections on Photography*, trans. Richard Howard (London: Hill and Wang, 1981), 57.
95. Kleege, "Audio Description Described," 94.
96. Lord, "Shared Resources (Contractual Obligations)," 5.
97. Dolmage argues that audio description "add[s] artistic and rhetorical value, not simply transposing or distilling meanings" while Mills proposes that audio description be viewed alongside captioning, fansubbing, voice-over, and "twin-vision" braille/print books as a "translation overlay" practice that adds alternative content to source material by integrating a new track without creating a new work. See Jay Dolmage, *Disability Rhetoric* (Syracuse, NY: Syracuse University Press, 2016), 5; Mara Mills, "Listening to Images: Audio Description, the Translation Overlay, and Image Retrieval." *Cine-Files* 8 (2015). https://www.thecine-files.com/listening-to-images-audio-description-the-translation-overlay-and-image-retrieval/.
98. Erika Balsom, *Ten Skies* (Melbourne: Fireflies, 2021), 53.
99. See Dublon and Zavitsanos, "Dependency and Improvisation," 52.
100. Kathryn Bond Stockton, "Growing Sideways, or Versions of the Queer Child," in *Curiouser: On the Queerness of Children*, ed. Steven Bruhm and Natasha Hurley (Minneapolis: University of Minnesota Press, 2004), 311.

101. Chion introduces the term *athorybos* for "any object or movement in the image that could, either in reality or in the imagination, produce sound but which is not accompanied by any sound," adding that "*all* the writing we read in a film image that is not accompanied by an utterance ... merits this term." The athorybal status of closed or option captions for D/deaf or hard of hearing audiences, which Chion does not address, is a topic requiring a separate discussion. See Michel Chion, *Words on Screen*, trans. Claudia Gorbman (New York: Columbia University Press, 2017), 60.
102. Quote from Lazard in Lazard, Zavitsanos, Jordan Lord, Deborah Lord, and Albert Lord, panel discussion at NYU Center for Disability Studies, May 7, 2020. Lazard's comments remind me of Devva Kasnitz's reflections on the slowness and effort of managing a revoicer she requires for her speech disability and an ASL interpreter while trying to teach a classroom full of students. Kasnitz muses, "I tell myself that the mere routine exposure to so much proximate disability expertise to apprehend IS the lesson." See Kasnitz, "The Politics of Disability Performativity," S22.
103. Dublon and Zavitsanos, "Dependency and Improvisation," 53.
104. John Lee Clark, "Against Access," *McSweeney's* 64: The Audio Issue, https://audio.mcsweeneys.net/transcripts/against_access.html, accessed July 5, 2022.
105. Phone conversation with Abby Sun, Wednesday, April 3, 2024. Sun states, "The refusal to accept burnt in subtitles was a policy change by Prime Video after [streamer] wrote to make an offer of licensing, but before we received the contract. After we received the contract, I wanted to make sure the contract included the open captions because I had previously identified it as a potential issue. But that also alerted [streamer] to the issue."
106. Phone conversation with Jordan Lord, Friday, June 7, 2024.
107. Story, "How Does it End?" 85.

3. LISTENING LIKE AN ABOLITIONIST

1. Nicole R. Fleetwood, *Marking Time: Art in the Age of Mass Incarceration* (Cambridge, MA: Harvard University Press, 2020), 25.
2. See Brian Wallis, The Sound of Defiance: How Can Listening to Images Reveal the Histories of the African Diaspora? Interview with Tina M. Campt," *Aperture*, October 25, 2017, https://aperture.org/editorial/tina-campt-conversation-brian-wallis/. In one case, Campt traces the discards of vernacular identification photos of Ugandan migrants fleeing war to a gallery in New York that displayed the larger prints from which rectangles had been

cut out. See Tina Campt, *Listening to Images* (Durham, NC: Duke University Press, 2017), 19–23.
3. Fleetwood, *Marking Time*, 15.
4. Story elaborates, "The bus to prison can itself be understood as a carceral space, insofar as its very existence is contingent on the coerced geographic removal of prisoners from their families, social networks, and communities. It exists because the prison system exists. The conditions it imposes on its riders echo the conditions of incarceration. In circulating, over long periods of time and across vast physical distances the mothers, sisters, wives, and girlfriends primarily tasked with the work of caregiving across the deep fissures produced by the prison regime, the bus functions as a holding space in which these women serve time in uncomfortable conditions, enduring the erosion of their bodies, psyches, and resources." See Brett Story, *Prison Land: Mapping Carceral Power Across Neoliberal America* (Minneapolis: University of Minnesota Press, 2019), 6; see also Brett Story, "Against a 'Humanizing' Prison Cinema," in *The Routledge International Handbook of Visual Criminology*, ed. Michelle Brown and Eamonn Carrabine (New York: Routledge, 2017), 458.
5. Fleetwood, *Marking Time*, 26.
6. See Sharon Sliwinski, *Human Rights in Camera* (Chicago: University of Chicago Press, 2011), 4; Thomas Keenan, "Getting the Dead to Tell Me What Happened: Justice, Prosopopoeia, and Forensic Afterlives," in *Forensis: The Architecture of Public Truth*, ed. Forensic Architecture (Berlin: Sternberg Press and Forensic Architecture, 2014), 42–43. Historians of witnessing have pushed back against Felman and Laub's exceptionalization of the Holocaust by bringing into focus other mass-mediated disasters, genocidal conflicts, and atrocities that have shaped aesthetic judgement and concepts of the political, including the 1755 Lisbon earthquake, the Bosnian and Rwandan genocides (Sliwinski), the Armenian genocide, the crisis in Darfur (Torchin), 9/11, and the beating of Rodney King by Los Angeles police (Guerin and Hallas); see Sliwinski, *Human Rights in Camera*; Leshu Torchin, *Creating the Witness: Documenting Genocide on Film, Video, and the Internet* (Minneapolis: University of Minnesota Press, 2012); and Frances Guerin and Roger Hallas, "Introduction," in *The Image and the Witness: Trauma, Memory, and Visual Culture*, ed. Frances Guerin and Roger Hallas (London: Wallflower, 2007), 1–22.
7. See Shoshana Felman and Dori Laub, *Testimony: Crises of Witnessing in Literature, Psychoanalysis, and History* (New York: Routledge, 1992), 206. Felman elaborates: "To bear witness is to take responsibility for truth: to speak, implicitly, from within the legal pledge and the juridical imperative of the witness's oath.

To testify—before a court of law or before the court of history and of the future; to testify, likewise, before an audience of readers or spectators—is more than simply to report a fact or an event or to relate what has been lived, recorded and remembered. Memory is conjured here essentially to *address* another, to impress upon a listener, to *appeal* to a community. To testify is always, metaphorically to take the witness stand, or to take the position of the witness insofar as the narrative account of the witness is at once engaged in an appeal and bound by an oath. To testify is thus not merely to narrate but to commit oneself, and to commit the narrative, to others: *to take responsibility*—in speech—for history or for the truth of an occurrence, for something which, by definition, goes beyond the personal, in having general (nonpersonal) validity and consequences" (204).

8. Laliv Melamed has noted, in an excellent revisionist history of the mass-mediated testimonial and the scholarly and public currents that contributed to its primary affiliations with trauma and crisis, that Felman's analysis of the Nuremberg trials in *The Juridical Unconscious* (2002) connects the formation of the traumatic subject with the reconceptualization of international law as the means of universal justice and the emergence of "humanity" as a justification for humanitarian intervention. See Laliv Melamed, *Sovereign Intimacy: Private Media and the Traces of Colonial Violence* (Berkeley: University of California Press, 2023), 166, 251 (note 56).

9. See Felman and Laub, 6, 204–6.

10. Ryan Watson, "In the Wakes of Rodney King: Militant Evidence and Media Activism in the Age of Viral Black Death," *Velvet Light Trap* 84 (2019): 34–49; and Stella Bruzzi, "Making a Genre: The Case of the Contemporary True Crime Documentary," *Law and Humanities* 10, no. 2 (2016): 249–80 deal, respectively, with the rise of activist media collectives and human rights watchdog organizations, and justice-driven true crime, as examples of accountability-based documentary practices. Story and I discuss the phenomenal rise of justice-driven true crime documentary media over the last several decades and the complicity of this genre with bipartisan criminal justice reform projects that leave intact the bedrock legitimacy of the carceral state in Pooja Rangan and Brett Story, "Four Propositions on True Crime and Abolition," in "Beyond Story," special issue, ed. Alexandra Juhasz and Alisa Lebow, *World Records* 5 (2021): 1–8.

11. See Joshua Malitsky, "Introduction," in *A Companion to Documentary Film History*, ed. Joshua Malitsky (Hoboken, NJ: Wiley-Blackwell, 2021), especially xv–xvi, for an account of how questions around documentary's underlying legitimacy led to the development of the subfield of documentary studies.

3. LISTENING LIKE AN ABOLITIONIST   219

12. Visible Evidence, an itinerant gathering that has come to serve as the de facto professional conference for the documentary field, held its inaugural meeting in 1993, the year after the Los Angeles riots. For many in the documentary field, George Holliday's tape of Rodney King's beating by Los Angeles police represented the vexed but critical status of the documentary image as a battleground for meaning, as well as the emancipatory potential of continuing to speak truth to power even in the face of legal setbacks. Linda Williams captures this sentiment in an essay published in the same year (1993) when she writes that Holliday's home video "might be taken to represent the other side of the postmodern distrust of the image: here the camera tells the truth in a remarkable moment of *cinema verité* which then becomes valuable (though not conclusive) evidence in accusations against the L.A. Police Department's discriminatory violence." See Linda Williams, "Mirrors Without Memories: Truth, History, and the New Documentary (1993)," in *The Documentary Film Reader: History, Theory, Criticism*, ed. Jonathan Kahana (New York: Oxford University Press, 2016), 795. I discuss the trial of Rodney King's assailants in the next section of this chapter.

13. See James E. K. Parker, *Acoustic Jurisprudence: Listening to the Trial of Simon Bikindi* (Oxford: Oxford University Press, 2015), 3. As elaborated later, Parker is interested in what he calls the law's sonic imagination, understood as the diverse ways in which legal institutions conceive sound for the purposes of coming to judgment, at the level of evidentiary rhetoric, argumentative strategies, and the types of juridical attitudes or commitments engaged (3, 7).

14. Didier Fassin and Mariella Pandolfi, "Introduction," in *Contemporary States of Emergency: The Politics of Military and Humanitarian Interventions* (New York: Zone, 2010), 12–13; Angela Y. Davis, *Are Prisons Obsolete?* (New York: Seven Stories, 2003), 12. As Ben-Moshe more recently notes, despite being home to just 5 percent of the world's population, the United States holds 25 percent of the world's imprisoned population. See Liat Ben-Moshe, *Decarcerating Disability: Deinstitutionalization and Prison Abolition* (Minneapolis: University of Minnesota Press, 2020), 7.

15. Ben-Moshe, *Decarcerating Disability*, 111.

16. Ben-Moshe, *Decarcerating Disability*, 15.

17. See Michelle Brown, *The Culture of Punishment: Prison, Society, and Spectacle* (New York: New York University Press, 2009), 112–13, 121. Brown has in mind the cultural scripts and meanings about punishment communicated through popular cultural forms and activities such as television news, prison tours, immigration debates, and military service, which explicitly or implicitly invite

viewers to produce justifications for the existence of prisons, detention centers, and other carceral enclosures.
18. Brown, *The Culture of Punishment*, 110, 112.
19. Tina Campt, "Black Visuality and the Practice of Refusal," in "Performing Refusal/Refusing to Perform," special issue, ed. Lilian G. Mengesha and Lakshmi Padmanabhan, *Women and Performance* 29, no. 1 (2019), https://www.womenandperformance.org/ampersand/29-1/campt.
20. Audra Simpson, "The Ruse of Consent and the Anatomy of 'Refusal': Cases from Indigenous North America and Australia," *Postcolonial Studies* 20, no. 1 (2017): 29.
21. Darat Al-Fanun. "Fellow Talk: Witnessing as Worldbuilding in Palestinian Visual Culture—Kareem Estefan," Facebook Live, November 23, 2021, https://www.facebook.com/daratalfunun/videos/3002036443458602/; LaCharles Ward, "Black Redaction, Black Evidence: Another Testimony of Black Life," in *A Site of Struggle: American Art Against Anti-Black Violence*," ed. Janet Dees (Princeton, NJ: Princeton University Press, 2022), 87–99.
22. Angela Y. Davis, Gina Dent, Erica R. Meiners, and Beth E. Richie, *Abolition. Feminism. Now.* (Chicago: Haymarket, 2022), 5–7; Mariame Kaba, *We Do This 'Til We Free Us: Abolitionist Organizing and Transforming Justice* (Chicago: Haymarket, 2021), 62, 148–49.
23. Mia Mingus, "Transformative Justice: A Brief Description," *Leaving Evidence* (blog), January 9, 2019, https://leavingevidence.wordpress.com/2019/01/09/transformative-justice-a-brief-description/.
24. Carole McGranahan, "Theorizing Refusal: An Introduction," *Cultural Anthropology* 31, no. 3 (2016): 319.
25. See Nadia Yaqub, "Introduction," In *Gaza on Screen*, ed. Nadia Yaqub (Durham, NC: Duke University Press, 2023), 14–16.
26. I follow Alexandrowicz's convention in referring to Maia Levy by her first name. I am also using the acronym IDF, rather than the more politically pointed IOF (Israeli Occupation Forces), because the insistence on defense is part of the discursive framing of Israeli victimhood under interrogation in this chapter.
27. Lisa Guenther, "Seeing Like a Cop: A Critical Phenomenology of Whiteness as Property," in *Race as Phenomena: Between Phenomenology and Philosophy of Race*, ed. Emily S. Lee (London: Rowman & Littlefield, 2019), 189, 196.
28. Campt, "Black Visuality and the Practice of Refusal."
29. Leopold Lambert, "Making Abolition Geography in California's Central Valley: Interview with Ruth Wilson Gilmore," *The Funambulist*, December

3. LISTENING LIKE AN ABOLITIONIST   221

18, 2018, https://thefunambulist.net/magazine/21-space-activism/interview-making-abolition-geography-california-central-valley-ruth-wilson-gilmore.

30. The forty videos were presented to Maia on a Vimeo channel with their original titles and logos but without extended textual descriptions; Alexandrowicz has said that if Maia had asked to see the descriptions of any of the videos as presented on YouTube (she did not), he would have shown them to her. Alexandrowicz's only other intervention was adding English subtitles to "five or six" videos (mostly not from B'Tselem) that were not translated. Information from a conversation with Alexandrowicz, October 1, 2022.

31. See Jasbir Puar, *The Right to Maim: Debility, Capacity, Disability* (Durham, NC: Duke University Press, 2017), 108–11.

32. See Amnesty International, "'You Feel Like You Are Subhuman': Israel's Genocide Against Palestinians in Gaza," December 5, 2024, https://www.amnesty.org/en/documents/mde15/8668/2024/en/, accessed December 7, 2024; United Nations General Assembly, *Report of the Special Committee to Investigate Israeli Practices Affecting the Human Rights of the Palestinian People and Other Arabs of the Occupied Territories*, 79th session, Agenda Item 50, UN Doc A/79/363 (September 20, 2024).

33. See Loveday Morris, Lorenzo Tugnoli, and Sufian Taha, "In Israeli-Occupied Hebron, Palestinians Describe Living in 'a Prison,'" *Washington Post*, February 28, 2024, https://www.washingtonpost.com/world/2024/02/28/west-bank-hebron-israel-occupation/.

34. Ra'anan Alexandrowicz, "Maia and the Boundaries of the Frame," in "In the Presence of Others," special issue, ed. Nicolas Gamso and Jason Fox, *World Records* 4 (2020): 16.

35. Morris's Interrotron (a portmanteau of the words "terror" and "interview") projects a live video feed of his face onto a teleprompter connected to a camera during interviews. He has described the setup, which creates the impression, for interviewees, of speaking directly to Morris, and for spectators, the uncanny effect of being spoken to directly by the interview subjects, as a device that "creates greater distance *and* greater intimacy." See Errol Morris, "The Fog of War: 13 Questions and Answers on the Filmmaking of Errol Morris by Errol Morris," *FLM* (2004), archived at https://www.errolmorris.com/content/eyecontact/interrotron.html, accessed July 27, 2022.

36. Laliv Melamed and Ra'anan Alexandrowicz, postscreening conversation at the Visible Evidence conference, Frankfurt, December 2021.

37. See B'Tselem, https://www.btselem.org/ and WITNESS, https://www.witness.org/, accessed July 28, 2022.

38. Ra'anan Alexandrowicz, "50 Years of Documentation: A Brief History of the Audiovisual Documentation of the Israeli Occupation," in *Visual Imagery and Human Rights Practice*, ed. Sandra Ristovska and Monroe Price (Cham, Switzerland: Palgrave Macmillan, 2018), 23. Alisa Lebow notes that B'Tselem staff would edit activist video clips, sometimes adding verbal or textual commentary in English or Hebrew. These clips were then sent out as press packages to international news outlets such as BBC, CNN, and Al Jazeera, compiled on themed DVDs, and shared on social media. See Alisa Lebow, "Shooting with Intent: Framing Conflict," in *Killer Images: Documentary Film, Memory, and the Performance of Violence*, ed. Joram ten Brink (New York: Columbia University Press, 2013), 52; 56.
39. These are terms developed by Watson; see Watson, "In the Wakes of Rodney King," 36. Also see Lebow, "Shooting with Intent," 56.
40. Alexandrowicz, "50 Years of Documentation," 31.
41. See Darat-Al-Fanun, "Fellow Talk: Witnessing as Worldbuilding in Palestinian Visual Culture—Kareem Estefan"; Yves Bois, Michael Feher, and Hal Foster, "On Forensic Architecture: A Conversation with Eyal Weizman," *October* 156 (2016): 136.
42. Thomas Keenan, "Mobilizing Shame," *South Atlantic Quarterly* 103, no. 2/3 (2004): 435; Rebecca L. Stein, "The Boy Who Wasn't Really Killed: Israeli State Violence in the Age of the Smartphone Witness," *International Journal of Middle East Studies* 53 (2021): 620–38.
43. Al-Haq. "Al-Haq Calls on Third States to Publicly Condemn and Call for the Full Rescinding of Israel's Designation of Palestinian Human Rights NGOs as 'Terrorist Organisations,'" October 24, 2021, https://www.alhaq.org/advocacy/19050.html; Puar, *The Right to Maim*, 129, 136. Puar notes, "The target here is not just life itself, but resistance itself" (135).
44. Forensic Architecture's work belongs in this tradition; see Forensic Architecture, ed. *Forensis: The Architecture of Public Truth* (Berlin: Sternberg Press and Forensic Architecture, 2014). Taking stock of the failure of videos documenting police brutality to spur legal accountability and justice, Ryan Watson nonetheless expresses faith in the cumulative *affective*—if not legally effective—force of documentary witnessing and its tactical deployment by activist agencies such as WITNESS and B'Tselem (Watson, "In the Wakes of Rodney King, 36). Erika Balsom defends neo-observational documentary as a corrective to what she sees as a collusion between the postmodern, essayistic turn in documentary and "a dangerous relativism that annuls a distinction between truth and falsity that we might rather want to fight for"; see Erika

3. LISTENING LIKE AN ABOLITIONIST 223

Balsom, "The Reality-Based Community," *e-flux* 83 (2017), https://www.e-flux.com/journal/83/142332/the-reality-based-community/.
45. The Arab media scholar Kareem Estefan refuses the limitations of "traumatic realism" as counterevidentiary practice of correcting the historical record, offering "reparative fabulation as a mode of narrating suppressed histories amid archival absences"; see Kareem Estefan, "Narrating Living and Looted Palestinian Archives: Reparative Fabulation in Azza El-Hassan's *Kings and Extras*," *Feminist Media Histories* 8, no. 2 (2022): 48. The documentary scholar Toby Lee has argued against the idealization of reality implicit in its recuperation by scholars such as Balsom in favor of the "radical potential of the unreal" as an aesthetic and political expression of Indigenous and trans experience; see Toby Lee, "The Radical Unreal: Fabulation and Fantasy in Speculative Documentary," *Film Quarterly* 74, no. 4 (2021): 10.
46. Keenan, "Getting the Dead to Tell Me What Happened," 52.
47. Alexandrowicz, "50 Years of Documentation," 30–31; Alexandrowicz, "Maia and the Boundaries of the Frame," 17–18; Jeffrey Skoller, "iDocument Police: Contingency, Resistance, and the Precarious Present," in "The Documentary Camera," special issue, ed. Jason Fox, *World Records* 1 (2017): 2; 5. Skoller describes happenstance films as a "cinema of present-time" because of the sense of urgency produced by their rough, unedited quality: "Often the filmers have little time to pay attention to their recording's composition, exposure, focus, coverage of the scene, or sound quality" (2).
48. Alexandrowicz writes, "For Maia, videos portraying Palestinian suffering under Israeli occupation seem to be hostile images, because they threaten some of her fundamental beliefs by portraying asymmetrical Israeli aggression. She is, if to slightly distort Stuart Hall's original term, an *oppositional viewer* of the B'tzelem videos. Arguably, for B'tzelem, as well as for myself, oppositional viewers like Maia are actually preferred viewers." Alexandrowicz, "Maia and the Boundaries of the Frame," 19.
49. Melamed and Alexandrowicz, postscreening conversation.
50. See "Soldiers Enter Hebron Homes at Night, Photograph Kids, 24/02/15," posted March 29, 2015, by btselem, YouTube, 8 min., https://www.youtube.com/watch?v=oHRj-GF5dwg&ab_channel=btselem, accessed August 10, 2022.
51. Alexandrowicz, "Maia and the Boundaries of the Frame," 19–20. B'Tselem's description of the video, presented in its original form with Hebrew and English subtitles on YouTube, follows similar contours: "Late at night on 23 Feb. 2015 Israeli troops entered 10 neighboring apartments in Hebron. B'Tselem camera volunteer Nayef Da'ana lives in one of the apartments and filmed

the incident in his home. The soldiers demanded that the children be awakened, asked them their names and photographed them. The military cannot treat civilians—and certainly not children—as potential criminals. Not only is this policy of entering Palestinian homes by night unjust and terrifying. It illustrates how casually and arbitrarily the lives of Palestinians under occupation are disrupted and their rights violated. B'Tselem calls on the military to discontinue this policy without delay."

52. As Lebow notes, the very fact that B'Tselem has been allowed to continue its work uncensored functions as a cover for Israel's benevolence; see Lebow, "Shooting with Intent," 56. In an anonymous conversation a member of the Ramallah-based Palestinian human rights organization Al-Haq (founded ten years prior to B'Tselem in 1979) expressed that there is significant skepticism among Palestinians regarding what they described as an "extractive relationship" between Israeli human rights organizations (including B'Tselem) and the Palestinian community. They elaborated that B'Tselem relies on Palestinian field workers in order to generate their data, but Palestinians don't have reciprocal access to data about settlements without permission from B'Tselem.

53. See Stein, "The Boy Who Wasn't Really Killed," 633. Stein traces the evolution of this script through smear campaigns mounted around watershed videos from 2000 (shooting of Muhammad al-Durrah), 2008 (shooting of Asraf Abu Rahma), and 2014 (shooting of Nadim Nawara and Muhammad Salama), respectively.

54. Stein, "The Boy Who Wasn't Really Killed," 625.

55. Alexandrowicz develops the phrase "ambush for an ambush" through a reading of a video shot by a Palestinian B'Tselem field worker who patiently keeps his camera focused on an empty corner as an ambush for a scene of violence so familiar that is correctly anticipated: In time, two Israeli soldiers come along, and one of them assaults a Palestinian child without cause. See Alexandrowicz, "50 Years of Documentation," 30.

56. See Stein, "The Boy Who Wasn't Really Killed," 621–22, 630.

57. Stein, "The Boy Who Wasn't Really Killed," 625, 637.

58. See Watson, "In the Wakes of Rodney King," 44. Watson quotes the WITNESS founder Peter Gabriel: "Sometimes, documenting a human rights crime doesn't directly lead to justice. But it can galvanize a movement. It can be proof regardless of what a jury decides. Most importantly, it can transform public opinion as well as national and international policies. We may not see

the outcome we want when we want it, but there is power in arming truth with evidence" (Peter Gabriel, "Video Will Bring Us Justice in the Long Run," *Time*, May 16, 2017, https://time.com/4781418/peter-gabriel-video-justice/.)

59. "Thomas Keenan. Watching Without Seeing: Police Violence and Eyewitness Video. 2017," posted January 22, 2018, by European Graduate School Video Lectures, YouTube, 36 min., https://www.youtube.com/watch?v=D3-347PCXUA&ab_channel=EuropeanGraduateSchoolVideoLectures, accessed August 9, 2022. For an overview of scholarship on the King trial and aftermath, see both Keenan and Watson, "In the Wakes of Rodney King."

60. Skoller, "iDocument Police," 7.

61. Kimberlé Crenshaw and Gary Peller, "Reel Time/Real Justice," in *Reading Rodney King/Reading Urban Uprising*, ed. Robert Gooding-Williams (London: Taylor and Francis, 1993), 64.

62. Hall uses the term "oppositional" to designate the interpretative stance of a reader whose social situation leads them to reject the dominant hegemonic code embedded in a given text and produce an alternative, subversive reading. See Stuart Hall, "Encoding/Decoding," in *Culture, Media, Language*, ed. Stuart Hall, Dorothy Hobson, Andrew Lowe, and Paul Willis (London: Routledge, 1980), 127.

63. See Hamid Naficy, "King Rodney: The Rodney King Video and Textual Analysis," in *The End of Cinema as We Know It: American Film in the Nineties*, ed. Jon Lewis (New York: New York University Press, 2001), 10.

64. Crenshaw and Peller, Naficy, and Williams (see "Mirrors Without Memories") all offer versions of this critique.

65. Stein, "The Boy Who Wasn't Really Killed," 624.

66. Alexandrowicz, "Maia and the Boundaries of the Frame," 22; Melamed and Alexandrowicz, postscreening conversation.

67. See European Graduate School Video Lectures, "Thomas Keenan."

68. Carol Clover, "Law and the Order of Popular Culture," in *Law in the Domains of Culture*, ed. Austin Sarat and Thomas R. Kearns (Ann Arbor: University of Michigan Press, 1998), 104.

69. Clover, "Law and the Order of Popular Culture," 100–4.

70. See Tory Jeffay, "Fatty Arbuckle's Fingerprints: Race, Photographic Evidence, and the Smudge," *Journal of Cinema and Media Studies* 64, no. 2 (2025): 97–98.

71. Clover, "Law and the Order of Popular Culture," 105.

72. Scott Krzych has made an argument along these lines in the context of U.S. right wing media cultures. He describes conservative media as a hysterical

mode of political discourse in the Lacanian sense, one that "sustains and reproduces noise as a defensive maneuver or mechanism that drowns out other voices, resists change or compromise, and substitutes a parody of democratic engagement for the real thing." For Krzych, hysterical noise is effective only as a "defensive weapon" or "deflective shield" against progressive political agendas. See Scott Krzych, *Beyond Bias: Conservative Media, Documentary Form, and the Politics of Hysteria* (New York: Oxford University Press, 2021), 22, 221.

73. Melamed and Alexandrowicz, postscreening conversation.
74. See Simpson, "The Ruse of Consent and the Anatomy of 'Refusal,'" 19, 23; Darat-Al-Fanun, "Fellow Talk: Witnessing as Worldbuilding in Palestinian Visual Culture—Kareem Estefan." I am indebted to Estefan for his reformulation of Simpson's politics of refusal in these terms.
75. Thomas Keenan and Eyal Weizman, *Mengele's Skull: The Advent of a Forensic Aesthetics* (Berlin: Sternberg, 2012), 13.
76. For more on Weizman's early work and his book *Hollow Land*, see Bois, Feher, and Foster, "On Forensic Architecture," 118.
77. See Eyal Weizman, *Forensic Architecture: Violence at the Threshold of Detectability* (New York: Zone, 2017), 94.
78. See Emily Watlington, "When Does Artistic Research Become Fake News? Forensic Architecture Keeps Dodging the Question," *Artnews*, March 15, 2023, https://www.artnews.com/art-in-america/features/forensic-architecture-fake-news-1234661013/.

   Also see Anika Marschall and Ann-Christine Simke, "Forensic Architecture in the Theater and the Gallery: A Reflection on Counterhegemonic Potentials and Pitfalls of Art Institutions," *Theater Research International* 47, no. 2 (2022): 142–59; Tania Osorio Harp, "Is Forensic Architecture the New Muralism of the Mexican State? A Reflection on Racialized Violence and the Construction of Mexican Identity," *Journal of Urban Cultural Studies* 5, no. 3 (2018): 371–80. Weizman has countered that FA's factual aesthetics seek to reconcile the domains of art and science, which have been disciplinarily sundered and positioned in opposition in the Enlightenment era and onward. See Eyal Weizman, "Open Verification." *e-flux* (2019), https://www.e-flux.com/architecture/becoming-digital/248062/open-verification/.
79. Sekula uses this term, whose definition and ethos Keenan adopts, in Allan Sekula, "Photography and the Limits of National Identity," *Culturefront* 2, no. 3 (1993): 54–55. "The history of human rights forensics," writes Keenan, "is marked by this asymmetrical reversal of state policing techniques into

3. LISTENING LIKE AN ABOLITIONIST

tactics for resisting and challenging injustice"; see Thomas Keenan, "Counterforensics and Photography," *Grey Room* 55 (2014): 71. Weizman adds that "counterforensics turns the state's own means against the violence it commits," describing the agency's work as "an engaged civil practice that seeks to articulate public claims using architecture"; see Weizman, *Forensic Architecture*, 64; also see 53.

80. Weizman, *Forensic Architecture*, 65.
81. Keenan and Weizman begin theorizing the forum in *Mengele's Skull* (see 25–30); Weizman further develops their initial proposal to reassert the public, political element of *forensis* in Weizman, *Forensic Architecture*, esp. 65.
82. Keenan and Weizman, *Mengele's Skull*, 28.
83. See Robert Bevan, "Turner Prize-Shortlisted Forensic Architecture's Eyal Weizman: 'I Want to Win Cases – Not Art Prizes.'" *Evening Standard*, July 3, 2018. https://www.standard.co.uk/culture/turner-prizeshortlisted-forensic-architectures-eyal-weizman-i-want-to-win-cases-not-prizes-a3877746.html.
84. See Kate Lacey, *Listening Publics* (Cambridge: Polity, 2013), viii.
85. For instance, even in FA's highly publicized Saydnaya project (https://saydnaya.amnesty.org/en/saydnaya.html), a web commission for Amnesty International for which the audio investigator and artist Lawrence Abu Hamdan collected "earwitness testimony" from survivors to reconstruct a model of the secret Syrian torture prison, the main attraction is not sound but a 3D model of the site that functions as a visual interface and navigation device.
86. See Weizman, *Forensic Architecture*, 217–27; Forensic Architecture, "Ground Truth: The Al-Araquib Museum of Struggle," https://forensic-architecture.org/programme/exhibitions/ground-truth-the-al-araqib-museum-of-struggle, accessed September 2, 2022; also see Toby Lee, "Occult Operations: Notes Toward a Politics of Operativity," lecture presented at Brown University, Providence, RI, March 17, 2023; Bevan, "I Want to Win Cases – Not Art Prizes."
87. Weizman, *Forensic Architecture*, 66.
88. See Keenan and Weizman, *Mengele's Skull*, 28. So far, the major scholarly elaborations of counterforensics have largely been proffered by affiliates of the agency, who have tended to focus either on the legal implications of emerging categories of material evidence (Schuppli) or the aesthetic implications of forensic modes of looking, listening, and noticing, that is, of making evidence evident (Fuller and Weizman; Abu Hamdan). See Susan Schuppli, *Material Witness: Media, Forensics, Evidence* (Cambridge, MA: MIT Press, 2020); Matthew Fuller and Eyal Weizman, *Investigative Aesthetics: Conflicts and Commons in the Politics of Truth* (New York: Verso, 2021); and Lawrence

Abu Hamdan, *[inaudible]: A Politics of Listening in 4 Acts* (Berlin: Sternberg, 2016).

89. Eyal Weizman, "Introduction: Forensis," in *Forensis: The Architecture of Public Truth*, ed. Forensic Architecture (Berlin: Sternberg Press and Forensic Architecture, 2014), 9.

90. See for instance Emerson Goo, "Remains to Be Seen: The Video Work of Forensic Architecture," *Mubi*, May 11, 2021, https://mubi.com/en/notebook/posts/remains-to-be-seen-the-video-work-of-forensic-architecture; and Watlington, "When Does Artistic Research Become Fake News?" Goo expresses concern that by trying to make art that is legally effective, FA runs the risk of accomplishing neither, while Watlington worries that some of FA's works call more attention to technological innovation than to human rights violations.

91. I am grateful to Lachlann Kermode for speaking with me on Monday, October 10, 2022, about his work with FA as a software researcher during the period when the Harith Augustus investigation was underway, for providing valuable context, and for his assistance with fact-checking my claims in this section.

92. Mariame Kaba, "Police 'Reforms' You Should Always Oppose," *Truthout*, December 7, 2014, https://truthout.org/articles/police-reforms-you-should-always-oppose/.

93. See Ruth Wilson Gilmore, *Golden Gulag: Prisons, Surplus, Crisis, and Opposition in Globalizing California* (Berkeley: University of California Press, 2007), 242; André Gorz, *Strategy for Labor: A Radical Proposal* (Boston: Beacon, 1967), 7.

94. The complexity of these negotiations arguably requires more extended consideration than I can offer here about what it means to deploy counterforensic methods devised in response to anti-Palestinian violence for resisting anti-Black violence in an altogether distinct carceral context. Developing this critique is beyond the scope of this chapter, but I take it up further in a forthcoming interview-based essay written in collaboration with Laliv Melamed, Rachel Nelson, and members of Al-Haq's Forensic Architecture Investigation Unit.

95. Ward, "Black Redaction, Black Evidence," 91, 93.

96. Ward, "Black Redaction, Black Evidence," 95, 97.

97. See Saidiya V. Hartman, *Scenes of Subjection: Terror, Slavery, and Self-Making in Nineteenth-Century America* (New York: Oxford University Press, 1997), 19, 22–23; Campt, "Black Visuality and the Practice of Refusal."

98. Jamie Kalven and Eyal Weizman, "How Chicago Police Created a False Narrative After Officers Killed Harith Augustus," *Intercept*, September 19, 2019, https://theintercept.com/2019/09/19/harith-augustus-shooting-chicago-police/.

3. LISTENING LIKE AN ABOLITIONIST   229

99. As Halpern notes, the discourse of data visualization equates the usefulness of data with its aesthetic properties or "beauty," and in doing so it draws attention away from the political economy of mining and crafting data to make it valuable. See Orit Halpern, *Beautiful Data: A History of Vision and Reason Since 1945* (Durham, NC: Duke University Press, 2014), 5. In July 2023, following just a few short hours of deliberation, a jury ruled against Harith Augustus's family in a wrongful death lawsuit naming Halley, other officers involved in the incident, then-Superintendent Eddie Johnson and the city of Chicago. See Kade Heather, "Jury rules in favor of CPD officers in 2018 fatal shooting of barber Harith Augustus in South Shore," *Chicago Sun-Times*, July 7, 2023, https://chicago.suntimes.com/crime/2023/7/7/23787787/jury-rules-in-favor-of-cpd-officers-in-2018-fatal-shooting-of-barber-harith-augustus-in-south-shore.

100. For an extensive methodological discussion of FA's use of 3D modeling and audio-visual synchronization in the Harith Augustus investigation, see Patrick Brian Smith and Ryan Watson, "Mediated Forensics and Militant Evidence: Rethinking the Camera as Weapon," *Media, Culture, and Society* 45, no. 1 (2023): 36–56.

101. See Alex Vitale, *The End of Policing* (New York: Verso, 2017), 21.

102. See chapter 1 of Vitale, *The End of Policing*, especially pages 16–17, 20–24; Kaba, "Police 'Reforms' You Should Always Oppose." Davis et al. elaborate: "Civilian and accountability watchdog organizations have had, at best, a negligible impact on reducing the violence of policing. While these strategies may result in an individual police officer potentially losing their employment or being punished, the prosecution of a police officer neither undoes the system nor exposes the underlying logics and structures that perpetuate harm." See Davis et al., *Abolition. Feminism. Now.*, 153.

103. See Bernard E. Harcourt, *Illusion of Order* (2001), 129, quoted in Guenther, "Seeing Like a Cop," 195; James Q. Wilson and George L. Kelling, "Broken Windows," *Atlantic*, March 1982, https://www.theatlantic.com/magazine/archive/1982/03/broken-windows/304465/.

104. See Guenther, "Seeing Like a Cop," 194–95. Guenther quotes from both Wilson and Kelling's article "Broken Windows" and Wilson's precursor book, *Varieties of Police Behavior: The Management of Law and Order in Eight Communities* (Cambridge, MA: Harvard University Press, 1968) in offering the following examples of the kinds of people that Wilson and Kelling deem threats: "panhandlers, drunks, addicts, rowdy teenagers, prostitutes, loiterers, the mentally disturbed" (quoted in Wilson and Kelling, "Broken Windows"), and "a Negro wearing a 'conk rag,'" "girls in short skirts,'" "interracial couples" and "boys in long hair parked in a flash car talking loudly to friends" (quoted in Wilson, *Varieties of Police Behavior*, 39–40).

105. Guenther, "Seeing Like a Cop," 189.
106. See Jeffay, "Fatty Arbuckle's Fingerprints," 97; 81–86.
107. European Graduate School Video Lectures, "Thomas Keenan."
108. I once again have Sasha Crawford-Holland to thank for pointing this out.
109. See Parker, *Acoustic Jurisprudence*, 3, 37, 40.
110. Ward, "Black Redaction, Black Evidence," 90.
111. Email conversation with Crawford-Holland, June 3, 2022; also see the discussion of Reynolds-Tyler's vocal disagreement with calls for community-based policing in Maxwell Evans, "5 Shots on 71st Street: New Investigation Challenges Police Narrative of Harith Augustus Death," *Block Club Chicago*, October 3, 2019, https://blockclubchicago.org/2019/10/03/5-shots-on-71st-street-new-investigation-challenges-police-narrative-of-harith-augustus-death/.
112. Kaba, *We Do This 'Til We Free Us*, 98–99.
113. Quincy T. Mills, *Cutting Along the Color Line: Black Barbers and Barber Shops in America* (Philadelphia: University of Pennsylvania Press, 2013), 3, 7. Also see 216–47.
114. Dylan Robinson, *Hungry Listening: Resonant Theory for Indigenous Sound Studies* (Minneapolis: University of Minnesota Press, 2020), 43–45.
115. Robinson, *Hungry Listening*, 70–71.
116. Paraphrase of Ardythe Wilson, quoted in Robinson, *Hungry Listening*, 70; also see 69.
117. Robinson, *Hungry Listening*, 72.
118. Ward, "Black Redaction, Black Evidence," 91.

CODA: LISTENING WITHOUT IMPACT

1. As a case in point, the 2022 iteration of the Non-Fiction Core Application, launched collaboratively in 2016 by grantors in collaboration with the LA-based International Documentary Organization (IDA), requires applicants to specify their impact strategy, goals, and plans toward developing an impact campaign (the original iteration acknowledged that "not all films are suited for social engagement"). See v.2022 and v.2016 of International Documentary Organization, The Non-Fiction Core Application Project, https://www.documentary.org/nonfiction-core-application-project, accessed August 11, 2024.
2. The Global Impact Producers Alliance, a community-led network and resource for impact producers, states, "An impact campaign is not another word for marketing and public relations for independent films, this is a social justice centered practice created strategically with care, collaboration and

organization in order to spark social change through ethical storytelling," https://globalimpactproducers.org/faqs/, accessed August 11, 2024.

3. These comments are based on anonymous conversations that I had with six filmmakers and impact producers who share investments in formally daring and politically committed filmmaking.

4. See Sonya Childress and Natalie Bullock-Brown, "The Documentary Future: A Call for Accountability," *Documentary*, July 2, 2020, https://www.documentary.org/feature/documentary-future-call-accountability. Recommendations developed by FWD-Doc and by the Documentary Accountability Working Group helmed by Bullock-Brown have now been folded into the accessibility and accountability requirements of the revised Non-Fiction Core Application.

5. See FWD-Doc, in association with Doc Society, supported by Netflix, "A Toolkit for Inclusion & Accessibility: Changing the Narrative of Disability in Documentary Film," https://www.fwd-doc.org/toolkit, accessed August 8, 2024; POV, "North By Current Discussion Guide," https://www.pbs.org/pov/resources/north-current-discussion-guide/, accessed August 12, 2024.

6. Chris Lorenz, "If You're So Smart, Why Are You under Surveillance? Universities, Neoliberalism, and New Public Management," *Critical Inquiry* 38, no. 3 (2012): 599–600, quoted in Rey Chow, *A Face Drawn in Sand: Humanistic Inquiry and Foucault in the Present* (New York: Columbia University Press, 2021), 8. Lorenz argues that post-1980s neoliberal policy discourses in public sector fields such as higher education show similarities to the managerial discourses of former Communist states.

7. See Lorenz, "If You're So Smart, Why Are You Under Surveillance?" 618, 625.

8. Bruce Charlton, "Audit, Accountability, Quality, and All That: The Growth of Managerial Technologies in UK Universities," in *Education! Education! Education! Managerial Ethics and the Law of Unintended Consequences*, ed. Stephen Prickett and Patricia Erskine-Hill (Thorverton, UK: Imprint Academic, 2002), 17.

BIBLIOGRAPHY

Abu Hamdan, Lawrence. "Aural Contract: Forensic Listening and the Reorganization of the Speaking Subject." In *Forensis: The Architecture of Public Truth*, ed. Forensic Architecture, 65–82. Berlin: Sternberg Press and Forensic Architecture, 2014.
———. *[inaudible]: A Politics of Listening in 4 Acts*. Berlin: Sternberg, 2016.
Aitken, Ian. *Film and Reform: John Grierson and the Documentary Film Movement*. London: Routledge, 1990.
Aldarondo, Cecilia, and Samara Chadwick. "All That Glitters: Reflections on the Not-So-Golden Age of Documentary Storytelling." In "Beyond Story," special issue, ed. Alexandra Juhasz and Alisa Lebow, *World Records* 5 (2021): 91–100.
Alexander, Neta. "The Right to Speed Watch (or, When Netflix Discovered Its Blind Users)." In *Interface Frictions: How Digital Debility Reshapes Our Bodies*. Durham, NC: Duke University Press, 2025.
Alexandrowicz, Ra'anan. "50 Years of Documentation: A Brief History of the Audiovisual Documentation of the Israeli Occupation." In *Visual Imagery and Human Rights Practice*, ed. Sandra Ristovska and Monroe Price, 15–34. Cham, Switzerland: Palgrave Macmillan, 2018.
———. "Maia and the Boundaries of the Frame." In "In the Presence of Others," special issue, ed. Nicolas Gamso and Jason Fox, *World Records* 4 (2020): 15–25.
Al-Haq. "Al-Haq Calls on Third States to Publicly Condemn and Call for the Full Rescinding of Israel's Designation of Palestinian Human Rights NGOs as 'Terrorist Organisations.'" October 24, 2021. https://www.alhaq.org/advocacy/19050.html.
Amnesty International. "'You Feel Like You Are Subhuman': Israel's Genocide Against Palestinians in Gaza." December 5, 2024. https://www.amnesty.org/en/documents/mde15/8668/2024/en/.

Anderson, Joel Neville. "Cinema's Prosthesis: (Dis)ability and the Politics of Hara Kazuo and Kobayashi Sachiko's Personal Documentary Practice," 1–32. Unpublished manuscript, June 17, 2019, typescript.

Aneesh, A. *Neutral Accent: How Language, Labor, and Life Became Global.* Durham, NC: Duke University Press, 2015.

Anthony, Scott. "An Introduction to the GPO Film Unit." In *We Live in Two Worlds: The GPO Film Unit Collection Volume Two*, 1–7. London: British Film Institute, 2009.

Apter, Emily. "Shibboleth: Policing by Ear and Forensic Listening in Projects by Lawrence Abu Hamdan." *October* 156 (2016): 100–15.

Arrington, Celeste L. "Disabled People's Fight for Rights in South Korea and Japan." *Current History* 120, no. 827 (2021): 233–39.

Ascheid, Antje. "Speaking Tongues: Voice Dubbing in the Cinema as Cultural Ventriloquism." *Velvet Light Trap* 40 (1997): 32–41.

Aufderheide, Pat, Peter Jaszi, and Mridu Chandra. "Honest Truths: Documentary Filmmakers on Ethical Challenges in Their Work." *Center for Media and Social Impact* (2009): 1–26. https://cmsimpact.org/resource/honest-truths-documentary-filmmakers-on-ethical-challenges-in-their-work/.

Bailey, Stephanie. "Art as Evidence as Art." *Art Monthly* 443 (2021): 6–10.

Balsom, Erika. "The Reality-Based Community." *e-flux* 83 (2017). https://www.e-flux.com/journal/83/142332/the-reality-based-community/.

——. *Ten Skies*. Melbourne: Fireflies, 2021.

Barthes, Roland. *Camera Lucida: Reflections on Photography.* Trans. Richard Howard. London: Hill and Wang, 1981.

Baugh, John. "Linguistic Profiling." In *Black Linguistics: Language, Society, and Politics in Africa and the Americas*, ed. Sinfree Makoni, Geneva Smitherman, Arnetha F. Ball, and Arthur K. Spears, 155–68. New York: Routledge, 2003.

Benjamin, Walter. "The Work of Art in the Age of Its Technological Reproducibility: Third Version." In *Selected Writings of Walter Benjamin, Vol. 4*, ed. Howard Eiland and Michael W. Jennings, 251–83. Cambridge, MA: Harvard University Press, 2002.

Ben-Moshe, Liat. *Decarcerating Disability: Deinstitutionalization and Prison Abolition.* Minneapolis: University of Minnesota Press, 2020.

Berlant, Lauren. "In a Nutshell: On Her Book *Cruel Optimism.*" *Rorotoko*, June 5, 2012. https://www.rorotoko.com/11/20120605-berlant-lauren-on-cruel-optimism.

Bevan, Robert. "Turner Prize–Shortlisted Forensic Architecture's Eyal Weizman: 'I Want to Win Cases–Not Art Prizes.'" *Evening Standard*, July 3, 2018. https://www.standard.co.uk/culture/turner-prizeshortlisted-forensic-architectures-eyal-weizman-i-want-to-win-cases-not-prizes-a3877746.html.

Bois, Yves, Michael Feher, and Hal Foster. "On Forensic Architecture: A Conversation with Eyal Weizman." *October* 156 (2016): 116–40.
Bookman, Mark Ross. "Politics and Prosthetics: 150 Years of Disability in Japan." PhD dissertation. University of Pennsylvania, 2021.
British Film Institute. "GPO Film Unit (1933–1940)." *ScreenOnline*. http://www.screenonline.org.uk/film/id/464254/index.html. Accessed November 11, 2020.
Brown, Michelle. *The Culture of Punishment: Prison, Society, and Spectacle*. New York: New York University Press, 2009.
Bruzzi, Stella. "Making a Genre: The Case of the Contemporary True Crime Documentary." *Law and Humanities* 10, no. 2 (2016): 249–80.
Bull, Michael, and Les Back. "Introduction Into Sound . . . Once More with Feeling." In *The Auditory Culture Reader*, 2nd ed., ed. Michael Bull and Les Back, 1–20. New York: Routledge, 2020.
Cachia, Amanda. "The Politics of Creative Access: Guidelines for a Critical Disa/Ability Curatorial Practice." In *Interdisciplinary Approaches to Disability: Looking Toward the Future, Volume 2*, ed. Katie Ellis, Rosemarie Garland-Thomson, Mike Kend, and Rachel Robertson, 99–108. London: Routledge, 2019.
Calhoun, Craig. "The Idea of Emergency: Humanitarian Action and Global (Dis)Order." In *Contemporary States of Emergency: The Politics of Military and Humanitarian Intervention*, ed. Didier Fassin and Mariella Pandolfi, 29–58. New York: Zone, 2010.
Callus, Anne-Marie. "The Poetics of Touch: Mediating the Reality of Deafblindness in *Planet of Snail*." In *Documentary and Disability*, ed. Catalin Brylla and Helen Hughes, 145–58. London: Palgrave Macmillan, 2017.
Campana, Andrew. "You Forbid Me to Walk: Yokota Hiroshi's Disability Poetics." *positions: asia critique* 30, no. 4 (2022): 735–62.
Campt, Tina M. *Listening to Images*. Durham, NC: Duke University Press, 2017.
——. "Black Visuality and the Practice of Refusal." In "Performing Refusal/Refusing to Perform," special issue, ed. Lilian G. Mengesha and Lakshmi Padmanabhan, *Women and Performance* 29, no. 1 (2019). https://www.womenandperformance.org/ampersand/29-1/campt.
Carillo Rowe, Aimee, Sheena Malhotra, and Kimberlee Pérez. *Answer the Call: Virtual Migration in Indian Call Centers*. Minneapolis: University of Minnesota Press, 2013.
Carrasco, Nicolás. "Interview: Kazuo Hara and Sachiko Kobayashi." *Desistfilm*, August 28, 2019. https://desistfilm.com/interview-kazuo-hara-sachiko-kobayashi/.
Crenshaw, Kimberlé, and Gary Peller. "Reel Time/Real Justice." In *Reading Rodney King/Reading Urban Uprising*, ed. Robert Gooding-Williams, 56–70. London: Taylor and Francis, 1993.

Chamarette, Jennifer. "Backdating the Crip Technoscience Manifesto: Stephen Dwoskin's Digital Activism." *Film Quarterly* 76, no. 2 (2022): 16–24.

Charlton, Bruce. "Audit, Accountability, Quality, and All That: The Growth of Managerial Technologies in UK Universities." In *Education! Education! Education! Managerial Ethics and the Law of Unintended Consequences*, ed. Stephen Prickett and Patricia Erskine-Hill, 13–28. Thorverton, UK: Imprint Academic, 2002.

Chase, Alisia. "Learning to Be Human: An Interview with William Pope.L," *Afterimage* 33 no. 4 (2006): 20–23.

Chen, Nancy N. "'Speaking Nearby': A Conversation with Trinh T. Minh-ha." *Visual Anthropology Review* 8, no. 1 (1992): 82–91.

Childress, Sonya. "Beyond Empathy." *Firelight Media*, March 20, 2017. https://firelightmedia.medium.com/beyond-empathy-ad6b5ad8a1d8.

Childress, Sonya, and Natalie Bullock-Brown. "The Documentary Future: A Call for Accountability." *Documentary*, July 2, 2020. https://www.documentary.org/feature/documentary-future-call-accountability.

Chion, Michel. *Audio-Vision: Sound on Screen*. Trans. Claudia Gorbman. New York: Columbia University Press, 1994.

———. *The Voice in Cinema*. Trans. Claudia Gorbman. New York: Columbia University Press, 1999.

———. *Words on Screen*. Trans. Claudia Gorbman. New York: Columbia University Press, 2017.

Chow, Rey. "After the Passage of the Beast: 'False Documentary' Aspirations, Acousmatic Complications." In *Rancière and Film*, ed. Paul Bowman, 34–52. Edinburgh: Edinburgh University Press, 2013.

———. *Not Like a Native Speaker: On Languaging as a Postcolonial Experience*. New York: Columbia University Press, 2014.

———. *A Face Drawn in Sand: Humanistic Inquiry and Foucault in the Present*. New York: Columbia University Press, 2021.

Clark, John Lee. "Against Access." *McSweeney's* 64: The Audio Issue. https://audio.mcsweeneys.net/transcripts/against_access.html. Accessed July 5, 2022.

Clover, Carol. "Law and the Order of Popular Culture." In *Law in the Domains of Culture*, ed. Austin Sarat and Thomas R. Kearns, 97–120. Ann Arbor: University of Michigan Press, 1998.

Connor, Steven. *Dumbstruck: A Cultural History of Ventriloquism*. Oxford: Oxford University Press, 2001.

Corner, John. *The Art of Record: A Critical Introduction to Documentary*. Manchester: Manchester University Press, 1996.

———. "Performing the Real: Documentary Diversions." *Television and New Media* 3, no. 3 (2002): 255–69.

Couldry, Nick. *Why Voice Matters: Culture and Politics After Neoliberalism.* London: Sage, 2010.

Cox, Geoffrey and John Corner. *Soundings: Documentary Film and the Listening Experience.* Huddersfield: University of Huddersfield Press, 2018.

Daston, Lorraine, and Peter Galison, *Objectivity.* New York: Zone, 2007.

Davé, Shilpa. *Indian Accents: Brown Voice and Racial Performance in American Film and Television.* Urbana-Champaign: University of Illinois Press, 2013.

Davis, Angela Y. *Are Prisons Obsolete?* New York: Seven Stories, 2003.

Davis, Angela Y., Gina Dent, Erica R. Meiners, and Beth E. Richie, *Abolition. Feminism. Now.* Chicago: Haymarket, 2022.

Deleuze, Gilles. *Foucault.* Minneapolis: University of Minnesota Press, 1988.

Dolar, Mladen. *A Voice and Nothing More.* Cambridge, MA: MIT Press, 2006.

Dolmage, Jay. *Disability Rhetoric.* Syracuse, NY: Syracuse University Press, 2016.

———. *Academic Ableism: Disability and Higher Education.* Ann Arbor: University of Michigan Press, 2017.

Dublon, Amalle, and Constantina Zavitsanos. "Dependency and Improvisation: A Conversation with Park McArthur." In "Disability and the Politics of Visibility," special issue, ed. Emily Watlington, *Art Papers* 42, no. 4 (2018/2019): 52–54.

Dyson, Frances. "The Genealogy of the Radio Voice." In *Radio Rethink: Art, Sound, and Transmission,* ed. Daina Augaitis and Dan Lander, 167–86. Banff, AB: Banff Center, 1994.

Eidsheim, Nina Sun. *The Race of Sound: Listening, Timbre, and Vocality in African American Music.* Durham, NC: Duke University Press, 2019.

———. "Re-writing Algorithms for Just Recognition: From Digital Aural Redlining to Accent Activism." In *Thinking with an Accent: Toward a New Object, Method, and Practice,* ed. Pooja Rangan, Akshya Saxena, Ragini Tharoor Srinivasan, and Pavitra Sundar, 134–50. Berkeley: University of California Press, 2023.

Egoyan, Atom, and Ian Balfour. "Introduction." In *Subtitles: On the Foreignness of Film,* ed. Atom Egoyan and Ian Balfour, 3–13. Cambridge, MA: MIT Press, 2004.

———, ed., *Subtitles: On the Foreignness of Film.* Cambridge, MA: MIT Press, 2004.

Ellcessor, Elizabeth. *Restricted Access: Media, Disability, and the Politics of Participation.* New York: New York University Press, 2016.

Ellis, Katie. *Disability and Digital Television Cultures: Representation, Access, and Reception.* New York: Routledge, 2019.

Estefan, Kareem. "Narrating Living and Looted Palestinian Archives: Reparative Fabulation in Azza El-Hassan's *Kings and Extras*." *Feminist Media Histories* 8, no. 2 (2022): 43–69.

Evans, Maxwell. "5 Shots on 71st Street: New Investigation Challenges Police Narrative of Harith Augustus Death." *Block Club Chicago*, October 3, 2019. https://blockclubchicago.org/2019/10/03/5-shots-on-71st-street-new-investigation-challenges-police-narrative-of-harith-augustus-death/.

Fabian, Johannes. *Time and the Other: How Anthropology Makes Its Object*. New York: Columbia University Press, 1983.

Farocki, Harun. "Phantom Images." *Public* 29, no. 1 (2004): 13–22.

Fassin, Didier, and Mariella Pandolfi. "Introduction." In *Contemporary States of Emergency: The Politics of Military and Humanitarian Interventions*. New York: Zone, 2010.

Felman, Shoshana, and Dori Laub. *Testimony: Crises of Witnessing in Literature, Psychoanalysis, and History*. New York: Routledge, 1992.

FitzSimons, Trish. "Braided Channels: A Genealogy of the Voice of Documentary." *Studies in Documentary Film* 3, no. 2 (2009): 131–46.

Fleetwood, Nicole R. *Marking Time: Art in the Age of Mass Incarceration*. Cambridge, MA: Harvard University Press, 2020.

Flores, Nelson, and Jonathan Rosa. "Undoing Appropriateness: Raciolinguistic Ideologies and Language Diversity in Education." *Harvard Educational Review* 85, no. 2 (2015): 149–71.

Forensic Architecture, ed. *Forensic: The Architecture of Public Truth* (Berlin: Sternberg Press and Forensic Architecture, 2014).

French, Lisa. *The Female Gaze in Documentary Film: An International Perspective*. New York: Palgrave Macmillan, 2021.

Fuller, Matthew, and Eyal Weizman. *Investigative Aesthetics: Conflicts and Commons in the Politics of Truth*. New York: Verso, 2021.

Furuhata, Yuriko. *Cinema of Actuality: Japanese Avant-Garde Filmmaking in the Season of Image Politics*. Durham, NC: Duke University Press, 2013.

FWD-Doc, in association with Doc Society, supported by Netflix. "A Toolkit for Inclusion & Accessibility: Changing the Narrative of Disability in Documentary Film." https://www.fwd-doc.org/toolkit. Accessed August 8, 2024.

Gabriel, Peter. "Video Will Bring Us Justice in the Long Run." *Time*. May 16, 2017. https://time.com/4781418/peter-gabriel-video-justice/.

Garland-Thomson, Rosemarie. "Ways of Staring." *Journal of Visual Culture* 5, no. 2 (2006): 173–92.

———. "The Story of My Work: How I Became Disabled." *Disability Studies Quarterly* 34, no. 2 (2014). https://dsq-sds.org/article/view/4254/3594.
Gilmore, Ruth Wilson. *Golden Gulag: Prisons, Surplus, Crisis, and Opposition in Globalizing California*. Berkeley: University of California Press, 2007.
Ginsburg, Faye, and Rayna Rapp. *Disability Worlds*. Durham, NC: Duke University Press, 2024.
Gitelman, Lisa. *Always Already New: Media, History, and the Data of Culture*. Cambridge, MA: MIT Press, 2006.
Global Impact Producers Alliance. "Frequently Asked Questions." https://globalimpactproducers.org/faqs/. Accessed July 23, 2024.
Goo, Emerson. "Remains to Be Seen: The Video Work of Forensic Architecture." *Mubi*, May 11, 2021. https://mubi.com/en/notebook/posts/remains-to-be-seen-the-video-work-of-forensic-architecture.
Gorz, André. *Strategy for Labor: A Radical Proposal*. Boston: Beacon, 1967.
Greenberg, Slava. "(Dis)abling the Spectator: Embodying Disability Experience in Animated Documentary." In *Documentary and Disability*, ed. Catalin Brylla and Helen Hughes, 129–44. London: Palgrave Macmillan, 2017.
Grigely, Joseph, and Emily Watlington. Conversation, New York University Center for Disability Studies, April 9, 2021.
Guenther, Lisa. "Seeing Like a Cop: A Critical Phenomenology of Whiteness as Property." In *Race as Phenomena: Between Phenomenology and Philosophy of Race*, ed. Emily S. Lee, 189–206. London: Rowman & Littlefield, 2019.
Guerin, Frances, and Roger Hallas. "Introduction." In *The Image and the Witness: Trauma, Memory, and Visual Culture*, ed. Frances Guerin and Roger Hallas, 1–22. London: Wallflower, 2007.
Guilford, Josh, and Toby Lee. "Introduction: Documentary World-Making." In "Documentary World-Making," dossier, ed. Josh Guilford and Toby Lee, *World Records* 4 (2020): 163–69.
Gulliver, Katrina. "Catfishing in the Ivory Tower." *Arc Digital*, September 21, 2020. https://arcdigital.media/identity-fraud-26e05a72fd82.
Hall, Jeanne. "Realism as a Style in *Cinema Vérité*: A Critical Analysis of *Primary*." *Cinema Journal* 30, no. 4 (1991): 24–50.
Hall, Stuart. "Encoding/Decoding." In *Culture, Media, Language*, ed. Stuart Hall, Dorothy Hobson, Andrew Lowe, and Paul Willis, 117–27. London: Routledge, 1980.
Halpern, Orit. *Beautiful Data: A History of Vision and Reason Since 1945*. Durham, NC: Duke University Press, 2014.
Hamraie, Aimi. *Building Access: Universal Design and the Politics of Disability*. Minneapolis: University of Minnesota Press, 2017.

Hara, Kazuo. *Camera Obtrusa: The Action Documentaries of Hara Kazuo.* Trans. Pat Noonan and Takuo Yasuda. New York: Kaya, 2009.

Harp, Tania Osorio. "Is Forensic Architecture the New Muralism of the Mexican State? A Reflection on Racialized Violence and the Construction of Mexican Identity." *Journal of Urban Cultural Studies* 5, no. 3 (2018): 371–80.

Hartman, Saidiya V. *Scenes of Subjection: Terror, Slavery, and Self-Making in Nineteenth-Century America.* New York: Oxford University Press, 1997.

Hayashi, Reiko, and Masako Okuhira. "The Disability Rights Movement in Japan: Past, Present, and Future." *Disability and Society* 16, no. 6 (2001): 855–69.

Heather, Kade. "Jury rules in favor of CPD officers in 2018 fatal shooting of barber Harith Augustus in South Shore." *Chicago Sun-Times*, July 7, 2023. https://chicago.suntimes.com/crime/2023/7/7/23787787/jury-rules-in-favor-of-cpd-officers-in-2018-fatal-shooting-of-barber-harith-augustus-in-south-shore.

Hendren, Sara. *What Can a Body Do?* New York: Riverhead, 2020.

Heyer, Katharina. *Rights Enabled: The Disability Revolution from the US, to Germany and Japan, to the United Nations.* Ann Arbor: University of Michigan Press, 2015.

Honess Roe, Annabelle. "Playing God: Film Stars as Documentary Narrators." In *Vocal Projections: Voices in Documentary*, ed. Annabelle Honess Roe and Maria Pramaggiore, 11–27. New York: Bloomsbury Academic, 2018.

Honess Roe, Annabelle, and Maria Pramaggiore, ed. *Vocal Projections: Voices in Documentary.* New York: Bloomsbury Academic, 2018.

Hou, Lynn, and Rezenet Moges. "'SORRY HARD UNDERSTAND STRONG ACCENT!': Racial Dynamics of Deaf Scholars of Color Working with White Female Interpreters." In Rangan et al., *Thinking with an Accent*, 151–72.

International Documentary Organization. The Non-Fiction Core Application Project. https://www.documentary.org/nonfiction-core-application-project. Accessed August 11, 2024.

Iversen, Gunnar. *Beyond the Visual: Sound and Image in Ethnographic and Documentary Film.* Aarhus: Intervention, 2010.

Jackson, Lauren Michele. "The Layered Deceptions of Jessica Krug, the Black Studies Professor Who Hid That She Is White." *New Yorker*, September 12, 2020. https://www.newyorker.com/culture/cultural-comment/the-layered-deceptions-of-jessica-krug-the-black-studies-professor-who-hid-that-she-is-white.

Jaikumar, Priya. *Where Histories Reside: India as Filmed Space.* Durham, NC: Duke University Press, 2019.

Johnston, Gordon, and Emma Robertson. *BBC World Service: Overseas Broadcasting, 1932–2018.* London: Palgrave Macmillan, 2019.

Jeffay, Tory. "Fatty Arbuckle's Fingerprints: Race, Photographic Evidence, and the Smudge." *Journal of Cinema and Media Studies* 64, no. 2 (2025): 78–101.

Jesty, Justin. "Image Pragmatics and Film as a Lived Practice in the Documentary Work of Hani Susumu and Tsuchimoto Noriaki." In "Developments in the Japanese Documentary Mode," special issue, ed. Marcos Centeno and Michael Raine, *Arts* 8, no. 41 (2019): 1–18. https://www.mdpi.com/2076-0752/8/2/41.

Juhasz, Alexandra, and Alisa Lebow. "Introduction: Beyond Story." In "Beyond Story," special issue, ed. Alexandra Juhasz and Alisa Lebow, *World Records* 5 (2021): 9–13.

Juhasz, Alexandra, and Alisa Lebow. "Beyond Story: An Online, Community-Based Manifesto." In "Ways of Organizing," special issue," ed. Jason Fox and Laliv Melamed, *World Records* 2 (2018): 1–5.

Kaba, Mariame. "Police 'Reforms' You Should Always Oppose." *Truthout*, December 7, 2014. https://truthout.org/articles/police-reforms-you-should-always-oppose/.

———. *We Do This 'Til We Free Us: Abolitionist Organizing and Transforming Justice*. Chicago: Haymarket, 2021.

Kafer, Alison. *Feminist, Queer, Crip*. Bloomington: Indiana University Press, 2013.

Kahana, Jonathan. "Introduction to Section 1." In *The Documentary Film Reader*, ed. Jonathan Kahana, 13–15. Oxford: Oxford University Press, 2016.

Kalven, Jamie, and Eyal Weizman. "How Chicago Police Created a False Narrative After Officers Killed Harith Augustus." *Intercept*, September 19, 2019. https://theintercept.com/2019/09/19/harith-augustus-shooting-chicago-police/.

Kang, Edward B. "On the Praxes and Politics of AI Speech Emotion Recognition." *FAccT* (June 12–15, 2023): 455–66.

Kasnitz, Devva. "The Politics of Disability Performativity: An Autoethnography." *Current Anthropology* 61, supp. 21 (2020): S16–S25.

Keenan, Thomas. "Getting the Dead to Tell Me What Happened: Justice, Prosopopoeia, and Forensic Afterlives." In Forensic Architecture, *Forensis*, 35–55.

———. "Counter-forensics and Photography." *Grey Room* 55 (2014): 58–77.

———. "Mobilizing Shame." *South Atlantic Quarterly* 103, no. 2/3 (2004): 435–49.

Keenan, Thomas, and Eyal Weizman. *Mengele's Skull: The Advent of a Forensic Aesthetics*. Berlin: Sternberg, 2012.

Kessler, Sarah. "The Voice of Mockumentary." In *Vocal Projections: Voices in Documentary*, ed. Annabelle Honess Roe and Maria Pramaggiore, 137–52. New York: Bloomsbury Academic, 2018.

Khosravi, Shahram. "Doing Migration Studies with an Accent." *Journal of Ethnic and Migration Studies* 50, no. 9 (2024): 2346–58.

Kim, Jina B. "Cripping the Welfare Queen: The Radical Potential of Disability Politics?" Lecture, University of Minnesota Critical Disability Studies Research Colloquium, October 9, 2020.

Kim, Jina B., and Sami Schalk. "Reclaiming the Radical Politics of Self-Care: A Crip-of-Color Critique." *South Atlantic Quarterly* 120, no. 2 (2021): 325–42.

———. "Integrating Race, Transforming Feminist Disability Studies," *Signs* 46, no. 1 (2020): 31–55.

Kleege, Georgina. "Audio Description Described: Current Standards, Future Innovations, Larger Implications." *Representations* 135 (2016): 89–101.

Kozloff, Sarah. *Invisible Storytellers: Voice-Over Narration in American Fiction Film*. Berkeley: University of California Press, 1988.

Krzych, Scott. *Beyond Bias: Conservative Media, Documentary Form, and the Politics of Hysteria*. New York: Oxford University Press, 2021.

Sadato, Kuniko. *Kansai shōgaisha undō no gendaishi—Osaka aoi shiba no kai o chūshin ni* ("Modern History of Disability Movement in Kansai Area: Focusing on Osaka Aoi Shiba no Kai") (2011). http://www.arsvi.com/o/aoi-e.htm. Accessed April 19, 2024.

Lacey, Kate. *Listening Publics*. Cambridge: Polity, 2013.

Lambert, Leopold. "Making Abolition Geography in California's Central Valley: Interview with Ruth Wilson Gilmore." *The Funambulist*, December 18, 2018. https://thefunambulist.net/magazine/21-space-activism/interview-making-abolition-geography-california-central-valley-ruth-wilson-gilmore.

Lazard, Carolyn, Constantina Zavitsanos, Jordan Lord, Albert Lord, and Deborah Lord, Panel Discussion, New York University Center for Disability Studies, May 7, 2020.

Lebow, Alisa. "Shooting with Intent: Framing Conflict." In *Killer Images: Documentary Film, Memory, and the Performance of Violence*, ed. Joram ten Brink, 41–62. New York: Columbia University Press, 2013.

Lee, Li-Young. *The Winged Seed: A Remembrance*. New York: Simon & Schuster, 1995.

Lee, Toby. "The Radical Unreal: Fabulation and Fantasy in Speculative Documentary." *Film Quarterly* 74, no. 4 (2021): 9–18.

———. "Occult Operations: Notes Toward a Politics of Operativity." Lecture, Brown University, Providence, RI, March 17, 2023.

Lee, Toby, Laliv Melamed, Pooja Rangan, Paige Sarlin, and Benjamín Schultz-Figueroa. "Documentary (adj.): Keywords and Provocations." In "Dossier on 'Documentary' (Adj.)," *Millennium Film Journal* 74 (2021): 82.

Leimbacher, Irina. "Hearing Voice(s): Experiments with Documentary Listening." In "Documentary Audibilities," special issue, ed. Pooja Rangan and Genevieve Yue, *Discourse* 39, no. 3 (2017): 292–318.

Liboiron, Max. *Pollution Is Colonialism*. Durham, NC: Duke University Press, 2021.

Linton, Simi. *Claiming Disability: Knowledge and Identity*. New York: New York University Press, 1998.

Lipari, Lisbeth. *Listening, Thinking, Being: Toward an Ethics of Attunement*. University Park: Pennsylvania State University Press, 2014.

Lippi-Green, Rosina. *English with an Accent: Language, Ideology, and Discrimination in the United States*, 2nd ed. New York: Routledge, 2012.

Lord, Jordan. "Shared Resources (Contractual Obligations)." MFA thesis. City University of New York School of Arts and Sciences, 2019.

Lorenz, Chris. "If You're So Smart, Why Are You Under Surveillance? Universities, Neoliberalism, and New Public Management." *Critical Inquiry* 38, no. 3 (2012): 599–629.

Lovell, Alan, and Jim Hillier. *Studies in Documentary*. London: Secker and Warburg for the British Film Institute, 1972.

MacDonald, Scott. *A Critical Cinema: Interviews with Independent Filmmakers, Vol. 3*. Berkeley: University of California Press, 1988.

Maitra, Ani. "The Persistence of the Other: Revisiting the (Post-)Colonial Scene of Fragmentation," 1–8. Paper presented at the American Comparative Literature Association Conference, Utrecht University, June 7, 2017.

Malitsky, Joshua. "Introduction." In *A Companion to Documentary Film History*, ed. Joshua Malitsky, xi–xx. New Jersey: Wiley-Blackwell, 2021.

Mansell, James G. "Rhythm, Modernity, and the Politics of Sound." In *The Projection of Britain: A History of the GPO Film Unit*, ed. Scott Anthony and James G. Mansell, 161–67. London: British Film Institute, 2011.

Marschall, Anika, and Ann-Christine Simke. "Forensic Architecture in the Theater and the Gallery: A Reflection on Counterhegemonic Potentials and Pitfalls of Art Institutions." *Theater Research International* 47, no. 2 (2022): 142–59.

McEnany, Tom. "This American Voice: The Odd Timbre of a New Standard in Public Radio." In *The Oxford Handbook of Voice Studies*, ed. Nina Sun Eidsheim and Katherine Meizel, 97–124. Oxford: Oxford University Press, 2019.

McGranahan, Carole. "Theorizing Refusal: An Introduction." *Cultural Anthropology* 31, no. 3 (2016): 319–25.

McRuer, Robert. *Crip Theory: Cultural Signs of Queerness and Disability*. New York: New York University Press, 2006.

Melamed, Laliv. "Operative Imaginaries." *NECSUS* (2021). https://necsus-ejms.org/operative-imaginaries/#_ednref2.

———. *Sovereign Intimacy: Private Media and the Traces of Colonial Violence*. Berkeley: University of California Press, 2023.

Melamed, Laliv, and Ra'anan Alexandrowicz. Postscreening conversation, Visible Evidence Conference, Frankfurt, December 2021.

Mills, Mara. "Listening to Images: Audio Description, the Translation Overlay, and Image Retrieval." *Cine-Files* 8 (2015). https://www.thecine-files.com/listening-to-images-audio-description-the-translation-overlay-and-image-retrieval/.

———. "Lessons in Queer Voice." *Amodern 9: Techniques and Technologies* (2020). https://amodern.net/article/queer-voice/.

Mills, Mara, and Neta Alexander. "Scores: Carolyn Lazard's Crip Minimalism." *Film Quarterly* 76, no. 2 (2022): 39–47.

Mills, Mara, and Rebecca Sanchez, with Constantina Zavitsanos. "Giving It Away: Constantina Zavitsanos on Disability, Debt, Dependency." In "Disability and the Politics of Visibility," special issue, ed. Emily Watlington, *Art Papers* 42, no. 4 (2018/2019): 62–65.

Mills, Quincy T. *Cutting Along the Color Line: Black Barbers and Barber Shops in America*. Philadelphia: University of Pennsylvania Press, 2013.

Mingus, Mia. "Access Intimacy, Interdependence, and Disability Justice." *Leaving Evidence*, April 12, 2017. https://leavingevidence.wordpress.com/2017/04/12/access-intimacy-interdependence-and-disability-justice/.

———. "Transformative Justice: A Brief Description." *Leaving Evidence*, January 9, 2019. https://leavingevidence.wordpress.com/2019/01/09/transformative-justice-a-brief-description/.

Mitchell, David T., and Sharon L. Snyder. *The Biopolitics of Disability: Neoliberalism, Ablenationalism, and Peripheral Embodiment*. Ann Arbor, MI: University of Michigan Press, 2015.

———. "Talking About Talking Back: Afterthoughts on the Making of the Disability Documentary *Vital Signs: Crip Culture Talks Back*." *Michigan Quarterly Review* 37, no. 2 (1998): 316–36.

Mithout, Anne-Lise. "Sayōnara CP: The First Filmic Representation of the Japanese Dis/ability Rights Movement." In *Dis/ability in Media, Law and History: Intersectional, Embodied and Socially Constructed?* ed. Micky Lee, Frank Rudy Cooper, and Patricia Reeve, 134–49. New York: Routledge, 2022.

Morris, Errol. "The Fog of War: 13 Questions and Answers on the Filmmaking of Errol Morris by Errol Morris." *FLM* (2004). Archived at https://www.errolmorris.com/content/eyecontact/interrotron.html. Accessed July 27, 2022.

Morris, Loveday, Lorenzo Tugnoli, and Sufian Taha. "In Israeli-Occupied Hebron, Palestinians Describe Living in 'a Prison.'" *Washington Post*, February 28, 2024. https://www.washingtonpost.com/world/2024/02/28/west-bank-hebron-israel-occupation/.

Mowitt, John. *Sounds: The Ambient Humanities*. Oakland: University of California Press, 2015.

Mugglestone, Lynda. "Accent as a Social Symbol." In *The Handbook of English Pronunciation*, ed. Marnie Reed and John M. Levis, 19–35. London: Wiley, 2015.

Murray, Rona. "British women documentary filmmakers 1930–1955, 5 April 2019: one day symposium at the London School of Economics." *Media Practice and Education* 20, no. 3 (2019): 297–301.

Naficy, Hamid. *An Accented Cinema: Exilic and Diasporic Filmmaking*. Princeton, NJ: Princeton University Press, 2001.

———. "King Rodney: The Rodney King Video and Textual Analysis." In *The End of Cinema as We Know It: American Film in the Nineties*, ed. Jon Lewis, 300–304. New York: New York University Press, 2001.

Naficy, Hamid. "Epistolarity and Textuality in Accented Films." In *Subtitles: On the Foreignness of Film*, ed. Atom Egoyan and Ian Balfour, 132–51. Cambridge, MA: MIT Press, 2004.

Nagib, Lúcia. "Filmmaking as the Production of Reality: A Study of Hara and Kobayashi's Documentaries." In *Realism and the Audiovisual Media*, ed. Lúcia Nagib and Cecilia Mello, 193–209. New York: Palgrave Macmillan, 2009.

Nichols, Bill. "The Voice of Documentary." *Film Quarterly* 36, no. 6 (1983): 17–30.

———. *Representing Reality*. Bloomington: Indiana University Press, 1991.

———. *Speaking Truths with Film: Evidence, Ethics, Politics in Documentary*. Oakland: University of California Press, 2016.

———. *Introduction to Documentary*, 3rd ed. Bloomington: Indiana University Press, 2017.

Nichols, Bill, with Jaimie Baron. *Introduction to Documentary*, 4th ed. Bloomington: Indiana University Press, 2024.

Nicholson, James. "Vocal Hierarchy in Documentary." In *Vocal Projections: Voices in Documentary*, ed. Annabelle Honess Roe and Maria Pramaggiore, 219–33. New York: Bloomsbury Academic, 2019.

Nornes, Abé Markus. "For an Abusive Subtitling." *Film Quarterly* 52, no. 3 (1999): 17–34.

———. "The Postwar Documentary Trace: Groping in the Dark." *Positions* 10, no. 1 (2002): 39–78.

———. "Private Reality: Hara Kazuo's Films." In *Rites of Realism*, ed. Ivone Margulies, 144–63. Durham, NC: Duke University Press, 2003.

Okada, Jun. "Hara Kazuo and *Extreme Private Eros: Love Song 1974*." In *Exploiting East Asian Cinemas: Genre, Circulation, Reception*, ed. Ken Provencher and Mike Dillon, 171–87. New York: Bloomsbury Academic, 2018.

O'Reilly, Sean. "'Disarmed': Disability, Trauma, and Emasculation in Contemporary Japanese Cinema." *Arts* 7 no. 1 (2018): 1–10.

Osamu, Nagase. "Development of Disability Studies in Japan: A Brief Outline." *Disability Studies Quarterly* 28, no. 3 (2008): https://dsq-sds.org/index.php/dsq/article/view/116/116.

Padios, Jan M. *A Nation on the Line: Call Centers as Postcolonial Predicaments in the Philippines.* Durham, NC: Duke University Press, 2018.

Parikka, Jussi. "Operational Images: Between Data and Light." *eflux* 133 (2023). https://www.e-flux.com/journal/133/515812/operational-images-between-light-and-data/.

Parker, James E. K. *Acoustic Jurisprudence: Listening to the Trial of Simon Bikindi.* Oxford: Oxford University Press, 2015.

Pfeifer, Michelle. "Data and Borders: Tracking Media Technologies of Migration Control in Europe." PhD dissertation. New York University, 2022.

———Pfeifer, Michelle. "'The Native Ear': Accented Testimonial Desire and Asylum." In Rangan et al., *Thinking with an Accent*, 192–207.

———. "Your Voice is (Not) Your Passport." *Sounding Out* (June 12, 2023). https://soundstudiesblog.com/author/mitchpfeifer/.

Piepzna-Samarasinha, Leah Lakshmi. *Care Work: Dreaming Disability Justice.* Vancouver: Arsenal Pulp, 2019.

POV. "North By Current Discussion Guide." https://www.pbs.org/pov/resources/north-current-discussion-guide/. Accessed August 12, 2024.

Price, Margaret. "Time Harms: Disabled Faculty Navigating the Accommodations Loop." In "Crip Temporalities," special issue, ed. Ellen Samuels and Elizabeth Freeman, *South Atlantic Quarterly* 120, no. 2 (2021): 257–77.

Puar, Jasbir. *The Right to Maim: Debility, Capacity, Disability.* Durham, NC: Duke University Press, 2017.

Ramjattan, Vijay A. "Accent Reduction as Raciolinguistic Pedagogy." In Rangan et al., *Thinking with an Accent*, 37–53.

Rancière, Jacques. *The Politics of Aesthetics.* Trans. Gabriel Rockhill. London: Bloomsbury Academic, 2013.

Rangan, Pooja. "Audibilities: Voice and Listening in the Penumbra of Documentary." In "Documentary Audibilities," special issue, ed. Pooja Rangan and Genevieve Yue, *Discourse* 39, no. 3 (2017): 279–91.

———. *Immediations: The Humanitarian Impulse in Documentary.* Durham, NC: Duke University Press, 2017.

———. "Documentary Listening Habits: From Voice to Audibility." In *The Oxford Handbook of Film Theory*, ed. by Kyle Stevens, 403–20. Oxford: Oxford University Press, 2022.

Rangan, Pooja, and Brett Story. "Four Propositions on True Crime and Abolition." In "Beyond Story," special issue, ed. Alexandra Juhasz and Alisa Lebow, *World Records* 5 (2021): 1–8.

Rangan, Pooja, Akshya Saxena, Ragini Tharoor Srinivasan, and Pavitra Sundar. "Introduction: Thinking with an Accent." In Rangan et al., *Thinking with an Accent*, 1–20.

Rangan, Pooja, and Genevieve Yue, ed. "Documentary Audibilities," special issue, ed. Pooja Rangan and Genevieve Yue, *Discourse* 39, no. 3 (2017): 279–91.

Renov, Michael. "Bearing Witness: The Documentary Art of Testimony." Conference paper presented at Expanded Documentary: Extensions, Movements, and Reconfigurations, Paris, May 28–29, 2019.

Richards, Jeffrey. "John Grierson and the Lost World of the GPO Film Unit." In *The Projection of Britain: A History of the GPO Film Unit*, ed. Scott Anthony and James G. Mansell, 1–9. London: British Film Institute, 2011.

Robinson, Dylan. *Hungry Listening: Resonant Theory for Indigenous Sound Studies*. Minneapolis: University of Minnesota Press, 2020.

Rogers, Holly, ed. *Music and Sound in Documentary Film*. New York: Routledge, 2014.

Rony, Fatimah Tobing. *The Third Eye: Race, Cinema and Ethnographic Spectacle*. Durham, NC: Duke University Press, 1996.

Rosa, Jonathan, and Nelson Flores. "Do You Hear What I Hear? Raciolinguistic Ideologies and Culturally Sustaining Pedagogies." In *Culturally Sustaining Pedagogies: Teaching and Learning for Justice in a Changing World*, ed. Django Paris and H. Samy Alim, 175–90. New York: Teachers College, 2017.

Rosen, Philip. "Now and Then: On the Documentary Regime, Vertov, and History." In *A Companion to Documentary Film History*, ed. Joshua Malitsky, 187–206. Hoboken: Wiley-Blackwell, 2021.

Samuels, Ellen. "Six Ways of Looking at Crip Time." *Disability Studies Quarterly* 37, no. 3 (2017). https://dsq-sds.org/article/view/5824/4684.

Samuels, Ellen, and Elizabeth Freeman. "Introduction: Crip Temporalities." In "Crip Temporalities," special issue, ed. Ellen Samuels and Elizabeth Freeman, *South Atlantic Quarterly* 120, no. 2 (2021): 245–54.

Sandahl, Carrie. "Queering the Crip or Cripping the Queer? Intersections of Queer and Crip Identities in Solo Autobiographical Performance." *GLQ* 9, no. 1–2 (2003): 25–56.

Sarlin, Paige. "Documentary Value." In "Dossier on 'Documentary' (Adj.)," *Millennium Film Journal* 74 (2021): 86–87.

Satō, Shigechika. "Arawaredeta nyū shinema gundan—Hara Kazuo kantoku 'Sayōnara CP'" ("Hara Kazuo's *Goodbye CP*: A New Cinema Group Has Appeared"). *Eiga Hyōron* 31, no. 4 (1972): 52–53.

Scarry, Elaine. *Thinking in an Emergency*. New York: Norton, 2011.

Schuppli, Susan. *Material Witness: Media, Forensics, Evidence*. Cambridge, MA: MIT Press, 2020.

Scott, James C. *Seeing Like a State: How Certain Schemes to Improve the Human Condition Have Failed*. New Haven, CT: Yale University Press, 1999.

Sekula, Allan. "Photography and the Limits of National Identity." *Culturefront* 2, no. 3 (1993): 54–55.

Shome, Raka. "Thinking Through Diaspora: Call Centers, India, and a New Politics of Hybridity." *International Journal of Cultural Studies* 9, no. 105 (2006): 105–24.

Siebers, Tobin. *Disability Theory*. Ann Arbor: University of Michigan Press, 2008.

———. *Disability Aesthetics*. Ann Arbor: University of Michigan Press, 2010.

Silverman, Kaja. *The Acoustic Mirror: The Female Voice in Psychoanalysis and Cinema*. Bloomington: Indiana University Press, 1988.

Simpson, Audra. "The Ruse of Consent and the Anatomy of 'Refusal': Cases from Indigenous North America and Australia." *Postcolonial Studies* 20, no. 1 (2017): 18–33.

Sinha, Amresh. "The Use and Abuse of Subtitles." In *Subtitles: On the Foreignness of Film*, ed. Atom Egoyan and Ian Balfour, 172–90. Cambridge, MA: MIT Press, 2004.

Skoller, Jeffrey. "iDocument Police: Contingency, Resistance, and the Precarious Present." In "In the Presence of Others," special issue, ed. Nicolas Gamso and Jason Fox, *World Records* 1 (2017): 1–17.

Sliwinski, Sharon. *Human Rights in Camera*. Chicago: University of Chicago Press, 2011.

Smith, Patrick Brian, and Ryan Watson. "Mediated Forensics and Militant Evidence: Rethinking the Camera as Weapon." *Media, Culture, and Society* 45, no. 1 (2023): 36–56.

Starosielski, Nicole. "Depth Mediators: Undersea Cables, Network Infrastructure, and the Deep Ocean." In *Deep Mediations: Thinking Space in Cinema and Digital Cultures*, ed. Karen Redrobe and Jeff Scheible, 262–85. Minneapolis: University of Minnesota Press, 2020.

Stein, Rebecca L. "The Boy Who Wasn't Really Killed: Israeli State Violence in the Age of the Smartphone Witness." *International Journal of Middle East Studies* 53 (2021): 620–38.

Sterne, Jonathan. *The Audible Past: Cultural Origins of Sound Reproduction*. Durham, NC: Duke University Press, 2003.

———. *Diminished Faculties: A Political Phenomenology of Impairment*. Durham, NC: Duke University Press, 2021.

Stockton, Kathryn Bond. "Growing Sideways, or Versions of the Queer Child." In *Curiouser: On the Queerness of Children*, ed. Steven Bruhm and Natasha Hurley, 277–315. Minneapolis: University of Minnesota Press, 2004.

Stoever, Jennifer Lynn. *The Sonic Color Line: Race and the Cultural Politics of Listening*. New York: New York University Press, 2016.

Stollery, Martin. "Voiceover/Commentary." In *The Projection of Britain: A History of the GPO Film Unit*, ed. Scott Anthony and James G. Mansell, 168–78. London: British Film Institute, 2011.

Story, Brett. "Against a 'Humanizing' Prison Cinema." In *The Routledge International Handbook of Visual Criminology*, ed. Michelle Brown and Eamonn Carrabine, 455–65. New York: Routledge, 2017.

———. *Prison Land: Mapping Carceral Power Across Neoliberal America*. Minneapolis: University of Minnesota Press, 2019.

———. "Artist-Run Documentary Studios: A New Form of Trust." *Documentary*, January 29, 2021. https://www.documentary.org/feature/artist-run-documentary-studios-new-form-trust.

———. "How Does It End? Story and the Property Form." In "Beyond Story," special issue, ed. Alexandra Juhasz and Alisa Lebow, *World Records* 5 (2021): 81–90.

Strathern, Marilyn. "Introduction: New Accountabilities." In *Audit Cultures: Anthropological Studies in Accountability, Ethics, and the Academy*, ed. Marilyn Strathern. New York: Routledge, 2000.

Sun, Abby and Jordan Lord. Q&A, The DocYard, Cambridge, May 14, 2021. https://thedocyard.com/screenings/shared-resources/.

Sundar, Pavitra. "Listening with an Accent, or How to Loeribari." In Rangan et al., *Thinking with an Accent*, 281–97.

Takahashi, Tess. "Digital Magnitude." Unpublished manuscript, July 8, 2021, typescript.

Tateiwa, Shin'ya. "Disability Movement/Studies in Japan 1–9." Trans. Hiragi Midori (2010). http://www.arsvi.com/ts/20100091-e.htm. Accessed March 28, 2021.

Torchin, Leshu. *Creating the Witness: Documenting Genocide on Film, Video, and the Internet*. Minneapolis: University of Minnesota Press, 2012.

Trinh, T. Minh-ha. *When the Moon Waxes Red*. New York: Routledge, 1991.

United Nations General Assembly. *Report of the Special Committee to Investigate Israeli Practices Affecting the Human Rights of the Palestinian People and Other*

Arabs of the Occupied Territories. 79th session, Agenda Item 50, UN Doc A/79/363, September 20, 2024.

Vitale, Alex. *The End of Policing.* New York: Verso, 2017.

Wallis, Brian. "The Sound of Defiance: How Can Listening to Images Reveal the Histories of the African Diaspora? Interview with Tina M. Campt." *Aperture*, October 25, 2017. https://aperture.org/editorial/tina-campt-conversation-brian-wallis/.

Waltham-Smith, Naomi. *Shattering Biopolitics: Militant Listening and the Sound of Life.* New York: Fordham University Press, 2021.

Ward, LaCharles. "Black Redaction, Black Evidence: Another Testimony of Black Life." In *A Site of Struggle: American Art Against Anti-Black Violence*, ed. Janet Dees, 87–99. Princeton, NJ: Princeton University Press, 2022.

———. *Black Forensis.* Forthcoming from Duke University Press.

Watlington, Emily. "The Radical Accessibility of Video Art (for Hearing People)." *Future Anterior* 16, no. 1 (2019): 110–21.

———. "Critical Creative Corrective Cacophonous Comical: Closed Captions." *Mousse Magazine* 68 (2019). https://www.moussemagazine.it/shop/mousse-68/. Accessed May 17, 2021.

———. "When Does Artistic Research Become Fake News? Forensic Architecture Keeps Dodging the Question." *Artnews*, March 15, 2023. https://www.artnews.com/art-in-america/features/forensic-architecture-fake-news-1234661013/.

Watlington, Emily, with Victor Cole. "Audio Description, Described." *Voices in Contemporary Art (VOCA)* 10 (2021). https://journal.voca.network/audio-description-described/. Accessed May 23, 2021.

Watson, Ryan. "In the Wakes of Rodney King: Militant Evidence and Media Activism in the Age of Viral Black Death." *Velvet Light Trap* 84 (2019): 34–49.

Waugh, Thomas. "Acting to Play Oneself: Notes on Performance in Documentary (1990)." In *The Documentary Film Reader*, ed. Jonathan Kahana, 815–28. Oxford: Oxford University Press, 2016.

Weizman, Eyal. "Introduction: Forensis." In Forensic Architecture, *Forensis*, 9–32.

———. *Forensic Architecture: Violence at the Threshold of Detectability.* New York: Zone, 2017.

———. "Open Verification." *e-flux* (2019). https://www.e-flux.com/architecture/becoming-digital/248062/open-verification/.

Weidman, Amanda. "Voice." In *Keywords in Sound*, ed. David Novak and Matt Sakakeeny, 232–45. Durham: Duke University Press, 2015.

Williams, Linda. "Mirrors Without Memories: Truth, History, and the New Documentary (1993)." In *The Documentary Film Reader: History, Theory, Criticism*, ed. Jonathan Kahana, 794–806. New York: Oxford University Press, 2016.

Wilson, James Q. *Varieties of Police Behavior: The Management of Law and Order in Eight Communities*. Cambridge, MA: Harvard University Press, 1968.

Wilson, James Q., and George L. Kelling. "Broken Windows." *Atlantic*, March 1982. https://www.theatlantic.com/magazine/archive/1982/03/broken-windows/304465/.

Whittaker, Tom, and Sarah Wright, eds. *Locating the Voice in Film: Critical Approaches and Global Practices*. Oxford: Oxford University Press, 2017.

Winston, Brian. *Claiming the Real II—Documentary: Grierson and Beyond*, 2nd ed. London: Palgrave Macmillan, 2008.

———. "The Marginal Spectator." In *A Companion to Documentary Film History*, ed. Joshua Malitsky, 421–36. Hoboken, NJ: Wiley-Blackwell, 2020.

Wolfe, Charles. "Historicising the 'Voice of God': The Place of Vocal Narration in Classical Documentary." *Film History* 9, no. 2 (1997): 149–67.

Yamashita, Sachiko. "Being Involved in Care for People with Disabilities as a Healthy Person: Focusing on the Ideology of the Able-Bodied People Movement in the 1970s Liberation Movement for People with Disabilities." Presentation, 51st National Conference of the Japanese Society of Social Welfare for Persons with Disabilities, October 13, 2003. http://www.arsvi.com/2000/031013ys.htm. Accessed April 19, 2024.

Yaqub, Nadia. "Introduction." In *Gaza on Screen*, ed. Nadia Yaqub, 1–28. Durham, NC: Duke University Press, 2023.

Zdenek, Sean. "Which Sounds Are Significant? Toward a Rhetoric of Closed Captioning." *Disability Studies Quarterly* 31, no. 3 (2011). https://dsq-sds.org/article/view/1667/1604.

INDEX

Pages numbers in *italics* refer to figures

6:30 Collection (GPO), 21, 38, 43, *44*
ableism, 22, 23, 81, 114, 120, 165, 210n53; and design, 98, 101; and the documentary audit, 8, 22, 78, 80, 82, 88, 120–21, 186n29; and *Goodbye CP* (Hara and Kobayashi), 23, 88, 95, 98; and *Shared Resources* (Lord), 23, 88, 107, 114, 117; and staring, 102; values of, 80, 81, 82, 87
Abu Hamdan, Lawrence, 22, 25, 34, 35, 51, 64–76; *The Freedom of Speech Itself*, 21, 34, 51, 64–76
accent, 17, 25, 29, 31, 35; analysis, 35, 70; fake, 27, 31; discrimination, 74–76; documentary, 32, 38, 75; exporting of, 39; in *The Freedom of Speech Itself* (Abu Hamdan), 69–70, 72–74; hierarchies of, 32, 39, 76; justice, 26; as metaphor, 33; monetizing of, 21, 34, 75; monitoring of, 21, 34, 53, 75; in *Nalini by Day, Nancy by Night* (Gulati), 51, 55–56, 58, 60–66, 69; neutralization, 9, 21, 32, 33, 34, 51,

53–55, 63, 76, 197n67; relationality of, 17, 72; training, 33, 76. *See also* accented interlistening; listening: for an accent; listening: with an accent
accent studies, 17, 18, 35, 88
accented interlistening, 20, 51, 64, 65, 74, 75, 76, 88, 181
access, 9, 18, 22, 82–83; activism, 18–19, 79, 213n82; as commodity v. public good, 9, 82, 109; disentitled, 93, 100, 104; fatigue, 118; features, 18, 22, 61, 80, 86, 106, 112, 113, 116, 210n62, 214n90; *Goodbye CP* (Hara and Kobayashi), 23, 79, 83–84, 87–89, 93, 95, 98, 100, 102–105, 121–23; intimacy, 22, 87, 107, 111–12, 114, 115–16, 119, 178, 180; norms, 78, 84, 88; obstacle, 100-101, 121; in *Shared Resources* (Lord), 23, 79, 88–89, 106–109, 111–13, 115–23. *See also* accommodations; audio description; captions; disability; disability justice

accommodations, 19, 93, 99, 100–101, 107–108, 114; textual, 99. *See also* access

accountability, 7–8, 172, 178; abolitionist, 133; and auditing, 7–8, 177–78; critique of, 132; and documentary, 2, 18, 20, 24, 83, 128, 131, 172, 173, 174, 176–78, 218n10; and impact, 176–77; of listening, 1–2, 122; logic of, 110; media, 155, 181; in *Shared Resources* (Lord), 108, 111. *See also* auditing

activism: abolitionist, 132; access, 18–19, 79, 213n82; against police violence, 162, 164, 169; disability, 9, 18, 22, 23, 83, 87, 94–97, 101, 112, 120, 204n25, 205n35, 205n36, 206n42, 212n81, 213n82; documentary, 20; human rights, 24, 133, 137, 147, 154–55. *See also* Aoi Shiba no Kai ("Green Grasses" group)

aesthetics: carceral, 125; disability, 114; forensic, 155, 156, 158; of operational images, 196n52; realist, 98

Aitken, Ian, 192n26

Aldarondo, Cecilia, 176

al–Durrah, Muhammad, 148, 224n53

Alexander, Neta, 26, 211n67, 213n82

Alexandrowicz, Ra'anan, 26, 134, 136–53, 174; *The Law in These Parts*, 134, 11, 53; *The Viewing Booth*, 24, 133–53, 173–75

Al-Haq (Palestinian human rights organization), 141, 181

Americans with Disabilities Act (ADA), 86, 93, 101

Anderson, Joel Neville, 11, 12k 99, 101, 102, 211n64

Aneesh, A.: on the "neutral accent," 54

Anstey, Edgar: *Housing Problems*, 46

Aoi Shiba no Kai ("Green Grasses" group), 22, 84, 89, 93, 96-98, 204n25, 210n53

Apter, Emily, 71, 200n86

Arrington, Celeste L., 205n36

audibility, 1, 12, 20, 79, 126, 167

audio description, 22, 23, 80, 86, 101, 107, 111-13, 116-17, 123, 139

auditing, 6–7, 28–29, 36–37, 39, 50–51, 68, 75, 178–79; in the documentary field, 178–79; in higher education, 178. *See also* documentary audit, the

Balsom, Erika: on ekphrasis, 117; on neo–observational documentary, 222n44

Barthes, Roland: the "blind field," 214n94

Baugh, John: on linguistic profiling, 65

Benjamin, Walter: on the "optical unconscious," 78, 201n4

Ben–Moshe, Liat: on "carceral enclosures," 130–31, 219n14

Berlant, Lauren: on "cruel optimism," 8

Bombay Calling (Mallal and Addelman), 55

Bookman, Mark Ross, 208n50

Bourdieu, Pierre: on "habitus," 13, 31

British Film Institute (BFI), 38. *See also* General Post Office (GPO)

Brown, Michelle, 131

Bruzzi, Stella, 69

B'Tselem (Israeli human rights organization), 24, 128, 133, 134, 140–43, 146–47, 151, 153–54, 222n38, 222n44, 223n51, 224n52; *Shooting Back*, 140

Bullock–Brown, Natalie, 83, 178

INDEX 255

Cable Ship (GPO), 21, 38, *43*, 44–45
call centers, 9, 21, 34, 50–59, 62–63, 72, 76, 197n56; "call center voice," 51
Campana, Andrew, 206n39
Campt, Tina, 20, 126, 132, 136, 216n2
captions, 18, 22, 56, 61, 80, 101, 106, 112–13, 202n7, 215n90; closed, 61, 212n82, 216n101; open, 23, 86, 107, 111, 113–115, *119*, 123, 198n70, 213n84
Cavalcanti, Alberto, 36, 38, *42*
Childress, Sonya, 83, 178
Chion, Michael: on acousmatic voices, 120; on *athorybos*, 120, 216n101; on cinema sound, 185n20
Chow, Rey: on the call center agent, 54; on the indexicality of images, 16; on "transcendental guarantees," 16
Clark, John Lee: on rejecting access, 121
Clover, Carol: on the adversarial trial, 150
Coal Face (GPO), 36, *43*
Connor, Steven: on the "vocalic body," 190n3
Copwatch (network of activist organizations), 129, 180
Corner, John: on "documentary," 184n10
Couldry, Nick: on voice, 4
Cox, Geoffrey, 12
Crawford-Holland, Sasha, 169, 230n108
Crenshaw, Kimberlé: on "narrative disaggregation," 148
crip, 81; and access, 19, 78; crip-of-color critique, 18, 22, 80, 88, 98, 114, 120. *See also* "crip time"
Crip Camp (Newnham and LeBrecht), 178, 214n85
crip time, 14, 19, 22, 62, 79–82, 89, 99, 103, 104, 111, 118, 122, 123, 180

Davé, Shilpa: on accent, 201n2
Deleuze, Gilles: on visibility, 12
disability: activism, 9, 18, 22, 23, 83, 87, 94–97, 101, 112, 120, 204n25, 205n35, 205n36, 206n42, 212n81, 213n82; aesthetics, 114; and documentary, 79, 120; justice, 9, 18, 23, 26 82; law, 82; and narrative, 120. *See also* access; crip time; *Goodbye CP* (Hara and Kobayashi); *Shared Resources* (Lord)
Diverted to Delhi (Stitt), 55
documentary: auditory unconscious of, 78; comportment, 30; disability, 79, 120; early sound, 9, 20, 33, 39, 115–16; ethics, 3, 10; ethos, 12; expository turn of, 8; listening, 2, 5, 8, 9, 16, 22, 35, 75, 179–81, 186n28; marked, 15; neutral-accented commentator of, 179; raciolinguistic norms of, 9, 21, 36, 40, 44, 50, 51, 63; sound; testimonial turn of, 8, 10, 20; unmarked, 15; verité, 8, 9, 18, 79–80, 83, 97, 98, 101, 105, 115, 190n7, 207n47, 219n12. *See also* documentary audit, the; documentary listening; documentary studies
documentary audit, the, 1, 2, 6, 7, 15, 17, 18, 19, 75, 179–80; and ableism, 79, 121, 126; and abolition, 23, 127; and call centers, 21, 29, 33, 51, 55–56; and the carceral state, 127; and crip time, 19; and neutral listening, 28, 179; origins of, 20, 36–44, 50
documentary listening, 2, 5, 8, 9, 16, 22, 35, 75, 179–81, 186n28; and ableism, 22, 82; and auditing, 51; and carceral politics of, 20, 125–26, 133; coalitional politics of, 26; and

documentary listening (*continued*)
disability, 78; emancipatory role of, 9, 134; extractive logic of, 9, 19; and forensics, 68, 71; liberal politics of, 67–68, 179; logic of, 20, 64, 65; and neutrality, 17; and objectivity, 67; social relations of, 8, 19. *See also* documentary; documentary audit, the; listening

documentary studies, 3, 11, 14n7, 35, 38, 129, 218n11

Dolar, Mladen: on voice, 12, 186n27

Dolmage, Jay: on accommodations, 100, 211n74; on audio description, 117, 215n97

Drew, Robert, 68

Dublon, Amalle, 114, 120

Dyson, Frances: on "radio voice," 40

Eidsheim, Nina Sun, 16; on "accented listening," 31, 33; on "just recognition," 74, 201n97; on vocal essentialism, 187n33, 190n5

Ellcessor, Elizabeth: on access, 82

Ellis, Katie: on automated captions, 213n83; on D/deaf and blind audiences, 212n81, 213n84

Estefan, Kareem: on Palestinian testimony, 132, 141, 142; on refusal, 141, 153; on reparative fabulation, 223n45

Fabian, Johannes: *Time and the Other*, 205n32

Fairy of the Phone, The (GPO), 21, 38, 44, 47, *48*

Farocki, Harun, 51

Fassin, Didier: on "humanitarian intervention," 130

Felman, Shoshana: *Testimony*, 10, 127–28, 154, 217n6, 217n7

Fleetwood, Nicole: on carceral aesthetics, 125–26, 171

Flores, Nelson: on raciolinguistic ideologies, 40, 194n34

Forensic Architecture (research agency), 16, 24–25, 128, 133, 135, 142, 154, 156–59, 161, 166, 181, 228n20

forensics, 21, 24–25, 50, 66, 135, 151, 154, 156, 158; border, 21, 50; counter–, 150, 155, 156, 158, 227n79, 227n88; as state tool, 156. *See also* accountability: forensic; listening: forensic

Foucault, Michel, 12

Freedom of Speech Itself, The (Abu Hamdan), 21, 34, 51, 64–70, 73–74, 76; accent analysis in, 69–70, 72–74; juridical listening in, 65–66

Freeman, Elizabeth: on chrononormativity, 80

French, Lisa, 184n5

Garland-Thomson, Rosemarie: on "misfitting," 93; on staring, 102

General Post Office Film Unit (GPO), 8, 21, 33, 36–38, 39, 41, 44–50, 54, 75, 192n26, 195n42; *6:30 Collection*, 21, 38, 43, *44*; *Air Post*, 38; *Cable Ship*, 21, 38, *43*, 44–45; *Coal Face*, 36, *43*; *The Fairy of the Phone*, 21, 38, 44, 47, *48*; *On the Fishing Banks of Skye*, *43*; *A Job in a Million*, 38, 44, 47, 49; *Mony a Pickle*, 21, 38, *43*, 44, 46; *Night Mail*, 36; *The North Sea*, 38; raciolinguistic system of, 49–50; *Pett and Pott*, 38, 44, 47; *The Saving of Bill Blewitt*, 21, 38, 44, 46; *Song*

of *Ceylon*, *43*, *44*, *45*; *The Voice of Britain*, 40
Gilmore, Ruth Wilson, 136, 159
Ginsburg, Faye, 26; on disability arts, 204n27
Goo, Emerson, 228n90
Goodbye CP (Hara and Kobayashi), 23, 79, 83–85, 88–105, 108, 121, 123; crawling listening in, 100, 103, 104, 121; crip time in, 89, 99, 103, 104; disentitled access in, 93, 100, 104; liability in, 108; and staring-listening, 101–102, 104
Gorz, Andre, 159
Green, Adam, 169
Grierson, John, 8, 36, 37, 41, *42*, 75, 184n10, 195n42; on ethnographic film, 6
Grigely, Joseph, 210n62; *Inventory of Apologies*, 114
Guenther, Lisa: on "seeing like a cop," 135, 160, 165
Guilford, Josh: on "world-making" capacity of documentary, 15
Gulati, Sonali: *Nalini by Day, Nancy by Night*, 21–22, 34, 51, 52, 55–64, 75–76, 180, 198n73

Hall, Stuart: on "oppositional reading," 149
Halpern, Orit: on "beautiful data," 162, 229n99
Hamraie, Aimi: on ableist design, 101; on the "crip curb cut," 87
Hani, Susumu, 96
Hara, Kazuo, 22, 23, 79, 82–84, 87, 89–101, 103–104, 108, 121, 123, 204n26, 207n46, 207n47, 208n48, 208n49, 209n51, 210n55, 211n73; *Goodbye CP*, 23, 79, 83–85, 88–105, 108, 121, 123
Hartman, Saidiya: on Blackness and witnessing, 160
Hediger, Vinzenz, 26
Honess Roe, Annabelle, 12
humanitarianism, 4, 10, 19, 55, 130, 141, 218n8; impulses of, 55; structures of governance, 130; values of, 4
human rights, 20, 24, 34, 64, 127, 137, 141–42, 155, 201n97, 218n10, 224n52; cases, 66; and counterforensics, 154, 158; forensics, 226n79; violations, 19, 24, 128, 134, 135, 155, 158, 228n90; and witnessing, 135, 224n58. *See also* Al-Haq; B'Tselem; WITNESS

ideology: raciolinguistic, 9, 21, 34, 36, 40, 44, 50, 51, 54, 55, 62, 63, 67, 194n34
immediations, 5, 88
interview, 13, 32, 73, 221n35; in *The Freedom of Speech Itself* (Abu Hamdan), 65, 69, 70, 71, 73; and language analysis for the determination of origin (LADO), 66, 67; in *Nalini by Day, Nancy by Night* (Gulati), 56, 58, 61, 62; in *Shared Resources* (Lord), 109–11; in *The Viewing Booth* (Alexandrowicz), 153

Jaikumar, Priya: on British instructional films, 45, 193n28
Jeffay, Tory: on the "forensic gaze," 150, 165
Job in a Million, A (GPO), 38, 44, 47, *49*
John and Jane (Ahluwalia), 55
Johnston, Gordon, 194n36

Juhasz, Alexandra, 83
juridical listening, 8, 10, 19, 24, 67–68, 125, 127–28, 130–31, 133, 135, 139, 143, 150–51, 153, 173–74, 179; carceral logic of, 130–31
justice, 3–4, 10, 19, 24, 127, 129, 132, 135, 153, 209n3; accent, 26; carceral, 24, 133, 136; criminal, 10, 127, 129, 131, 140, 160, 167, 168, 218n10; decarceral, 26; disability, 18, 23, 26, 82; and documentary, 4, 9, 135; transformative, 20

Kaba, Marianne: on safety, 171–72
Kafer, Alison: on coalitional politics, 202n16; on crip time, 80; on disability, 82
Kang, Edward B.: on call centers, 197n59
Keenan, Thomas: on counterforensics, 150; on Forensic Architecture, 142; on the "forensic turn," 66, 154, 156, 158; on the Rodney King trial, 148, 167
Kelling, George L.: on "broken windows" policing, 165, 229n104
Khosravi, Shahram: on accented thinking, 192n19
*Killing of Harith Augustus, Th*e (Forensic Architecture and Invisible Institute), 25, 133, 135, 158–64, 167–75; "Days," 161, 162; "Hours," 161, 162, *163*; "Milliseconds," 161, 166, 168; "Minutes," 161, 162, 166, 167; "Seconds," 161, 162, *163*; testimony in, 169–70, 173; "Years," 168–70, 172–73, 175, 180
Kim, Christine Sun, 86; *[Closer Captions]*, 86; *Spoken on My Behalf*, 114
Kim, Jina B.: on crip time, 80l, on feminist-of-color disability studies, 203n16;

King, Rodney, 148–49, 217n6; trial of, 164. *See also* WITNESS
Kleege, Georgina: on audio description, 215n90
Kobayashi, Sachiko, 22, 23, 79, 82, 83, 84, 87, 95–97, 99, 108, 121, 123, 207n46, 207n47; 23, 79, 83–85, 88–105, 108, 121, 123
Krug, Jessica, 27–28, 30, 189n2
Krzych, Scott: on hysterical noise, 225n72

Lacey, Kate, 11, 157
language analysis for the determination of origin (LADO), 64–67, 69–72, 198n77
Laub, Dori: *Testimony*, 127, 128, 154
Lazard, Carolyn: *A Recipe for Disaster*, 86, 114, *115*, 120
Lebow, Alisa: on B'Tselem, 222n38, 224n52
Lee, Toby; on the potential of the unreal, 223n45; on "world-making" capacity of documentary, 15
Legg, Stuart: *BBC: The Voice of Britain*, 40
Leimbacher, Irina: on extractive listening, 69–70
Levinas, Emmanuel, 10
Liboiron, Max, 184n14
Lipari, Lisbeth, 16; on "interlistening," 31, 73; on "listening habitus," 13; on "otherwise" listening, 103
Lippi-Green, Rosina: *English with an Accent*, 54, 190n9
listening: like an abolitionist, 14, 24, 127, 133, 136, 171–72, 180; for an accent, 28, 73; with an accent, 35, 65, 73, 180; accented inter–; 20–22, 32, 51, 52, 64–65, 74–76, 88, 181; like a cop, 24,

135, 159, 168; crawling, 100, 103–104; in crip time, 81, 104, 121, 123, 180; defensive, 24, 151, 153; disentitled, 84; documentary, 2, 5, 8, 9, 16, 17, 19–20, 22, 26, 35, 51, 64–65, 67–68, 71, 75, 78, 82, 125–26, 133, 134, 179–81; entitled, 102; forensic, 21, 52, 64–65, 69; inter–, 73; juridical, 8, 10, 19, 24, 67–68, 125, 127–28, 130–31, 133, 135, 139, 143, 150–51, 153, 173–74, 179; and liberal–progressive values, 9; liberatory, 10, 127; neutral, 8, 9, 18, 20–21, 27–29, 32, 34, 37, 39, 50, 54–55, 62, 64, 74–76, 88; outlaw, 135; sideways; like a state, 22, 87, 107, 181; staring–, 102, 104. *See also* accented interlistening

Lord, Jordan, 23, 79, 82, 86, 87, 105–23, 180, ; *After . . . After . . . (Access)*, 108; *Shared Resources*, 23, 79, 86–88, 105–12, 115, 118–23, 180

Lorenz, Chris, 231n6

Lusztig, Irene, 176, 179

Mairs, Nancy, 202n13
Making a Murderer (series), 129
Marx, Karl: on primitive accumulation, 184n14; on use value, 8
Matsumoto, Toshio, 97, 208n48
McArthur, Park, 86, 114, 117; *PARA-SITES*, 114
McEnany, Tom, 40
McRuer, Robert, 81
Melamed, Laliv, 26, 51, 139, 218n8
Mills, Mara, 16, 26, 47, 117
Mingus, Mia: on "access intimacy," 82, 87, 107, 111
Minh-Ha, Trinh; 200n8, on "speaking nearby," 35; *When the Moon Waxes Red*, 5

Mitchell, David T., 97, 120, 214n85
Mony a Pickle (GPO), 21, 38, *43*, 44, 46
Morris, Errol, 97, 137, 209n51; Interrotron, 221n35; *The Thin Blue Line*, 129
Mowitt, John: on "audit," 7, 37
Mugglestone, Lynda: on accent, 193n31

Naficy, Hamid, 149, 192n19; on "accented cinema," 51, 74–75
Nagib, Lúcia, 98
Nalini by Day, Nancy by Night (Gulati), 21–22, 34, 51, 52, 55–64, 75–76, 180, 198n73; accented speech in, 51, 55, 56, 62, 63, 69; and the documentary audit, 51, 55, 56; subtitles in, 61–62
neutral listening, 8, 9, 18, 20–21, 27–29, 32, 34, 37, 39, 50, 54–55, 62, 64, 74–76, 88; myth of, 29, 64, 88
Nichols, Bill, 16; on documentary address, 2; on voice, 3
Night Mail (GPO), 36
North By Current (Minax), 178

objectivity, 9, 17, 67; critiques of, 31; as documentary value, 68; as liberal–progressive value, 9; and listening, 9, 68
Ogawa, Shinsuke, 96
Okada, Jun, 204n26

Padios, Jan M.: on the Filipino accent and call centers, 196n56, 197n63, 197n67
Pandolfi, Mariela: on "humanitarian intervention," 130
Parikka, Jussi: on operational images, 196n52
Parker, James: on law's sonic imagination, 167, 219n13

Peller, Gary: on "narrative disaggregation," 148
Pfeifer, Michelle: on LADO, 65,198n77, 199n79; on passports, 198n76
Piepzna-Samarasinha, Leah Lakshmi: on revolutionary love, 111
Pope.L, William: on crawling, 103
Pramaggiore, Maria, 12
Price, Margaret: on "time harms," 100
prison abolition, 127, 131, 133, 136, 158, 160, 164, 165, 171–75; feminist, 132; and reforms, 23, 133, 159, 165, 168; and refusal, 132
Prison in Twelve Landscapes, The (Story), 124–25
Puar, Jasbir, 141, 222n43

radio, 195n44; and General Post Office (GPO), 17, 39, 47, 50; and imperialism, 50; stations, 124, 126; voice, 40
Ramjattan, Vijay A.: on accent neutralization, 54
Rapp, Rayna: on disability arts, 204n28
Received Pronunciation (RP), 39. *See also* accent: neutralization
reform: criminal justice, 129, 168, 218n10; rhetoric of, 178
Renov, Michael, 16; on testimonial turn, 10
Rivera Andía, Juan Javier: *We Are Going to Record*, 1–2
Robertson, Emma, 194n36
Robinson, Dylan: on "hungry listening," 104; on "listening positionalities," 13; on witnessing, 173–74
Rosa, Jonathan: on raciolinguistic ideologies, 40, 194n34
Rotha, Paul: *Shipyard*, 41

Samuels, Ellen: on "crip time," 19, 80, 103
Sandahl, Carrie: on crip provocation, 81
Sarlin, Paige: on documentary's use value, 8
Satō, Shigechika: on *Goodbye CP* (Hara and Kobayashi),
Saving of Bill Blewitt, The (GPO), 21, 38, 44, 46
Saxena, Akshya, 25–26
Scarry, Elaine, 10
Schalk, Sami: on crip time, 80; on feminist-of-color disability studies, 203n16
Scott, James C.: on seeing like a state, 193n27
Sekula, Allan: on counterforensics, 155; on counterinsurgency, 226n79
Shared Resources (Lord), 23, 79, 86–88, 105–12, 115, 118–23, 180; access in, 23, 79, 88–89, 106–109, 111–13, 115–36; and disability, 107; redundancy in, 116–19; reflexivity of, 105; sideways listening in, 107, 119–20
Shoah (Lanzmann), 128
Siebers, Tobin; on disability aesthetics, 201n5
Silbey, Jessica: "evidence *verité*," 69
Silverman, Kaja: on gendered voices in cinema, 86n27
Simpson, Audra: on refusal, 132
Sinha, Amresh: on subtitles, 212n80
Skoller, Jeffrey: on "happenstance videos," 142, 148, 223n47
Smith, Patrick Brian: on media forensics, 229n100
Snowdon, Peter: *We Are Going to Record*, 1–2
Snyder, Sharon, 97

solidarity, 25; with disability, 82, 87, 103; in documentary, 180; and prison abolition, 15, 160; and sideways listening, 22, 107; in performance art, 103
Song of Ceylon (GPO), 43, 44, 45
sound: and crawling listening, 103; in cinema, 185n20, 212n81; documentary, 12, 13–14, 17, 32, 33, 79, 82, 120; in early film, 9, 20, 36, 39, 115; encultured, 187n33; in *Goodbye CP* (Hara and Kobayashi), 84, 95, 101; in GPO films, 20, 36, 39, 50; ideology of, 37; and image, 11, 16; in *The Killing of Harith Augustus*, (Forensic Architecture and Invisible Institute), 166, 175; and the law, 219n13; *Nalini by Day, Nancy by Night* (Gulati), 63; and objectivity, 9; in *The Prison in Twelve Landscapes* (Story), 124; in *Shared Resources* (Lord), 114, 115
sound studies, 17, 35
speech: accented, 28–29, 44, 51, 55, 56, 62–63, 69, 74–76; and call centers, 53–56, 60–63; disability-affected, 22, 23, 79, 84, 88, 90, 94–95, 100–101, 121, 123; documentary, 75, 78, 104; freedom of, 64, 65, 73; in *The Freedom of Speech Itself* (Abu Hamdan), 65–73; in *Goodbye CP* (Hara and Kobayashi), 84, 90, 94–95, 100, 102, 121, 123; and General Post Office (GPO) films, 40, 41, 44–45, 46, 50; and language analysis for the determination of origin (LADO), 65–67; and the law, 152, 156; in *Nalini by Day, Nancy by Night* (Gulati), 53–56, 60–63; testimonial, 10, 30, 68; in *We are Going*

to Record (Snowdon and Rivera Andía), 2. *See also* accent; voice
Srinivasan, Ragini Tharoor, 25
staring, 22, 84, 101–102; –listening, 102, 104
Starosielski, Nicole: on undersea cables, 195n44
Stein, Rebecca: on Zionist repudiation, 147
Stockton, Kathryn Bond: on "growing sideways," 119
Stoever, Jennifer Lynn: on the "listening ear," 7, 13, 41, 195n41
Stollery, Martin, 195n42
Story, Brett, 25, 26, 83, 110; *The Prison in Twelve Landscapes*, 124–26
Sundar, Pavitra, 26; on temporality of listening, 73
Sylvestre, Liza: *Captioned–Channel Surfing*, 114

Takahashi, Tess: on "marked" and unmarked documentary media, 15, 188n37
telephone: and the documentary audit, 50; in General Post Office (GPO) films, 21, 38, 45, 47–48; and language analysis for the determination of origin (LADO); and linguistics, 196n47; operators, 47. *See also* call centers
testimony, 10, 13, 28, 30, 66, 128, 132, 157; Black, 132, 160; in *The Freedom of Speech Itself* (Abu Hamdan), 69, 70; in *The Killing of Harith Augustus* (Forensic Architecture and Invisible Institute), 162, 167, 169, 173; Palestinian, 132, 142, 152, 181. *See also* Felman, Shoshana; Laub, Dori; witnessing

time. *See* crip time
Torchin, Leshu: on "witnessing publics," 10
Tsuchimoto, Noriaki, 96, 208n46

urban infrastructure: and disability, 89, 94

Viewing Booth, The, (Alexandrowicz), 24, 133–53, 173–75; and "happenstance videos," 142; juridical listening in, 133, 135, 139, 143, 150–51, 153, 173–74; reflexivity of, 137; and witnessing, 134–35, 140, 173–74
violence: anti-Black, 20, 132, 135, 136, 159–60, 169, 173, 228n94; anti-Palestinian, 24, 35, 134, 140–41, 151, 224n55, 228n94; police, 161, 229n102; carceral, 126, 132; settler, 35, 134–35, 137, 140; state, 20, 80, 133, 140–41, 155–56, 166, 173
visibility, 12; as commodity, 9; in documentary, 4; refusal of, 126
voice, 3, 158; call center, 51, 54–56; embodied, 17; "giving voice," 1, 3, 5–6, 11, 13, 50, 55, 66, 76, 88, 156; neutral, 40; and prosopopoeia, 66, 71, 76,156; radio, 40; as trope, 1, 4, 183n4. *See also* accent; sound; speech

Waltham-Smith, Naomi: on language analysis for the determination of origin (LADO), 199n79
Ward, LaCharles: on "Black evidence," 25, 132, 168; on "Black redaction," 160, 175

Watson, Ryan: on documentary witness, 225n58; on media forensics, 229n100
Waugh, Thomas: on presentational performance, 190n7
We Are Going to Record (Snowdon and Rivera Andía), 1–2
Weizman, Eyal, 141, 154, 161; on counterforensics, 155–57; on forensics, 65, 66, 69, 155
Williams, Linda: on Rodney King's beating, 219n12
Wilson, James Q.: on "broken windows" policing, 165, 229n104
Winston, Brian: on "social victims," 4–5
WITNESS (human rights organization), 24, 129, 140, 148
witnessing, 23, 128, 154, 217n7, 222n44; abolitionist, 20; critique of, 134, 140, 160, 173–74; expert, 71, 167; and human rights, 127; and juridical listening, 19; and listening, 10, 154; prosecutorial impulse of, 124, 135; video, 139. *See also* testimony

Yaqub, Nadia: on refusal, 133
Yokota, Hiroshi, 85, 89–95, 97–99, 102, 103, 108, 121, 206n40; manifesto of, 208n50
Yokotsuka, Kōichi, 89, 95, 97, 98, 99, 102, 108, 121, 208n50
Yue, Genevieve, 11

Zavitsanos, Constantina, 86, 114–15
April 4, 1980, 114
Zdenek, Sean, 214n90

GPSR Authorized Representative: Easy Access System Europe, Mustamäe tee
50, 10621 Tallinn, Estonia, gpsr.requests@easproject.com

www.ingramcontent.com/pod-product-compliance
Lightning Source LLC
Chambersburg PA
CBHW022042290426
44109CB00014B/951